NATIONAL
CONSCIOUSNESS,
HISTORY, and
POLITICAL CULTURE
in EARLY-MODERN
EUROPE

THE JOHNS HOPKINS SYMPOSIA
IN COMPARATIVE HISTORY

The Johns Hopkins Symposia in Comparative History are occasional volumes sponsored by the Department of History at The Johns Hopkins University and The Johns Hopkins University Press. Each considers, from a comparative perspective, an important topic of current historical interest and comprises original essays by leading scholars in the United States and other countries. The present volume is the fifth. Its preparation has been assisted by the James S. Schouler Lecture Fund.

NATIONAL CONSCIOUSNESS, HISTORY, and POLITICAL CULTURE in EARLY-MODERN EUROPE

Edited by
OREST RANUM

The Johns Hopkins University Press
Baltimore and London

The Johns Hopkins University Press, Baltimore, Maryland 21218
The Johns Hopkins University Press Ltd., London

Library of Congress Catalog Card Number 74-6837
ISBN 0-8018-1619-X

Library of Congress Cataloging in Publication data
will be found on the last printed page of this book.

CONTENTS

v

ACKNOWLEDGMENTS

The editor would like to express his thanks to Professor Michel Roublev, of the University of Pittsburgh, for agreeing to review the transcription of the Russian words in Professor Cherniavsky's chapter and to Patricia M. Ranum for her help in proofreading and in preparing the index.

CONTRIBUTORS

MICHAEL CHERNIAVSKY was Distinguished Professor in the Department of History at the State University of New York, Albany, at the time he presented the lecture which subsequently formed the basis for his chapter in this volume. He was Andrew W. Mellon Professor of History at the University of Pittsburgh when he completed it. His publication *Tsar and People: Studies in Russian Myths* (New Haven, 1961) is closely related to the themes of Russian national consciousness and political culture. Professor Cherniavsky died in July 1973.

WILLIAM FARR CHURCH is Professor of History at Brown University. Among his recent publications linking political thought and state-building is *Richelieu and Reason of State* (Princeton, 1972).

FELIX GILBERT is Professor of History at the Institute for Advanced Study, Princeton, N.J. His *Machiavelli and Guicciardini: Politics and History in Sixteenth-Century Florence* (Princeton, 1965) is one among many of his works on the themes of Italian national consciousness and history.

HELMUT KOENIGSBERGER was Professor of History at Cornell University until 1973, when he became Professor of History, King's College, University of London. His *The Government of Sicily under Philip II of Spain* (1st ed., London, 1951; 2d ed., Ithaca, 1969) is an exploration in detail of some of the relationships between Spanishness and non-Spanish populations in the Hapsburg Empire.

LEONARD KRIEGER was William R. Shepherd Professor of History at Columbia University until he accepted a university professorship at the University of Chicago in 1973. His *The Politics of Discretion: Pufendorf and the Acceptance of Natural Law* (Chicago, 1965) is among his more recent publications in the field of German political and intellectual history.

ix

JOHN POCOCK was William Eliot Smith Professor of History and Professor of Political Science at Washington University at the time he presented the lecture which subsequently formed the basis for his chapter in this volume. In 1974 he became Harry C. Black Professor of History at the Johns Hopkins University. His *Politics, Language, and Time* (New York, 1971) contains several essays which develop themes related to the subjects of English national consciousness and time.

OREST RANUM is Professor of History at the Johns Hopkins University. His *Paris in the Age of Absolutism* (New York, 1968) appeared in French translation in 1973.

INTRODUCTION

 OREST RANUM

The essays contained in this book are based on the 1973 Schouler Lectures, which were sponsored by the Department of History of The Johns Hopkins University. The authors were asked to consider the relationships among the concepts of national consciousness, history, and political culture in one of six nation-states during the early-modern era. The developments within these national monarchies beginning in the late fifteenth century seemed to make them particularly appropriate for a functional analysis of national consciousness and political culture. Centralized authority had begun to exert its power over provincial elites, and regularized administrative practices had resulted in the achievement of substantial fiscal, judicial, and military control over some peoples. Did this process promote a sense of national consciousness? Did the existence of some such sense and, more specifically, an awareness of a national past, a national language, imagery, and customs—in short, a peculiarly national political culture—provide strong identities for elites, lower social orders, and newly conquered peoples who had previously been untouched or barely influenced by the state? The Italian, French, German, English, Russian, and Spanish experiences provide some answers to these questions.[1]

The topics chosen for discussion in these essays are admittedly difficult and elusive. There was a recognized danger that the essays might be too

[1] The number of national examples might have been greater. In fact, the late Professor Rosalie Colie of Brown University had been invited to lecture on the Dutch. However, concentration on these six quite varied national experiences seems sufficient to elucidate the main implications of the general topics. An alternative scheme would have been to select fewer national examples, complementing them with lectures, say, on Neapolitan, Catalan, Scottish, or some other particularistic or subordinate national experience. This alternative was finally rejected because it might have led to increased emphasis on the conflicts between the "dominant" and the "dominated" nations, and on political parties, taxes, wars, and privileges, which are subjects potentially less illuminating for comparative analysis. As it turned out, in several instances the

diffuse or that they might be given over entirely to problems of definition. Neither occurred. The authors quickly develop useful definitions and then concentrate on analyzing the various national experiences. Some authors assert that these concepts could be more easily defined if applied to medieval or post-eighteenth-century history. But this may not, in fact, be the case. The increased documentation, development of new techniques of political organization, and the entry of hitherto nonexistent or inarticulate groups into the political arena would require a much broader focus and would render these concepts even more difficult to define for the period after 1800. In addition, general emphasis on the actions and thought of elite groups characterizes all these lectures and would not, of course, be as appropriate for discussing the national or even the historical components of popular culture for the nineteenth century. The old questions about the geographic origins of these peoples and of the differing ways they were acculturated by the Romans would deserve special attention again if these topics were discussed for the medieval period. But to go beyond what has already been learned by historians and philologists, it would be necessary to change the topics themselves, to pose the questions which cultural anthropologists ask about societies, and try to answer them as much by archaeological as textual evidence.

The authors emphasize some chronological periods more than others in order to analyze the critical conjunctions of institutions, ideas, and events in the formation of the six nation-states. These conjunctions did not, of course, occur simultaneously in the six states. In Italy and Germany, for example, the formative stage of the nation-state did not occur until the nineteenth century. It is particularly valuable, however, to note the presence in the early-modern period in Italy and Germany of many of the elements which seem to have acted as determinants in state-building in, for instance, France and Russia. But the papal and imperial claims to universal authority in the Italian and German political cultures, when combined with the regional identities, somehow distorted or weakened the development of a national consciousness which could in turn be supported by and reinforce bureaucratic centralization.

For the medieval period, places such as Fulda, Rheims, and Westminster, missionaries and saints of the stature of Augustine, Boniface, and James of Campostella, military heroes, miraculous events, and peoples and lands, whose names are usually obscure to those not brought up to

---

relationship between conflicting national and "local-national" identities is brought out in these essays, especially in the case of the Italians and the Germans.

In the main, these national examples demonstrate the predominant constitutional arrangements developed in the early-modern period, with the exception of the federation, for which the Dutch had been selected as the example.

venerate them, are examples of the diffuse and intangible elements which, as Michael Cherniavsky suggests for the Russians, provided some kind of identity, consciousness, or definition which preceded political organization into nation-states. Veneration for a land, one's own people, and one's own language; apparent marks of providential favor upon that land; and later, the development of a unique company of saints and ruling families produced a sense of identity and gave significance and form to social relationships. This knowledge transcended and gave general, though not cosmic, meaning to banal events of everyday life. Sometimes related to the Christianization of a "people" or to the conquest of territories, the early events, which would later form the broad relief of so many national histories, fused the pasts of dynasties and peoples with other elements of collective identity, some of which are explicitly psychological. The sense of separateness, even uniqueness, or of being "chosen" and subsequently sustained by divine favor infuses early-modern national histories, at least in some societies, and provides clues to the elements constituting collective identities in some very early histories, or at least histories of very early national events.

How did these historical elements become joined to psychological determinants of collective behavior? Historians lack the methods or analytical tools for conducting research on this question. They must proceed step by step, as the authors of these essays have done, first to establish some definitions and then to work out rudimentary chronologies of the fundamental shifts in the modes of expression and precise content of the various national consciousnesses. The current state of knowledge is uneven at best. B. Guenées' summary of the scholarship on French "national sentiment" could probably be applied to most other contemporary national experiences:

> . . . What do we really know about national sentiment in France at the end of the Middle Ages? First of all, when did it appear? Did it exist all through the Middle Ages, as claimed by J. Huizinga? Did it originate only at the end of the Hundred Years' War, as suggested by H. Hauser? Or was it only later still, in the sixteenth century, that it can be unmistakably recognized as such, as is the view of F. Chabod? But the answer to our initial question brings up, or rather follows, a whole series of others. Above all, what precisely should we call "national sentiment"?[2]

The inclusion of the concept of history as one of the factors to be analyzed in these essays enables the authors to define the constituent parts of national consciousness and to discern fundamental shifts in their make-

---

[2] B. Guenée, "The History of the State in France at the End of the Middle Ages as Seen by French Historians," *The Recovery of France in the Fifteenth Century*, ed. P. S. Lewis (New York, 1971).

up. Perceptions of the past provide a manageable focus for studying national consciousness and for determining the nature of national consciousness itself.

The function of these perceptions in the changes in national consciousness varied not only from society to society, but also and perhaps more significantly from time to time within specific societies. Similarly, in some political cultures, especially those with political aims to "restore" the society to its pristine ways, be they Frankish or Anglo-Saxon, the more "remote" pasts seem to have played much more important roles than in other political cultures. Clearly, after 1500 the study of national origins in Europe and the concept of pastness this pursuit represented were connected with the development of defined national political cultures. As Felix Gilbert points out, the failure except in literary matters to integrate a perception of Italy as unified under the ancient Romans into the national consciousness is indicative of the power of the various political cultures of the city-states in the late Middle Ages; consciousness could not be inspired by evoking early Roman, that is republican, history. These "origins" had, in a sense, been associated with elements in subsequent political cultures, which made early Roman history dysfunctional in early-modern Italian political culture. The association with the universal imperial Roman history of antiquity and the still very real associations of Rome with both imperial and papal political cultures thus relegated the history of Italian "origins" to the poets and philosophers.

The atomization of European social and political systems after the disintegration of the Carolingian Empire had been accompanied by the rise to dominance of the religious in intellectual life. Monks provided the ceremonials of political cultures as well as the sense of the past which lay at their heart, no matter how slight or how powerful the secular authority. Therefore, it is not surprising to find religious elements receiving heavy stress in the early formation of national identities.[3] Providential favor upon a ruling family or people gave some events a heightened significance. God's intervention was always recorded, for the events in which He participated were somehow more meaningful or, for medieval minds, "truer" than those involving men alone. This is not to say, of course, that all the elements of national identity, say in Germany or France, were formed by the influence of the religious in the political cultures, as the historical residue of dynastic wars and papal-monarchical

---

[3] This explains the difficulty which may be encountered in discerning the secular elements in national consciousness during the Middle Ages, for monks may simply have ignored or failed to include in their histories those secular elements hostile to their definition of political culture.

controversies attest. Nevertheless, churchmen remained primarily responsible for integrating both secular and religious events into a whole, with the names of peoples, places, and events forming a coherent perception of the past. The names of victorious battles, founders of dynasties, and leaders in crusades and the records of miraculous cures by kings had an increasingly preponderant place in the histories being written, though it was not until the later Middle Ages that monarchies began to separate themselves from the aegis of the religious, who alone possessed the rhetorical and theatrical skills needed to recreate ancient Roman-Byzantine rites and to join the *gestae* of reigning monarchs or cities to those tropes about the deeds of Alexander the Great, Charlemagne, Troy, and Athens.

By 1500 senses of the past among elite groups had clearly become a major if not predominant element in various political cultures of Europe, but the national elements had not been given primordial status or recognition except in France, England, and to a certain extent, Russia. Indeed, the conflict within and among all European societies over competing claims of universal, national, and local political power—each claim representing a separate identity and history—continued to have intellectual ramifications in the various political cultures. The political cultures laying the greatest claims to universal authority, the empire and papacy, would eventually prove to be incapable of integrating the elements of national consciousness, including the historical, embodied within them. Thus Germany and Italy would not be united. The counterbalance, of course, was also true; where the universal authorities were most strongly defended, again in Germany and Italy, local authorities and even the particular consciousness of great city-states, such as Florence and Milan or Hamburg and Würtemburg, would continue to survive down into the nineteenth century.

At this level of definition, the study of national consciousness poses few problems. It is not difficult to observe themes in late medieval literature and art which served to elevate the sense of loyalty to constituted authority and to unite peoples in support of that authority. Like the priests of the early Middle Ages who participated in the miraculous events involving St. Boniface, St. Augustine, St. Denis, and others, the writers of history began in the High Middle Ages to provide a canon of historical and mythical elements which could rally peoples and give them a sense of uniqueness and pride. Their intimate affiliation with constituted authorities, first as priests and more gradually as secular writers patronized by both crown and republic, gave the writers an opportunity to weave a fabric of ideas capable of stimulating emotional responses and political action out of otherwise little-known or insignificant—even mythical—events.

Taken together, were these early expressions of identity, so often couched in a mythical past, qualitatively different from the elements constituting national identities in the nineteenth and twentieth centuries? By asking this question, Cherniavsky takes us indirectly to another question: Can we use modern historical science to recover modes of thought and political behavior far outside the range of issues and thinking of twentieth-century historians without being hopelessly anachronistic? When it is discovered that a myth is indeed a myth, the temptation may be simply to call it that and stop, instead of attempting to study the relationships of particular myths to political cultures. Dare we try to reconstruct what could be called national modes of perceiving the past in medieval political cultures? Cherniavsky answers that we can sense what those identities were in medieval societies, but that we can do so only by carefully respecting the contexts in which the elements of national identity are found. Here still another difficulty emerges, because it would seem that no element of political culture can be ignored even though it has no place in the definition of national identity. Thus the problem is not one of determining whether these identities existed in the Middle Ages, but one of discerning what their components and functions were at various times and how the perception of the past changed as a result of its relationship to the other elements in political cultures.

Then, too, is not the perception of the past the least difficult element for twentieth-century historians to reconstruct? Other perceptions, primarily oral or visual, may more easily elude us. Witness the specific intellectual context of the national style of St. Basil's Cathedral in Moscow. It seems that no sixteenth-century Russian, nor even any foreigner, attempted to put into words the architect's aims or to explain how he attempted to capture the Russian national identity in stone and paint.

In support of Cherniavsky's conclusion that we can, however, reconstruct the written elements is the fact that some medieval expressions of national identity remain familiar to populations down to modern times, as Koenigsberger observes in the case of Spain. Yet the intellectual and political contexts of these same medieval "survivals" must be scrutinized very closely, for they may have undergone drastic mutations. Frequently, their almost complete secularization as a consequence of the political and "historical" thinking of men of power and men of the pen in our own era has changed all but the labels. Indeed, the nineteenth-century wave of reconstructions of ideologies based on medieval national heroes and institutions is a case in point, and it is for this reason that the specific social and political links to and consequences of these perceptions of the past must be taken into account. Put another way, what are the motivating forces for changing these perceptions of the past? They may be preeminently intellectual, as in the case of the "historical revolution" of the sixteenth century; but in addition, social and political currents would always seem to have been at work in altering perceptions of the past and of national consciousness itself.

On a more fundamental level of analysis—that of explaining how emotional responses became linked to these elements providing for national identity—scholars have achieved very little. The problem posed by selecting the concepts of history, political culture, and national consciousness, then, is still one of establishing a framework of functional analysis which links the concepts logically to public events, institutions, and political perceptions.

In defining these concepts, the authors of these essays had three related but fundamentally different approaches available to them. The first was simply to draw upon the recent literature of social science for definitions and methods and then to proceed to delineate the similarities and differences which might conceivably be said to exist between recent experiences among the developing nations in the "third world" and the corresponding events and ideas found in the various European societies from 1500 to 1800.

A second approach was to draw upon the sophisticated analytical frameworks and definitions that have emanated from the various European national historiographies. Indeed, each of the European nations has developed a way of looking at itself. These ways invariably include philosophical and linguistic components which—as congeries of ideas and symbols, assumptions and prejudices—themselves constitute part of the subject of these essays.

The third possible approach was to modify the topics for any given national example and to endeavor to develop a mode of analysis appropriate for that example. This approach, if followed by all the authors, would have made comparative analysis by the reader much more difficult. Only in the English example, discussed by John Pocock, is there an attempt to develop an analytical framework that goes beyond the second approach, with all its ramifications. In the case of the English, who experienced their first modern revolution in the seventeenth century, it was necessary for the author to create analytical categories regarding the various senses of time developed by English radicals. Neither the sense of apocalyptic time nor the civic consciousness it helped to stimulate in revolutionary England obscures the similarities and differences in the English experience. Quite the contrary. Though these elements may also have been expressed in other European societies in the seventeenth century, they never supplied the dominant mood or gained acceptance by men of power as they did in England. In addition, it is interesting to note that both the Ancient Constitution and apocalyptic time as described by Pocock seem to have had greater impact on political culture than did the prevailing humanist historical thought, or the *ars historica*.

Dare we speak of history and national consciousness in the early-modern period, the case of the Russian peasants in revolt excepted, as generally legitimating systems of ideas and beliefs, rather than as forces which challenged conventional political behavior and thought? The English experience had, of course, precedents in the reforming societies of the sixteenth century, notably the Dutch and Swiss, and also in the Florence of Savanarola and Machiavelli. Pocock's elucidation of the very special achievement of the English allows us to perceive the effects of the Counter Reformation, as Gilbert notes, on the rest of western Europe. The power of a revived papacy and the monastic and educational regeneration in the Roman church inhibited the growth of national consciousness in Italy and impeded its evocation in historical writing in other predominantly Catholic societies. Indeed, history and national consciousness in the seventeenth-century Catholic states, like rooks in a game of chess, merely supported the knights and queens and scarcely entered the fray themselves. French historical thought of the seventeenth century, as William Church depicts it, supports this contention: serene as a literature of praise and/or erudition, it would provoke only occasional waves of controversy within the political culture, never revolt, because it sustained both absolutist and Gallican modes of political action.

The value of these various approaches merits brief discussion as possible direction for new research. The first approach, that of calling upon the methods and languages of the social sciences, involves at least two possible modes of analysis. The most obvious should not be excluded automatically, for the mere attempt to define the social mechanisms and beliefs of early-modern European societies within some of the various models and analytical frameworks of cultural anthropology, for example, would be no mean achievement. This strategy was not pursued by any of the authors, yet within the diffuse and rich field of cultural anthropology is much that historians might test on such difficult topics as history, political culture, and national consciousness. A case in point is the model study by A. Coupez and M. Kamanzi, *La Littérature de Cour au Rwanda* (Oxford, 1970). At once empirical and analytical, this work offers much more than interesting points of comparison between "early-modern" African and European monarchies. Functional relationships between thought and perceptions of dynasty, nation, and court are suggested which deserve to be examined comparatively in other "traditional" societies, notably those of early-modern Europe.

A second mode of analysis may strike historians as even more anachronistic, namely to adopt contemporary definitions of such ingredients of political culture as propaganda and centralization for testing on early-modern European societies. Here one very promising system of analytical tools is the literature about political culture itself, starting perhaps with the pioneering work of Gabriel Almond.[4] By beginning with broad categories and by defining political culture itself to include elements so frequently left out of studies of "political history," Almond is able to delineate the more autonomous elements of individual political cultures.[5] When combined with precise definitions of the groups which constitute the political nation, and of those which in fact do not, Almond's notion of a "measure of autonomy" might lead to a clarification of the specific links between elite and popular elements of a political culture, and it might help determine the common and elitist elements in any given national consciousness. These two modes of analysis, lumped together as derived from the social sciences, present some obvious dangers, but they deserve attention on the part of historians when they undertake to define such concepts as those under discussion here.[6]

The second approach, which was chosen by all the authors, has its dangers as well. The most important of these is parochialism, which would have been manifested if the authors had accepted claims to unique historical and cultural development implicit in any model drawn from a national historiography in order to explain and to define specifically national developments. The use of terms which were actually employed in the sixteenth and seventeenth centuries but which have since been given very different meanings by historiographical traditions creates an additional uneasiness. The word "state" is a case in point. *Within* each separate national historiographical tradition, the literature concerning its meaning is vast, indeed almost limitless; and yet we see it used here, albeit somewhat uncomfortably, to connote a variety of phenomena. We realize that we are able to compare societies and political cultures be-

---

[4] Useful introductions to this literature are L. W. Pye, Introduction to *Political Culture and Political Development*, ed. L. W. Pye and S. Verba (Princeton, 1965), and R. C. Tucker, "Culture, Political Culture, and Communist Society," *Political Science Quarterly*, Vol. 88, no. 2 (June 1973), pp. 170-90. Tucker's step-by-step approach in the application of these analytical tools might serve as a model for work on early-modern societies.

[5] "Comparative Political Systems," *Journal of Politics*, Vol. XIII (1956), pp. 396ff.

[6] An interesting example of the limits of one of these approaches is apparent in R. Rose, "England, a Traditionally Modern Political Culture," *Political Culture*, ed. Pye and Verba, pp. 83-129. The English perception of the past or its possible role in maintaining "traditional" value systems are not really discussed as components of English political culture.

cause this and other similar terms appear in the various essays; yet we know we must be cautious. Each of these essays must thus be perceived as possessing two overlapping and quite distinct analytical frameworks: the first being that of the specific national historiography of the society described, and the second being a more general, cosmopolitan, and later twentieth-century framework of assumptions and definitions. The joining of these two analytical frameworks has been a remarkable achievement on the part of the authors. Their essays make a significant contribution within the specific framework of national history and, at the same time, allow a comparison of developments across Europe.

In some instances these two frameworks also provide a valuable corrective to one another. The national historiographies might otherwise have tended to distort the assessments of "universal" institutions, such as the empire and the papacy, as well as local and ethnic aspects of each national experience. Here, if anywhere, the mid-twentieth-century historian has made an important correction in nineteenth-century national historiographical methods and assumptions. National historiographies have been tempered and refined, but not discarded; they may be perceived as operative in each of these essays. They are, of course, a product of the political cultures and national consciousness which are the principal subjects of the essays. The nineteenth-century additions to the early-modern perception of the "nation" might have been more precisely delineated. But perhaps this would be asking too much. In some instances, notably the Spanish, one senses that the historiographical framework has not yet developed an autonomy from other national elements in the political culture. Does this failure mean that the Spanish framework is a "survival" —in the general anthropological meaning of that term—of an early-modern political culture? The nineteenth-century elaborations of the idea of the nation and of the secularization and demythification of the state seem not to have occurred in Spain or, in any event, to have had little impact on the Spanish *ars historica*.

The third approach—developing new modes of analysis and descriptive language to clarify either national or all-European aspects of political culture—has attracted John Pocock. His task, it is true, has been a special one. The mechanisms which linked religious reform, senses of time, and radical attacks upon existing institutions had appeared in Germany and France, for example, in the sixteenth century. But they did not culminate in those societies in the triumph of new protestant, national political cultures as they did in England after 1640. For this reason Pocock has appropriately analyzed the makings of a new civic and national consciousness in revolutionary England.

The French, notably in the works of Hotman and his followers, also may have developed a coherent myth of an ancient constitution which would challenge the established order.[7] And similarly, apocalyptic thought was more or less present in the sixteenth century in Italian, German, and French political cultures.[8] Only in England in the seventeenth century, however, did these strands of thought, with different but logically related senses of time, provide the foundations for a revolutionary civic consciousness that reflected a clear idea of the nation as a foundation.

Leonard Krieger's analysis of the meanings of "pastness" aids in differentiating the senses of time which developed in England. Whether related to "origins" or to "continuity," to the senses of pastness in "ancient constitutions" or to the pastness of papal *traditio* and James I's divine-right theory, the dominant modes of thinking about the past were a potential link to a perspective of the future, at once utopian and apocalyptic. The analyses of the meanings of time in the essays by Pocock and Krieger are perhaps the most contemporary feature of the analytical frameworks developed in these lectures. Together they represent a twentieth-century achievement in historical thinking, for the national historiographical traditions, so strongly grounded in philology, cannot by philology alone be dissected to provide an assessment of the elements of which the historiographies themselves are constituted. Thus it is through these analyses of the senses of time that some general conclusions about the second approach may be made. Though it must be stated with the greatest possible caution, it would seem that the place of history in early-modern political cultures was that of "legitimator" and "codifier" of the internal and international institutional changes which occurred. History only rarely inspired new definitions of national consciousness and political power, but it did coherently depict recent institutional and intellectual shifts by changing the "canon" of accepted truths about the national past to reflect new political realities.

The German example, as described by Krieger, was an experiment the results of which, though negative, confirmed this general conclusion. Because no fundamental institutional or social transformation occurred in early-modern Germany, the definition and role of national consciousness neither effected a marked change in the political culture nor engendered a redefinition of the national past.

The French example was an experiment where all conclusions were

---

[7] See the editors' Introduction to Francois Hotman's *Francogallia*, ed. R. Giesey and J. H. M. Salmon (Cambridge, 1972), pp. 62-90.

[8] N. Cohn, *The Pursuit of the Millenium* (London, 1962), and S. L. Thrupp (ed.), *Millenial Dreams in Action* (The Hague, 1962), are standard works.

positive, given the relationship between the monarchy, Gallicanism, and national consciousness which had become well established by 1600. Yet neither subsequent social upheavals nor intellectual revolutions undermined the synthesis of the French past with seventeenth-century institutions and societies. The general process of historicizing the present had been established in late-medieval and sixteenth-century histories of the French monarchy, and being French meant loving and honoring French sovereigns and being wary of foreigners, be they from Rome or from Madrid.

Whether expressed by revolutionary Englishmen, *thèse-royaliste* Frenchmen, or Brunswickian Germans, the elements of national consciousness appear so overladen with religious and constitutional presuppositions and principles that it is difficult to assert that national consciousness held a primordial place in early-modern political cultures. Before reading these essays, the editor had taken "national consciousness" to mean the presence of an activist element in the political culture—a force with which statesmen occasionally had to reckon and, if they were artful, could use to gain support for their policies. These essays suggest a different conclusion: such a force rarely if ever manifested itself overtly in an age still dominated by court politics, localism, and imperial-papal universalism. True, the heaven to which the English Puritans aspired had English characteristics, in a sense, but Englishness was not the primary element in their apocalyptic view of the future. Perhaps Englishness, like the sense of being Russian, had already been worked out and articulated among the entire population. Without a social component—such as appealing to the entire populace by calling them equal because they were all of the same nation—the significance of national consciousness in political decisions might have been minor indeed. It would be there to engender outbursts of xenophobia, notably in England under Elizabeth and Charles I regarding the Spanish,[9] among the French *vis-à-vis* Italians and Spaniards in the 1580s and 1640s, and still more notably in the great schism between slavophiles and westernizers in imperial Russia. But was national consciousness more influential than the international implications of dynasticism among governing elites in the seventeenth century? The persistence of local consciousness and the attractiveness of universal ideals of Christendom, even among those living in Protestant cultures, are indications of the boundaries of national consciousness. A number of other exceptions are brought to mind, which brings us back to the prob-

[9] On the possible relationships between xenophobia and apocalyptic time, see the suggestive application of Weberian categories developed by R. Kaufman, *Millénarisme et Acculturation* (Brussels, 1964), Conclusion.

lems of definition. William Church has preferred to use the term patriotism, rather than national consciousness, and his reasons merit consideration. Despite the rather impressive territorial and administrative unification of the French state, which was built on top of a quite homogeneous social and cultural heritage, the specifically national elements in the political culture were still not delineated distinctly enough from the monarchy to justify using the term "national consciousness" before 1789. Furthermore, where was the popular component? This sense of the importance of the *peuple* and of citizens in arms, which is so essential to any definition of French national consciousness, raises doubts about employing the term to describe conditions prior to 1789. Indeed, the specific dating of a popular element is an implicit problem for the study of all European political cultures, because it affects the appropriateness of defining certain elements in these political cultures as national consciousness. The disjunctures between "elitist" and "popular" senses of national consciousness and perceptions of the past further complicate matters. Clearly, the question of the number in the populations affected by or acting upon some sense of national consciousness is particularly difficult. It might be useful to approach the issue of whether national consciousness was an active political force in the early-modern period by analyzing shifts of power from elite to popular political systems, or the reverse.

One of the principal characteristics of late-medieval and early-modern historical writing is the constancy of events recounted, the *gestae* considered worthy of recollection, from work to work. The ceaseless moralizing of humanist history in recounting the same miracles, battles, and other worthy deeds seems to flow from history to history with little change. There are occasional differences of detail, but far more important for us to discern are the reasons for the continuity of moods and events in these histories, for they may provide a clue to what the readers expected to find in histories. Like the listeners to Homeric tales in ancient Greece, or of the dynastic histories of Rwanda, the readers of early-modern histories may well have been already familiar with the events recounted and would have been upset either by the addition of too many unfamiliar events or by the omission of familiar ones. In addition to stylistic matters, these additions and omissions provided the foundation for historical criticism down into the eighteenth century. For people of the early-modern era, there was a well-established and well-known account of events about the history of the world, their monarchy, or their city. Almost like singing a psalm to a different tune, reading more histories gave them the comfortable feeling of participating in a familiar litany, different each time only because of changes in mood or style, which marked the unique contributions of the author-historian. Antiquaries ignored works of this kind; they never quite brought their critical powers sufficiently under control to make a frontal attack either on humanistic history as *ars historica* or on the public response to it. Early-modern historians, rhetoricians that they were, did everything they could to preserve and enhance the emotional responses evoked by reading *gestae*. For this reason we must turn to the less "revolutionary" historians of the sixteenth and seventeenth centuries for a glimpse into the patterns of treating events and emotions which history was thought to be. By the late seventeenth century the mood would gradually shift from a blending of the pietistic and sententious to one in which the latter, à la Livy, would predominate. The emotional responses, both pietistic and classicistic, indicate in literary form the contours of a civilization which was much more oral than ours. For this reason the authors of these essays have been able to rely on histories to discern the elements of national consciousness. Thanks to history, pride in the gifts bestowed on a ruler and his people by God could be felt in the hearts of subjects living centuries later.

The possible effects of the "historical revolution" upon this general configuration of history and national consciousness in the age of humanism deserve some mention, because so many historians throughout Europe took notice of the works of the innovators in sixteenth-century Italy and France who dared to challenge some of the principles of humanistic history.[10] Pocock, Krieger, and Gilbert note these influences and indirectly attempt to relate the historical revolution itself to changes in national consciousness.

Thanks to the impetus of the historical revolution, a new perspective on sources developed. Philology would help to change ideas about the past, and the search for "truth" took on a meaning quite different from the trope so dear to the humanists, who had grown quite comfortable in recounting the fantastic after solemnly opening their narratives with a promise to recount only the "truth." The work of the legal scholars and antiquaries throughout western Europe provided a new wealth of accurate and detailed evidence about the past which had hitherto been unknown.

However, with the exception of such pioneers as Pasquier and Selden, this wealth of detail was scarcely exploited to reconstruct "new" national histories. Genealogies of kings and their "actions" and accounts of the

---

[10] On the historical revolution and its influences see primarily J. G. A. Pocock, *The Ancient Constitution and the Feudal Law* (Cambridge, 1957); F. S. Fussner, *The Historical Revolution, English Historical Writing and Thought* (New York, 1962); and D. Kelley, *The Foundations of Historical Scholarship* (New York, 1970).

founding of cities and monasteries continued to be written in essentially the same pattern. These writings had been "canonized" as history by 1500. The number of national histories actually written, say in France, increased enormously during the late sixteenth and seventeenth centuries; yet, despite the flood of new evidence provided by local *érudits* and publishers of texts, this increase did not produce a concomitant enrichment of interpretations or even differences in emphasis from history to history.

This constancy of genre and of subject matter in national histories may help delineate the role of the historical revolution in defining national consciousness. Prior to the development of antiquarian historical methods, "change" in the canon of historical events had been largely motivated by political controversy, such as quarrels between popes and kings, or rivalries between monasteries or religious orders, courts of law, and great nobles. Did the historical revolution change this pattern? As Church points out, "So much of the power and prestige of the [French] monarchy stemmed from tradition, and an awareness of tradition depended upon a sense of history. . . ."

Étienne Pasquier's great *Recherches de la France* broke with the established canon of events to be recounted, and to a lesser degree so did the works of some of the other makers of the revolution. Their writings would also inspire English and German antiquaries to expand the scope of history to include a great variety of subjects which until that time had not been part of the canon. When compared with the works of their predecessors, Pasquier's, Selden's, and Leibniz' histories demonstrate a vastly increased range of subject matter, largely involving the origins of national institutions or specific ingredients of national culture. Thus the historical revolution, apart from its very significant role in the creation of myths about the "ancient constitution," would also have another long-range effect on the definition of the nation. Perhaps less politically potent at that moment, the recounting of the cultural accomplishments of the Italian, English, French, Swedes, and every other nation whose historians were influenced by the revolution nevertheless laid foundations for a greatly expanded perception of a glorified national past, and consequently resulted in broadening the scope of events to be included in national histories and the role of individuals previously considered unworthy of note. The humanists loved to boast about the poets and scholars who had preceded them in the long campaign to establish "good letters." The French experience was not atypical: Pasquier and his eighteen-century heirs, Père Daniel and Voltaire, added a cultural component to the canon of events called French history. In Voltaire's *Le Siècle de Louis XIV*, poets and architects would be joined to marshals and battles, though the poets and architects would be relegated to the back of the book. Even as late as 1750 it may have seemed improper to violate the canon of subjects—kings and battles—by fully integrating the cultural element into the work.

Prior to the development of philology and a new critical perspective on the past, political and religious controversy may have been the almost exclusive cause of "adjustment" of historical events to conform to changed political circumstances. The wave of pro-imperial, Gallican, and Anglican histories written in the Middle Ages offers remarkable testimony to these patterns of adjusting the canons of national past to undermine either mythical or historical claims of the papacy.

There is little evidence to suggest that the historical revolution halted this process of adjustment. In fact, some of the most eminent *érudits*—notably such Frenchmen as the Dupuy brothers, the Godefroys, and even the Duchesnes, father and son—continued to adjust the national past to conform to contemporary ideological, psychological, or social needs.[11] For example, while much more authoritative than the histories published in the late Middle Ages, the histories published in the seventeenth century concerning the Gallican or imperial claims made by the French monarchy were nevertheless ideologically linked to Louis XIV's campaign to wrest the imperial crown from the Hapsburgs, or to quarrels with the papacy. Thus, even in the French national experience of historical thinking which, as Gilbert, Pocock, and Krieger attest, inspired many imitators abroad, the historical revolution did not fundamentally undermine the deep-seated pattern of adjusting the past to serve contemporary political aims.[12] The political and legal controversies continued to be the dominant source for changing perceptions of the past as an element of national consciousness. But the historical revolution also set in motion another way of perceiving the past which would serve later generations of scholars as a model or pioneering effort to separate the study of the past from contemporary controversies in a political culture, to historical research for its own sake.[13] The outlook on the past familiarly known as "historicism" had been formulated in legal studies by Cujas and some of

---

[11] A. Du Chêne, *Histoire des Papes* (Paris, 1615), is a superbly researched history for its time, representing the mode of historical research born of the "historical revolution." Nevertheless, it is also an intensely Gallican history where the rights of the French monarchy are amply historicized. The past is adjusted to support French claims against papal authority.

[12] On the beginnings of the movement to separate history from any relevance to contemporary society, see Pocock, *The Ancient Constitution*, pp. 9-13, and J. H. Plumb, *The Death of the Past* (London, 1972), passim.

[13] Kelley, *The Foundations of Historical Scholarship*, passim.

his followers. But did not the attack upon the lack of relevance of Cujas's work for Roman law by Du Moulin, Hotman, and others partly derive from a growing and confining definition of national consciousness?[14] Roman law was dead; it could not be applied to French jurisprudence. The world of the sixteenth-century humanists would bring forth both "historicism" and a more coherent national consciousness through the works of Hotman, Pithou, and Pasquier. But this is not all it would accomplish.

The impetus of the historical revolution would not be reserved exclusively for extending the scope of national history and, through its influence on political cultures, of national consciousness. Indeed, in no other way were the political-cultural constraints upon historical researches to become more apparent than in the flowering of local history, which had localism or particularism and the historical revolution as its principal causes. In the still atomized political systems of sixteenth- and seventeenth-century Europe, the universal, but more especially the local or particularistic institutions—as well as the perceptions of the past which underlay them—also underwent refinement and extension at the hands of the antiquarian historians. The "common history" of man since the creation and of Christendom, the papacy, and the empire underwent new critical assessments, an expansion in matters of detail, and a new grounding in Biblical and early Christian historical scholarship based on philology.

But it would be primarily local history which would receive an enormous impetus. Often without much previous knowledge of the medieval history of their region or town, scholars eagerly began to examine charters and other local and more general records to write their local histories. Every region, town, and monastic foundation seemed to attract a little group of scholars who published massive tomes of often poorly digested factual material on local families, rights, and political events. Pride in Bamberg, Naples, Angers, and Lincoln was always lying beneath the surface of the sea of detail. Thus these essays suggest that while the historical revolution may have stimulated much greater interest among political elites than had been the case when theology had been the queen of the sciences, it did not fundamentally alter the complex balance of universal, national, and local perceptions of the past in favor of one, the national. The psychological-political motivations which led antiquaries to select their topics for research—universal, national, or local—had preceded the more intellectual aspects of a historian's commitment to his subject. This seems evident in the German historians' willingness to work

[14] *Ibid.*

at all three simultaneously, a state of affairs not unfamiliar to many other antiquaries throughout Europe in the early-modern period.[15]

In conclusion let us return to the problem of definitions, particularly to the concept "political culture." The latter failed to appeal to the authors as an analytical device. It appears in some of the essays, but none of the authors attempts to define it in ways which would help in characterizing the place or function of national consciousness in political cultures. Two different reasons may be advanced to explain why this topic failed to stimulate interest.

The first reason is each author's assumption that his readers possess a significant body of information about the politics of each nation. The decision to place their analyses within the frameworks of the various national historiographies inevitably led to what could perhaps be called an over-reliance upon the conventionally established assumptions about the politics of one nation or another. This remark should not be interpreted as a criticism in the obvious or negative meaning of the word. Each essay in itself represents a *tour de force*. Had the authors been obliged to formulate analyses of political cultures, the discussions of history and national consciousness would have been less complete. Nevertheless, it must be remembered that reliance on the national historiographies enabled the authors to take short-cuts regarding the meanings of such crucial terms as monarchy, empire, estates, and administration. These terms provided a necessary shorthand for analyses of the various political cultures themselves.

Nevertheless, a second, related, and perhaps more important reason for the authors' failure to employ the concept of political culture more systematically is simply its complexity and vastness. The term encompasses all elements of the political process at all levels of political society, and as such is perhaps unwieldy as an analytical device. After exploring the meanings and relationships of history and national consciousness in early-modern Europe, the reader may find himself, all the same, returning to the concept of political culture as the great imponderable in these studies. By 1500, or in some instances much earlier, the *données* of political life would generally determine the place and character of national consciousness in the societies discussed here. Yet three very significant exceptions immediately come to mind. Changes in the English nation

---

[15] It would be interesting to attempt to pull together for purposes of a comparative study those historians—from France and England in particular—who wrote both national and local history with equal interest. Such combined efforts possibly may have created some sort of inner tension.

during revolution are difficult to compare with the possibly growing disparity between dynasty and nation in France or with the development of two national consciousnesses in Russia; yet, if anywhere, it is in these three phenomena that we see the limited value of placing complete emphasis on elite political cultures as determinants in national experience, for these three elements reveal a more modern, a more complex and variegated, world than that envisaged by the men of power and the writers of history in the three centuries which provide the temporal focus of these essays.

CHAPTER I

ITALY

FELIX GILBERT

This essay is concerned with the period of Italian history between the Renaissance and the Enlightenment. Benedetto Croce has pronounced a judgment of remarkable harshness on this period: "The histories written about Italian life during these centuries take the form of accounts of incidents of meanness, stupidity, sorrow and horror rather poorly relieved on occasions by a laugh of derision or a smile of irony." He added: "That century and one-half has acquired and still retains in our history books the designation of the decadence of Italy. The designation deserves to be kept. . . . From the middle of the Cinquecento up to about the close of the Seicento Italy was not truly alive."[1] This condemnation of a period of Italian history which produced Tasso and Bernini, Campanella and Galileo is startling; Croce's justification was that, while in the Renaissance a movement toward an Italian national consciousness and toward social and moral reform had begun, this movement had been halted and even reversed in the late sixteenth and the seventeenth centuries, and that, in this period, common aims and ideals had disappeared from Italian life.

Croce's views on the significance of these centuries in Italian history gain their full weight if they are placed into the framework of a debate which has been going on among Italian writers and scholars for a long time. When does Italian history begin? Can one trace the line of Italian national development back to the early Middle Ages, or does the lack of any common organization before the Risorgimento indicate that only after that time did the feeling of belonging to an Italian nation become a significant factor in Italian political and social life?

[1] In his article, "La Crisi Italiana del Cinquecento e il legame del Rinascimento col Risorgimento," *La Critica*, Vol. XXXVII (1939), pp. 401-11. I used the English translation of this article, published in *The Late Italian Renaissance 1525–1630*, ed. Eric Cochrane (New York: Harper Torchbooks, 1970), pp. 23-42. The quoted passages can be found on pp. 34, 36, 38.

The period with which we are concerned plays a crucial role in these considerations about the unity of Italian history.[2] These were the years in which, under foreign pressure, the various parts of Italy were drawn into distinct orbits and the differences among the various geographical regions of Italy were considerably increased. Moreover, in this period the Church tightened its grip over Italian intellectual life and created, or at least widened, the gap between religious and secular culture which formed one of the main obstacles for Italian national unification and is a threat to Italian national coherence up to the present day. The question whether the one and one-half centuries between Renaissance and Enlightenment contributed to the growth of Italian national consciousness has bearing upon the manner in which the entire course of Italian history ought to be interpreted.

In the late sixteenth and seventeenth centuries the states on the Italian peninsula were satellites of France or of the Hapsburgs; even the two buffer states in the north, Venice and Savoy, had to shape their course in accordance with the great powers, whose every move they anxiously watched. The pope, the ruler of the church-state, alone could claim to be more than a satellite and could follow an independent policy. But in the seventeenth century rule over Rome did not make the pope a protagonist of a primarily Italian policy; Rome was not the center of Italy but of the world. The colonnades which Bernini built on the Piazza San Pietro were decorated with statues of saints of all ages and all peoples; they opened their arms to pilgrims from all over the world. The river gods who rendered homage to the power of the Church on the new fountain of the Piazza Navona were the Nile and the Ganges, the Danube and the Rio de la Plata, not the Tiber or the Po or the Arno. The victories which were solemnly celebrated in Rome had been obtained in distant countries in the name of Christianity, not of a particular nation: Lepanto, St. Bartholomew, the Battle of the White Mountain.

From the late sixteenth into the seventeenth century the one Italian power of European standing, the papacy, had as the paramount concern of its policy the progress of the Counter Reformation. It cut off the roots of some of the developments toward Italian national-consciousness which had begun in the Renaissance. Certainly it would be anachronistic to ascribe to the Italians of the fifteenth or the sixteenth century a fully developed national feeling or even a longing for a firm political union among the inhabitants of Italy. Nor is it accurate to deny the existence of

[2] For a summary of discussions of this problem, see Alessandro Passerin d'Entrèves, "Riflessioni sulla Storia d'Italia," *Dante Politico e altri Saggi* (Turin, 1955), especially pp. 20-25.

national consciousness in the Renaissance. It is true that the appeals for the "liberation of Italy," for an alliance of all Italian states, usually were made when the state which issued them was threatened by Ultramontani and in need of allies; the same state had no hesitation to ally itself with a foreign power against an Italian power if such a move promised advantages. Nevertheless, these appeals to a common interest among all Italians, even if not successful or not systematically pursued, would have made no sense if they had not reflected the feeling that those living on the Apennine Peninsula were bound together in a special relationship and were different from peoples living on the other side of the Alps. How many went a step farther and recognized the need for common political action is impossible to estimate. Some did, as is evident in the writings of Guicciardini and Machiavelli. In his great work, Guicciardini described with sadness the gradual establishment of foreign rule over Italy, which he attributed to the shortsightedness of the Italian rulers and their incapacity or their unwillingness to place the common interest over personal advantage. Machiavelli, who died a decade before Guicciardini began to write his *History of Italy*, held till the end[3] to the conviction he had expressed in the last chapter of *The Prince*: that the Italian rulers should join forces to drive the foreigners out of Italy.

Machiavelli's exortation to "liberate Italy from the barbarians" ends with the famous lines from Petrarch:

"Vertú contra furore
Prenderá l'arme; e fia 'l combatter corto,
Ché l'antiquo valore
Ne l'italici cor non è ancor morto."

These lines indicate the sources which fed national consciousness and national pride in the period of the Renaissance. The sources were the notion of a secular political virtue[4] and it was the idea that the Italians of then and the Romans of classical times were the same people.

The Church of the Counter Reformation began to look upon pagan antiquity with distrust. For instance, in Marino's *Galeria* of 1619, Erasmus, the leader of a Christian humanism who once had warned "ne sub obtextu priscae litteraturae renascentis caput erigere conetur paganismus,"[5] was banned among the Negromanti and called "falso profeta"

---

[3] For a refutation of the view that Machiavelli abandoned such hopes in the last years of his life, see my article, "Machiavelli's *Istorie Fiorentine*, An Essay in Interpretation," *Studies on Machiavelli*, ed. Myron P. Gilmore (Florence, 1972), especially pp. 96-97.

[4] I prefer these terms to the concept of civic humanism. The influence which humanism exerted on political thought was not limited to republics, and the same humanist could in one work praise republics and in another, monarchies.

[5] P. S. Allen, *Opus Epistolarum Erasmi* (Oxford, 1906-58), Vol. II, p. 491.

whose "scienza chiara" concealed a "coscienza oscura."[6] A threat to the Christian religion began to be seen in the preoccupation with the literary and artistic legacy of the classical world because it might lead to a revival of paganism. On this the popes of the Counter Reformation agreed, though it depended on their personal inclinations whether they preferred to eliminate or to absorb all traces of classical influences.[7]

When the news of the victory of Lepanto reached the Eternal City, the Romans prepared a solemn reception for their victorious compatriot Marcantonio Colonna. He was to enter the city on a gilded chariot with a laurel wreath around his head. On command of Pope Pius V, however, these plans were abandoned. Colonna rode into the city behind the standard of Christ; practices of pagan antiquity which had been used on similar occasions in Rome throughout the period of the Renaissance were banned.

If the saintly Pius V tried to erase all pagan traditions, Sixtus V, the most powerful figure among the popes of the Counter Reformation, tried to subject antiquity to the Church and to use it for the glorification of Christianity. He was proudly conscious of the Roman heritage. He was aware that ancient Rome had been the city of the Seven Hills and he was eager that Rome reach beyond the low stretch along the Tiber, to which it had been confined in medieval and Renaissance times, and occupy its seven hills. The pope invested, therefore, a good amount of energy and money in building the aquaduct which conducted the water from the mountains to the Roman hills; Roman princes and cardinals could now build there the villas and gardens which until the end of the nineteenth century formed the pride of Rome. But, on the monumental fountains from which the waters of the aquaduct gushed, there rode no Neptune with his triton, but instead there stood the figure of Moses, whose staff indicated the opening for the outflow of the water. The columns of Trajan and Marcus Aurelius were crowned with the statues of the apostle princes, Peter and Paul, and a cross was placed on the tops of the ancient obelisks which had been excavated and re-erected with great ingenuity and immense effort. "Drizzando gli obelischi a la croce," Tasso said in a famous poem praising the works of Sixtus V.[8]

---

[6] Clearly, one of the reasons for the condemnation of Erasmus was the stimulus which his work had given to Luther and the Reformers. But the limited number of classical heroes, which are treated in Marino's collection of "portraits in poems," is striking. In the 1667 edition of Marino's La Galeria, the Negromanti will be found on pp. 138-42.

[7] For the facts, given in the following description of papal Rome, see L. Pastor, History of the Popes, especially Vols. XIX, XXI, XXII.

[8] Torquato Tasso, Opere, ed. Bruno Maier (Milan, 1964), Vol. II, nr. 1389, p. 112;

The change in attitude toward antiquity went beyond the field of religion. Art and literature show an ironic and irreverent application of classical materials. Classical mythology was used for satirizing human follies, for celebrating passion and love. The classical world is no longer seen as providing the norms and values for the conduct of life.[9] The classical stories which Marino celebrated in his poems were those of Adonis and Endymion, Ganymede and Galatea, Narcissus and Leander; Bernini gained his reputation by fixing in marble the fleeting moment in which Daphne, shying away from Apollo's embraces, is transformed into a laurel tree. On Carracci's frescoes in the Palazzo Farnese a noisy assembly of ancient gods celebrates the indomitable power of love. We are far removed from the Renaissance when, as on Raphael's *School of Athens*, the ancients were the messengers of eternal truth, or when, as in Michelangelo's *Brutus*, the example of Roman virtue is placed as an admonition before a base present.

The unlikelihood or impossibility of imagining a seventeenth-century work with the ethos of Michelangelo's *Brutus* shows the evanescence of the other element which had nourished national consciousness and pride: secular virtue and political heroism diminished in value and importance. If Machiavelli had been the main advocate of political *virtú* in the Renaissance, the manner in which his ideas were discussed in the political literature of the late sixteenth and seventeenth centuries provides a good indication for the change which took place in political thought and in the political climate.[10] In 1559 Machiavelli's name had appeared on the *Index Librorum Prohibitorum* as one of the authors "quorum libriet scripta omnia prohibentur." Despite this prohibition his work evidently continued to be read, but it is difficult to establish precisely what influence he exerted because the political writers of the Counter Reformation[11] had to use caution and concealment when they discussed Machiavelli's ideas. When they openly mentioned his name we can be

---

Tasso's numerous poems celebrating Rome's restoration by Sixtus V are characteristic of a new attitude toward antiquity.

[9] Fritz Saxl, *Antike Goetter in der Spaetrenaissance* (Studien der Bibliothek Warburg, Vol. VIII; Leipzig, 1927), has directed attention to the anti-classical trend in the period of the Counter Reformation; see particularly pp. 26-33. Since then, these tendencies have been frequently mentioned in general works on the period, but we still need a systematic study of this phenomenon.

[10] Rodolfo de Mattei, *Dal Premachiavellismo all' Antimachiavellismo* (Florence, 1969), is the most recent comprehensive survey of the discussions which Machiavelli's ideas provoked in the Italian political literature of the Cinquecento and Seicento.

[11] The concept "Counter Reformation" is a very dubious one. Here and in the following it is used in a purely chronological sense, designating the period between 1560 and 1625.

sure that they were vehemently condemning the Florentine secretary. When they embarked on a serious discussion of his ideas, they concealed their interest in the writings of this dangerous and diabolical man by referring to him somewhat mysteriously as "autor discursum," or they take up arguments and issues of The Prince or the Discorsi without mentioning Machiavelli's name. They dealt with issues which were prevalent in Machiavelli's writings: the part which Fortune and Virtue played in the rise of Rome,[12] the risks involved in pursuing a "middle course,"[13] or the need for maintaining traditional institutions in newly acquired territories.[14] The weight of Machiavelli's theories hangs heavily over the political discussions of this later period.

However, acceptance of the conceptual framework which Machiavelli had created did not mean that the later political writers were his followers or that they approved his theories. The religious climate in which they lived permeated their thinking, and they felt aversion to what they considered to be Machiavelli's amorality. Their political society differed basically from that which had existed before foreign powers, particularly Spain, had gained control. Machiavelli's chief work had been commentaries on Livy who had told the story of the foundation and rise of the Roman republic. The political writers of the Counter Reformation regarded Tacitus as the "primo principe della politica";[15] they expressed their views in comments on Tacitus,[16] who had written about Rome in the times of the emperors. They lived in a world of states ruled by princes; they looked upon politics from above, from the point of view of the ruler, his psychology, the court, and the rivalries among courtiers. These writers assumed a hierarchical structure of government in which promotions to a higher bureaucratic rank were to proceed from grade to grade, not by jumps. They had only contempt for the groups that were at the bottom of the social hierarchy. Ammirato wrote: "the masses are a lazy beast that is unable to distinguish truth from falsehood,"[17] and Boccalini calls the people "a herd of sheep."[18] In contrast to Machiavelli, who had asserted that the people possessed a *virtú* which made them a basic force

[12] Scipione Ammirato, *Discursus in Cornelium Tacitum* (Helenapoli: Schönwetti, 1609), p. 325; Ammirato calls Machiavelli "autor discursum."

[13] Giovanni Botero, *The Reason of State [Ragione di Stato]*, trans. P. J. Waley and D. P. Waley (London, 1956), p. 50.

[14] *Ibid.*, p. 51.

[15] Traiano Boccalini, *Ragguagli di Parnaso* (Bari, 1948), Vol. III (a cura di Luigi Firpo), p. 152.

[16] For instance, Scipione Ammirato, see note 12 above.

[17] "Est vulgus otiosa bestia, quae verum a falso non discernit." Ammirato, *Discursus*, p. 353.

[18] "Gregge di pecore." Boccalini, *Ragguagli*, Vol. I, p. 232.

in political life, the writers of the Counter Reformation regarded princes and rulers alone as the dominating and controlling factors in political life. Politics became an object of cautious calculation dependent upon the intelligence of the prince and his advisers. It is hardly possible to find a statement more alien to Machiavelli's views than Botero's sentence: "Greatly daring plans are dangerous because after bold and spirited beginnings they run into difficulties and troubles and end in misery and despair."[19]

The extent to which these writers, despite their interest in the questions which Machiavelli had raised, were remote from Machiavelli's deepest concerns emerges from an analysis of what is usually regarded as their main contribution to the history of political thought: their discussion of the notions of "reason of state"[20] and of "balance of power."[21] Clearly these notions presupposed acceptance of a basic Machiavellian assumption—existence of a separation of morals and politics. Hesitatingly, and with many reservations, these writers admitted that the observance of the rules of morality might be a hindrance to political success. Boccalini, for instance, first declared that the doctrine of reason of state was in contradiction to the laws of God and man, but he then admitted that it provided useful rules for politics.[22] Like Machiavelli they recognized the determining role of interest in politics but they drew very different conclusions from this insight. In Machiavelli's view, conflict among states was unavoidable because each state was guided by its own interest and survival in these struggles for power required a dynamic and expansionist policy. The political writers of the later period tried to analyze precisely what the interests of the various European powers were. They had subtle discussions about the course of action prescribed by the interests of each state, and they then tried to gauge the reactions which the move of one power might produce among all others. The aim of such considerations was not to discover how a state might augment its power and expand; rather, these writers tried to show how counter forces could be organized and mobilized against aggression and to demonstrate the futility of any action that might disturb the existing situation. The purpose to which the

[19] Botero, *Reason of State*, p. 50.

[20] The classical historical treatment of the development of this idea in sixteenth-century Italy is Friedrich Meinecke's *Idee der Staatsräson in der Neueren Geschichte* (Munich and Berlin, 1924).

[21] One of the most delightful discussions of the idea of "balance of power" will be found in Boccalini, *Ragguagli*, Vol. III, pp. 34-44; the chapter is entitled "Pesa de' stati di tutti i principi e monarchie d'Europe fatta da Lorenzo de' Medici."

[22] Boccalini, *Ragguagli*, Vol. II, pp. 289-92. On p. 290: "legge utile agli stati, ma in tutto contraria alla legge d'Iddio e degli uomini."

notions of reason of state and balance of power were applied was the maintenance of the status quo.

There is a striking example showing how these basic notions led to conclusions widely different from those of Machiavelli; that is, the admiration which the later writers had for Venice. For Machiavelli there was only one model for the conduct of policy: the Roman republic. For Venice and its policy he had only contempt.[23] The political writers of the Counter Reformation regarded Venice as a model. In their eyes the Venetians had wisely learned to manage the balance of power and thereby maintained the status quo. The reasons why Venetian policy seemed so attractive to these advocates of a rational and cautious policy were succinctly stated by Boccalini: "The Venetians have as the ultimate purpose of their existence peace, the Roman Senate only knew war. . . . For the Venetians it is enough to have territorial possessions large enough to assure Venice its freedom. They want to have power not out of ambition to command others but out of their striving not to become the subject of others."[24]

The lengthy reports which the Venetian ambassadors submitted to the Senate on their return from a diplomatic mission have always been regarded as testimonies of Venetian political sagacity; they can also be viewed as practical application of the theories developed at that time. Like the political writers of the Counter Reformation, the Venetian ambassadors considered a hierarchically structured monarchy as the model of a well-organized society. Their reports focused on a description and analysis of the character of the ruler, of the court and its influential personalities, and on the relations of the country with other powers. They started from the principle that "princes do not take any action if not for their own interest,"[25] though they are aware that princely resentments and ambitions can sometimes overcome useful interests. They described in detail the relationships which existed between the state to which they

---

[23] See my article "Machiavelli e Venezia," *Lettere Italiane*, Vol. XXI (1969), pp. 389-98.

[24] ". . . i senatori veneziani per ultimo scopo del viver loro aveano la pace, ove il senato romano solo ebbe la guerra . . . a lei solo bastava di posseder tanto imperio, che dalle armi degl'inimici stranieri assicurasse la libertà veneziana, e che ella non amava la grandezza dello Stato per ambizion di comandare, ma per gloria di non servire." Boccalini, *Ragguagli*, Vol. I, p. 292.

[25] ". . . i principi non si sogliano muover se non per propri interessi . . ." This is the beginning of Francesco Contarini's report after his mission to Mantua, October 31, 1588. The following quotations come from the reports on Savoy from Simon Contarini, dated August 3, 1601, and the reports on Tuscany from Francesco Contarini, dated June 1589. All these reports were edited by Eugenio Albèri in Vol. V of the second series of the *Relazioni degli Ambasciatori Veneziani* (Florence, 1839-63).

had been accredited and all other states, particularly the great powers of France and Spain and their small neighbors on the Italian peninsula. Venetian ambassadors admired rulers who, on the basis of accurate information, acted rationally and according to their interests; they were antagonistic to Italian princes who aimed at expansion and caused disturbances. They praised the grand duke of Tuscany who "studied to maintain good feelings among the princes of Italy," and they considered "continua pace et felicissima tranquillita" as the highest goal that a prince might achieve.

Two different, even rather divergent tendencies, can be observed in Italian political thought of the late sixteenth and seventeenth centuries. One group of political thinkers and writers had as its aim the discovery of the rational basis of political actions. This group concluded that the guiding principle was interest, as determined by geography, economic reasons, and prestige. Concepts like balance of power and reason of state were crucial because they provided the conceptual framework for a rational analysis of politics. In the view of these writers, the prerequisite for successful political action was a correct evaluation of the motives of others. Qualities required in a statesman were cleverness, intelligence, and foresight, and his main concern was diplomacy. These writers believed in the possibility of limiting the impact of such irrational factors as force, energy, enthusiasm, and passion. The aim of a statesman ought to be to avoid situations in which irrational factors had been let loose, because events might slide out of control. In such situations the outcome was no longer in the hands of men but of Fortune. These writers were thinking in terms of the existing situation, of its correct evaluation, and its preservation. When they looked upon the Italian scene, they regarded the existence of many independent states as a permanent feature of Italian political life, and they did not envisage changes which might result in a federation among the Italian powers or which might produce a certain amount of unification. Considerations of nationalism, even in an embryonic form, had no place in the system of these writers.

While the attention of these writers remained firmly fixed to the ground so that they could not perceive any wider community beyond the small one in which they lived, there was another group of political thinkers whose thoughts dwelt so high above reality that they too could not distinguish the existence of a national entity. In histories of Italian political thought the chapters dealing with the century of the Counter Reformation have sometimes been entitled "Gli utopisti del seicento."[26]

---

[26] On this genre, see Luigi Firpo, *Lo Stato ideale della Controriforma* (Bari, 1957). See also Paul F. Grendler, *Critics of the Italian World* (Madison, 1969), which contains a very comprehensive bibliography, though the writers with whom Grendler deals precede the period with which we are concerned.

Indeed, the depiction of a utopia became in this time a favorite form for the expression of political ideas. Certainly, the utopia was not a new form of political literature. After its emergence in the ancient world it had been revived in the Renaissance and it had served well for the expression of basic beliefs of this period. The utopias of the Renaissance taught that if life were organized according to man's natural reason the miseries and vices of the present—hunger, violence, envy—would disappear. The fundamental assumptions of the most important utopia of the seventeenth century, of Campanella's *Città del Sole*, were in direct opposition to those of the Renaissance utopias.[27] If the latter were constructed on the basis of an inquiry into the needs and desires of rational man, Campanella intended to demonstrate the possibility of a society established in obedience to the principles of religion and to explain the institutional forms needed for the attainment of this goal. For Campanella the world had two centers: the sun, which represents warmth and love, and the earth, which represents coldness and hatred. The society which he envisaged would serve to establish the reign of the sun. In such a society the world would be subjected to unified rule. Campanella's *Città del Sole* embraced the entire world. Campanella, like most of his contemporaries had been deeply shaken by the discovery of the new world which had revealed the existence of human beings who had never heard of Christ and never received the word of God. He imagined for his sun city a religion which was very similar to Christianity but not identical with that known to Europe. The sun city would possess a hierarchical structure; its head would be a priest-king, and directly below him in the hierarchy were priests and knights, the priests taking care to organize the lives of all men in such a way that the spiritual ends for which society existed would be achieved. The knights would protect society against outside enemies. Activities connected with the material needs of men were of low value; agriculture found somewhat more favor with Campanella than industry or trade.

The description of particular arrangements like the recommendation of communal property had aroused the interest of later generations in Campanella's work. In our context it may be enough to point out the prevailing idea of Campanella's work: the transformation of life into a city of God and the return to a divinely inspired and controlled social order. Campanella's work exemplifies the particular character of the political utopias of this period: despite its unorthodox character the strength of

[27] Of the rich and detailed literature on Campanella, the chapter "Giordano Bruno and Tommaso Campanella" in Frances A. Yates, *Giordano Bruno and the Hermetic Tradition* (London, 1964) is particularly relevant for us.

the religious element made it a product of the intellectual climate of the Counter Reformation.

The utopian tendency of Italian political thought in this period has two sources. It was stimulated by the rejection of a present in which the Italian peninsula was divided into small powerless states and subjected to foreign rule. However, the utopian political thinkers refrained from a concrete analysis of this situation because they were also inspired by the second source, the universalism of the Church of the Counter Reformation which hoped to regain control of the entire world. We find in literature and art the same counter-reformatory spirit which inspired the utopianism of political thought. Tasso's *Gerusalemme Liberata* proclaims the necessity of a divinely ordered European society by giving a poetic image of its existence in the past. And Borromini's creation of space and distance that deceived the eye expresses the same longing for a flight from the restricting conditions of the present to a differently ordered world. Neither acceptance nor rejection of the present offered the possibility of finding any political relevance in the notion of a national entity.

Neglect of the national element in the political literature of Italy in the late sixteenth and seventeenth centuries is astounding because the political situation in Italy was such that national feelings and reactions might well have been natural.[28] The period which we are examining was a time of foreign rule in Italy, and close contacts with foreigners, especially when contacts are of a hostile nature, have always stimulated the growth of national consciousness. The conclusion we have reached—namely, that the political literature was dominated by issues which stood in the way of a development of national consciousness—must be supplemented by the consideration of the following question: Why did the customary reaction to foreign rule—an upsurge of national feeling—*not* take place in Italy?

It must be admitted that, in the middle of the sixteenth century, when the Italian wars, which had begun with the invasion of Charles VIII of France in 1494, ended with the establishment of Spanish rule in Italy, we find many expressions of regret about the "infelici tempi" into which the "misera Italia" had fallen.[29] However, in the following decades, when the Spanish rule had secured stability and tranquility, the contrast between the happy past and the miserable present began to become less

[28] Alessandro Visconti, *L'Italia nell'Epoca della Controriforma*, Vol. VI of Arnoldo Mondadori's *Storia d'Italia* (Milan, 19—) is the best-known general survey of the period. For an outstanding analysis of social developments, see Giuliano Procacci, *History of the Italian People*, trans. Anthony Paul (New York, 1970).

[29] See Grendler, *Critics of the Italian World*, chap. III, entitled "La Misera Italia."

sharply felt. If from time to time ideas of federation aimed at driving the foreigners out of Italy reawakened, they were sudden outbursts provoked by special circumstances rather than indications of a constantly present and steadily growing trend.[30]

Such sporadic expressions of national feeling were primarily connected with the moves of Savoy, the one power whose rulers continued to harbor expansionist aims. The duke of Savoy, the first Carlo Emmanuele, wrote propagandistic poems in which he used a nationalistic appeal against the Spanish governor of Milan:

> Havemo el sangue zentil et no vilan
> Credemo in Dio, et si semo cristiani
> Ma sopra il tutto boni Italiani.

When Carlo Emmanuele dared to challenge the Spanish power and became involved in war with Spain, writers praised him as the defender of Italian liberty and tried to spur the other Italian powers to support him. Tassoni wrote the *Filippiche* in which, in a style reminiscent of the last chapter of Machiavelli's *Prince*, he complained that Italy was ruled by princes not "of our blood nor used to Italian customs"[31] and admonished the other northern Italian states, particularly Venice and Modena, to join Savoy in the attempt to get rid of foreign domination. Fulvio Testi wrote his "Pianto d'Italia" and stanzas in honor of Carlo Emmanuele—poems for which, because of their anti-Spanish content, Testi had to pay with exile from the court of Modena. Again, in the next decade when the extinction of the Gonzaga dynasty in Mantua drew the opposing powers of Spain and France into the Italian scene, writers of pamphlets and poems tried to encourage the duke of Savoy to pursue a policy which would liberate Italy from foreign domination.

But these writers were propagandists who followed the directions of the ruler whom they served. They tried to influence the court circles in other Italian states. Though he had appealed to nationalism in the *Filippiche*, other writings of Tassoni praised the Spanish monarch as the great protector of peace in Italy; and Testi, the author of the *Pianto d'Italia*, could express views in favor of the French king. Without denying that these poets and writers took a certain amount of patriotic pride in the Italian past, a program of Italian federation had no pre-eminent or permanent place in their political thinking.

[30] For the facts, see Vittorio di Tocco, *Ideali d'Indipendenza in Italia durante la Preponderanza Spagnuola* (Messina, 1926), though the exclusive concentration on expressions of national feeling gives a somewhat distorted picture of the general character of political thought.

[31] ". . . prencipi del nostro sangue, nati ed allevati con i costumi nostri d'Italia." Alessandro Tassoni, *Prose Politiche e Morali*, ed. G. Rossi (Bari, 1930), p. 353.

Passages in the *Filippiche*, the most important, literarily, of these national appeals, indicate a reason why the reactions against foreign rule and manifestations of national feeling were sporadic and never widespread. The author of the *Filippiche* stated that his appeal was directed to princes and nobles but not to the Italian people; the masses, he said, were cowardly by nature and in them every true feeling of courage and honor was dead.[32] These words point to a rift in Italian society, placing the upper class group in opposition to peasants and townspeople; thus the upper classes looked upon the foreign rulers not only as enemies but also as fellow aristocrats, allies, and protectors.

The political developments in those areas directly under Spanish control, Milan in the north and Naples and Sicily in the south, show this clearly. Italy in the seventeenth century was a restless country.[33] The revolutions of 1647 in Palermo and Naples were not isolated events but open expressions of widespread discontent and misery. In the course of these outbreaks some anti-Spanish slogans appeared, but these revolts were not directed against foreign rule. The people, in what might be regarded as the traditional attitude of lower class discontent in pre-industrial society, appealed to the King against his incompetent officials. In Palermo as well as in Naples the feelings of the masses were expressed in the slogan, "Long live the King, and down with the taxes and the bad government." The revolutions in Palermo and Naples[34] represented conflicts among social groups, in which peasants and the urban masses, sometimes also the urban middle classes, stood against the nobility. In these regions agriculture barely provided a minimal subsistence for peasants with small holdings; when bad harvests brought misery and starvation, they moved into the mountains and became brigands or migrated to the towns and swelled the number of the poor. The middle classes of the towns shared the discontent of the lower classes because administrative centralization encroached upon their rights to self-government. The wars in which Spain was involved since the beginning of the revolt of the Netherlands aggravated these tensions because of the increasing amount of taxes imposed by the Spanish government on Naples and Sicily. Frequently urban and rural localities could procure these taxes only by tak-

[32] ". . . la plebe, vile di nascimento e di spirito, ha morto il senso a qualsivoglia pungente stimolo di valore e di onore." Tassoni, *Prose*, p. 343. See also notes 17 and 18 above.

[33] J. H. Elliott, "Revolts in the Spanish Monarchy," *Preconditions of Revolution in Early Modern Europe*, ed. Jack P. Greene (Baltimore, 1970), provides an up-to-date statement of the events in southern Italy. "A Note on Further Reading," pp. 129-30, lists the relevant literature.

[34] For events in Naples, Rosario Vilari's *La Rivolta Antispagnola a Napoli* (Bari, 1967), is of fundamental importance. But see also the relevant articles in the *New Cambridge Modern History* (Cambridge, 1970), Vol. IV.

ing loans from merchants, financiers, and rich landlords. The small wealthy group that provided these loans was compensated in various ways by the Spanish rulers. Members of this group received extension of their jurisdiction over the peasants on their estates. They were entrusted with the levying of taxes, and they were raised in social status. At the beginning of the seventeenth century the Neapolitan titled nobility numbered 133 families; this was three times the number of 1675. The upper social group, composed of old, landowning noble families as well as newly nobilitated men of affairs, supported the Spanish regime against the discontented peasants and the urban poor and middle classes in the revolutions of 1647. The members of this upper group allied themselves with the Spanish officers because they wanted to preserve the privileges and advantages which the Spanish rulers had granted them. Social and economic contrasts within the populace of southern Italy prevented any real national movement against foreign rulers and their rule.

Though different in detail, the developments in the Spanish possessions in northern Italy followed the same general pattern. In the Duchy of Milan[35] both absentee rulership and control by Spain were novel phenomena. Tension between the governor, who was the representative of the Spanish king and a member of the high Spanish nobility, and the indigenous administrators and the Senate, composed of the Milanese patriciate and members of the landowning nobility, was unavoidable. This struggle had national undertones. A particularly vehement conflict developed over the appointment of the president of the Senate. The governor wanted this post filled by a Spaniard, but the Senate, claimed the position for one of its members. The Senate won a significant victory, which assured that from this time on under the regime of Philip II an equilibrium would be maintained between the governor and the Senate, between the decision-making power of Spain and the administrative and executive functions of the native patriciate. But at the beginning of the seventeenth century this equilibrium was broken. The economic situation deteriorated, and these difficulties were compounded by Spanish demands for higher taxes and by the stationing of troops in the pivotal area of northern Italy. The members of the ruling group in the Duchy of Milan felt economically threatened; they were eager to keep the available benefices to themselves. Non-nobles were excluded from holding offices. Only those whose ancestors had been nobles one hundred years ago were recognized as members of the nobility. In order to reinforce the separation of the nobility from the rest of the population, nobles were not allowed to engage in commercial activities. Accordingly, they invested their money in landed estates. The rest of the population resented the

[35] For events in Milan, see Ugo Petronio, *Il Senato di Milano* (Rome, 1972).

exclusiveness of the Senate nobles, who began to rely on the Spanish government for protection of their rights and claims. As in Naples, an alliance between the Spanish king and the upper group in the Milanese Duchy was forged, and a national front against Spanish rule never gained much impetus.

The widening of the gap between the ruling group and the rest of the population was not limited to the Italian possessions of the Spanish crown; the same process can be observed in all the states of the Italian peninsula. In all of them a hierarchically organized society was created in imitation of the dominant power of Spain; a wealthy upper group began to acquire landed estates and to form a nobility just below—and allied with—the princely ruler.

The most important of these territorial states was the Medici Grand Duchy of Tuscany.[36] Its size, situation, and economic strength enabled the Grand Duke to maintain close contacts with France, which limited his dependence on Spain. Nevertheless, when the first Grand Duke Cosimo was buried, the funeral was organized on the pattern of that of Charles V. The solemn processions at religious festivals, at weddings, and at burials were arranged strictly according to rank. The bankers and merchants who had created the wealth and the greatness of Florence, even though they did not abandon commercial activities, became courtiers and finally marquisses and counts. While many features of the traditional system of government were maintained, the executive functions were carried out by a bureaucracy which no longer resided in the old seat of government, the Palazzo della Signoria, but in the extended structure of the Uffizi which Vasari built next to it. This bureaucracy worked as the willing instrument of the Grand Duke, who resided in the Palazzo Pitti, distant from and above the Florentine populace. The Florentines of the Renaissance claimed that their government was based on the ideas of liberty and equality. Even if one takes such notions with a grain of salt, it is evident that social ideas and ideals had almost been reversed.

The one republic which still existed in Italy, Venice, was no exception to the general process.[37] From the fifteenth century on, the circle of the policy-making group in Venice had steadily narrowed. The Great Council

[36] See the two articles by Samuel Berner, "Florentine Society in the Late Sixteenth and Early Seventeenth Centuries," *Studies in the Renaissance*, Vol. XVIII (1971), pp. 203-46, and "Florentine Political Thought in the Late Cinquecento," *Pensiero Politico*, Vol. III (1970), pp. 177-99. In a subsequent article, "The Florentine Patriciate in the Transition from Republic to Principato," *Studies in Medieval and Renaissance History*, Vol. IX (1972), pp. 3-15, Berner emphasizes that the Florentine patriciate continued commercial activities throughout the sixteenth century.

[37] The most recent work on Venice in this period is William J. Bouwsma, *Venice and the Defense of Republican Liberty* (Berkeley, 1968), though my interpretation of this period in Venetian history is very different from his.

had receded into the background *vis-à-vis* the numerically smaller Senate. The Senate had become an obedient instrument of the Collegio, and during the sixteenth century the Office of the Ten had taken the crucial political decisions into their hands. Its grasp of governmental functions had been so ruthless that it had aroused opposition, and in 1582 its powers were reduced. But this was a temporary setback. The Ten soon reasserted their authority. The fight with the papacy which led to the Interdict and in which Fra Paolo Sarpi was one of the intellectual leaders was part of this development. It was not, as Protestants then and later were inclined to believe, a fight for freedom against authoritarianism. It was a jurisdictional struggle. The Venetian government refused all restrictions in its control over any of the inhabitants of the city; nor would it allow the pope to interfere in its conduct of foreign policy. As Sarpi argued,[38] if Venice wanted to exert, as it had in the past, "il fondamento principale d'ogni imperio e dominio," namely, "la vera religione e pietà," it had to keep the right to determine where churches and monasteries were to be built "per poter ricerverle e sostentarle" and had to be able to punish criminal ecclesiastics. The sovereignty of the state, and that meant particularly the unrestricted power of a small ruling group, was the issue.

If in the various Italian states power became concentrated in the hands of a small upper group dependent on and allied with princely rulers, the focal point of attention of all those who determined Italian politics was the individual state. The preservation of territorial independence and maintenance of the status quo became their guiding principle: they were not inclined to see far beyond the social body in which they lived. If political thinkers and writers regarded "peace and tranquility" to be the highest political values, they might have overlooked or disregarded the basic importance of the element of power to which Machiavelli had directed attention. But they remained close to—and reflected—the concrete needs and aims of the rulers of their time.

In the emergence of a hierarchically structured society and of an aristocratic upper group monopolizing the positions of power, the Spanish conflicts and the religious climate of the time both played their part. But these trends were reinforced by a third factor to which we have already alluded, namely, to the economic difficulties which beset Italy at this time.[39] In the evolution of the economic situation, two different stages

[38] The following quotations come from Sarpi's "Considerazioni sopra le Censure della Santità di Papa Paoli V," easily available in Paolo Sarpi, *Opere*, ed. G. Cozzi and L. Cozzi (Milano, 1969).

[39] See Carlo M. Cippola, "The Economic Decline of Italy," *Crisis and Change in Venetian Economy*, ed. Brian Pullan (London, 1968); this is the revised and translated version of an article which appeared first in *The Economic History Review*, 2nd series, Vol. V (1952).

can be distinguished. Throughout the sixteenth and the beginning of the seventeenth century, Italian economic decline was relative rather than absolute. First English and then Dutch ships appeared in the Mediterranean and took over portions of the trade with the east which previously had been an Italian monopoly. Moreover, Italian manufactured goods, especially textiles, now encountered serious competition in the European market, particularly since, because of the maintenance of traditional guild regulations, the prices of their goods remained high. Nevertheless, the Italian economic decline was slow and gradual; and the wealth that Italians had accumulated assured that Italian bankers would remain the financiers of Europe. In the 1720s, however, *pari passu* with general European trends, economic decline accelerated and economic stagnation set in. As it happens in such situations, the prices for industrial goods began to fall more sharply than those for agricultural goods. Foodstuffs remained in demand inside and outside Italy, and consequently, whenever possible, a shift from manufacture to agriculture took place. If the Spanish government had favored the feudal nobility in Naples and Sicily for political reasons, this social group now acquired a strengthened economic basis as well. In southern Italy an almost medieval feudalism not only survived but became the dominant force of social life. The existence of a variety of independent states had created sharp divisions, but added to this was an even deeper-reaching division: the contrast between south and north, if not well defined at that time, at least became so great that it has remained a problem for Italian national thought and national consciousness until the present.

Antonio Gramsci noted that the role the middle class played in other countries was taken over by the intellectuals in Italian political development. This observation was primarily aimed at developments in later centuries. However, the ground for what happened later was laid in the period with which we deal.

The crucial fact to which we have frequently directed attention was that Italy was the center of the Counter Reformation and remained tied to the Roman Catholic Church. In countries that broke with the pope, church and state were brought together in a close relationship in which the same person—the prince—was the head of both church and state. However, a complex and often tense situation fraught with the possibility of friction arose in Roman Catholic countries where a papal lordship, extending its claims and interests over the entire world, encountered a prince, primarily or exclusively concerned with a strictly limited territory and everyday problems. In the jurisdictional conflict between Venice and the papacy, which placed Venice from 1605 to 1607 under the Interdict, this tension came into the open. But in the other Italian states, the princely rulers were equally concerned with preventing the papacy and the Church from encroaching on what they considered the secular spheres of their government. The decades after the Council of Trent were full of disputes between the Church and the Italian rulers. For example, the Farneses insisted on the right to tax the clergy; and the Senate in Milan denied Carlo Borromeo the right to call laymen before ecclesiastical tribunals.

The struggle of the princes against the far-reaching claims of the papacy presupposed preservation of a certain amount of intellectual freedom. The rulers would not go so far as to protect heretics or those with views which clashed directly with the teaching of the Church; yet the princes had a strong interest in furthering intellectual activities free from Church interference. They would be particularly pleased if the artists or scholars whom they protected would glorify their deeds or those of their ancestors. But beyond that, princely patronage of art and literature, of scholarship and science, had the advantage of providing defense by the secular government against papal dogmatism. Princely patronage demanded a reorganization of intellectual activities. Italian rulers could no longer rely on the universities in which the traditional spirit of the Middle Ages was still dominant and which had become stagnant in Italy. The new centers of intellectual exchange were the academies established all over Italy, some of them on the initiative of a ruler or prince, some of them by the scholars or scientists themselves.[40] In addition to the most well known, such as the academies of the Lincei in Rome or the Cimento or the Crusca in Florence, there were the Otiosi, the Intronati, the Erranti, and the Dogliosi. The ironical flavor in these names indicates that these academies included not only professionals but also dilletantes. The nobility and the wealthier men of the bourgeoisie formed an audience for scholarly writings and scientific discoveries. Achievements in these fields became known all over Italy, and princes and towns competed for the services of distinguished *literati* who moved from one town to another or from one court to another.

Precondition for the creation of a wider audience was the use of the vernacular language, thereby giving an impetus to the movement for the use of the Italian language which Bembo had initiated in the first half of the sixteenth century. But dangers were perceived in the use of the vernacular for literary and scholarly purposes. It might lead to carelessness in the use of language and to its disintegration into a variety of

---

[40] For the establishment of academies in general, see Visconti, *L'Italia*, pp. 567-70, and in particular, Stillman Drake, "The Academia dei Lincei," *Galileo Studies* (Ann Arbor, 1970).

dialects. This issue gave importance to the Crusca and its great enterprise, the Dictionary of the Italian Language. The academicians of the
Crusca tried to establish a code for good linguistic usage. As Florentines
they were convinced that the language in which the great Florentine
writers of the Trecento had written ought to be the model—though their
concept of the "buon secolo" soon became extended to the entire Renaissance. They were strict: they were not willing to recognize Tasso's vo-
cabulary as a model because he introduced innovations that went beyond
Ariosto. The decision against Tasso did not stick, however, and the
academicians of the Trusca reluctantly gave Tasso a solemn reception
when he visited Florence.

This was the intellectual world in which Galileo moved, from Pisa to
Padua, to Venice, to Florence, and to Rome, and to which, in spite of his
uniquie scientific genius, he remained bound in a variety of ways. His
Dialogo sopra i due Massimi Sistemi del Mondo was addressed to the
groups assembled in the academies—to the "discreto lettore," the interested laymen; accordingly it was written in Italian.[41] In the Foreword,
Galileo stated that he wanted "foreign nations to realize that Italians
understood this matter as much as the Transalpine (*oltramontana*) mind
could imagine."[42] These words express pride in the cultural achievements
and cultural mission of Italy; they testify to the strength of the feeling
that, though a political organization encompassing the entire Italian
peninsula did not exist, there was, below or above the external forms of a
political and social bond, a bond comprised of culture, language, and
literature. The contribution this period made to the development of Italian national consciousness lies in the firm establishment of the view that
an outstanding and singular Italian culture existed.

This view drew its justification and strength from the achievements of
the Renaissance. The basic assumption of the Crusca—that the language
of the Renaissance was to serve as the model of the Italian language—is a
demonstration of the paradigmatic importance which the Renaissance
had gained in the Italian mind. Previously the classical world has been
regarded as the only existing golden age. Now the Renaissance took its
place next to the golden age of a remote past. The ancient world un-
avoidably became somewhat diminished in value. We have mentioned

---

[41] Like Angeli di Costanzo, who, in his *Istoria del Regno di Napoli*, Vol. I, p. xliii,
stated: "Ho voluto scriverla in lingua comune Italiana, a tal che possaessere letta e
intesa da tutti"; it does not matter that it will not come "a notizia di nazioni esterne."

[42] ". . . mostrare alle nazioni forestieri, che di questa materia se ne sa tanto in
Italia, e particolarmente in Roma, quanto possa mai averne imaginato la diligenza
oltramontana . . ." From our point of view, the fact that this foreword was written in
compliance with ecclesiastical requests is irrelevant.

that in the period of the Counter Reformation the veneration of the classical world was regarded as a danger for Christianity; the recognition of the normative nature of the Renaissance had the same effect of weakening the hold of the classical world over the minds of men. Because the attainments of the Renaissance had proved that a new cultural highpoint could be reached even in the post-classical world, it also became evident that one needed not only to look backward toward a golden age of the past but that one could also look forward to a golden age in the future. All this involved a change in the conceptual scheme which had been placed on the past. Italy began to emerge from its subordination to the greatness of Rome. In the work of the historians this new image of Italy, which implied a recognition of a past national history, began to take shape.

If this essay had dealt exclusively with the development of historiography it might have been entitled "From Guicciardini to Muratori." Insofar as the development of historiography is concerned, the period with which we are dealing is an *inter regnum*. This *inter regnum* began after the composition of the greatest historical work of the Renaissance, Guicciardini's *History of Italy*, which was also the last such work in which Italy was presented as an independent entity in European politics. And it ended with the publication of the great documentaries which embraced the whole of Italy.

The names Guicciardini and Muratori also suggest something of the changes in concepts and methods that took place during this period. Until the emergence of modern critical history in the nineteenth century, and perhaps even up to the present, there have always been two different types of historical works: histories written by participants, by statesmen-historians, and learned histories composed by professors or professional *literati*. Guicciardini was a statesman-historian, one of the greatest; it is indicative of Italian political decadence that no other Italian statesmen-historians emerged in the later centuries. Muratori is the outstanding example of a learned historian who absorbed and perfected that which took place since the sixteenth century.

No Italian writer or scholar played a significant part in the development which brought about new critical methods to the writing of history and to the awareness of the distinctiveness and the differences among historical periods. The major advances in historical criticism and understanding of the sixteenth century were primarily the work of French scholars;[43] their work was largely the result of applying legal and philo-

[43] See Donald Kelley, *Foundations of Modern Historical Scholarship, Language, Law and History in the French Renaissance* (New York, 1970).

logical methods of research to wider historical problems. In Italy legal history contributed little toward the formation of a new historical outlook. In countries with a strong central power, research in legal history helped promote national feeling, while in Italy legal studies had the opposite effect—that of deepening divisions by reinforcing the claims of the various rulers against each other. Philology and archaeology, however, greatly influenced the Italian view of the past. Classical scholarship revealed the particular conditions of life in ancient Rome, showed the connection between religion and institutions, and stressed the distance which separated the classical world from later times. The Romans became different people rather than patterns for all times.

The most impressive and most striking testimony of an attitude which divided ancient Rome from Italy was the medieval history of Italy which Sigonius published under the title *De regno Italiae*. Sigonius distinguished two forms of government in Italy: the *imperium* and the *regnum*.[44] The *imperium*, which of course is the Roman Empire, had been exhaustively studied and was well known; but the *regnum*, which originally had been introduced by foreign people—the Langobards, the Franks, and the Germans—was almost unknown and needed to be investigated. In Sigonius the interest of the philologist was combined with that of a legal historian. Clearly, the legal historian's concern with institutional continuity aroused his interest in the chronicles and documents of medieval Italy and resulted in his description of the gradual development of Italy as an individual and autonomous social body. Sigonius' story ended with the liberation of the Italian towns from foreign rule in the thirteenth century, that is, with the beginning of the Renaissance.

Sigonius' treatment of Italian history is based on presuppositions which deserve to be spelled out. The highpoint to which his description leads is the Renaissance, but he considers the Renaissance as the outcome of a long development of which the liberation from the subjection to foreign powers and the emergence of a society of free republics formed an integral part. The Renaissance therefore is not the sudden, miraculous rebirth of a golden age long past. The process which brought it forward and from which it emerged at a felicitous moment began long ago in earlier times and will continue into the future. The Renaissance was not a mirror of Rome but an Italian creation, and Italy lived before and after the Renaissance. What Sigonius shows is the connection between the pride in the cultural achievements of the Renaissance, which permeated

---

[44] See particularly the programmatic statements at the beginning of the first book of Caroli Sigonii, *Historiarum De Regno Italiae Libri Quindecim* . . . (Venice, 1574; Frankfurt, 1591).

the thinking of the intellectuals, the *literati*, and the growth of national consciousness.

As a sequel to Sigonius' history, Muratori (who opens the period of Italian intellectual history which led to the Risorgimento) initiated his own work. For Muratori, Sigonius with his *De Regno Italiae* was the first to lay "the ground on which later generations could build."[45] It was in the spirit of Sigonius that Muratori in his Preface to the *Rerum Italicarum Scriptores* wrote those moving sentences in which awareness of a sad Italian past is combined with hopes for the future: "It is a sign of arrogance and of insolence, even of ingratitude, to limit oneself to a knowledge of Italy when she was victorious and triumphant, and to turn away from her, when she is defeated and subjected to foreign nations. Italy remains our mother whether victorious or defeated, and it is the duty of her sons to acknowledge the obligation which they owe her, in good and in evil times."[46]

It is certainly true that scholars of other countries also delved into the dark ages in search of the roots of their national past. But the efforts that were made in Italy gained their importance from the fact that the notion of a national culture and of a national past was maintained in a period when outside forces—Spain, the Church, a shift to the Atlantic—impinged upon the social, economic, and intellectual foundations of Italian life. This might explain why the guardians of national consciousness in this period were a small group of scholars and *literati*. This might also help to explain the political leadership which intellectuals have held more recently after the Italian nation was formed.

[45] ". . . primi magnifica aedificia a fundamentis erexere quibus posteri quippe deinde superstruere potuerunt." Ludovico Muratori, "Vita Caroli Sigonii," *Raccolta delle Opere Minori* (Naples, 1757-64), Vol. XVII, p. 16.

[46] "È, infatti di un animo troppo orgoglioso e schififtoso, dirò anzi ingrato, voler conoscere l'Italia soltanto vittoriosa e trionfante, e distogliere lo guardo da lei vinta e assoggettata dalle nazioni stranieri. E sempre la madre nostra, nell'uno e nell'altro stato e spetta sopratutto ai figli conoscerne non meno la buone che l'aversa fortuna."

CHAPTER II

FRANCE

WILLIAM F. CHURCH

The concept of patriotism, as it was understood in France during the early-modern period, has been variously defined. When analyzing the elements of this amorphous but potent intellectual phenomenon, French historians call attention to the leadership and mystique of the monarchy, its relatively early acquisition of dominion over a large, compact territory, and the massive body of tradition that stemmed from cumulative historical experience. In addition, such factors as language, religion, and even an incipient idea of race are frequently mentioned. Surely the best definition holds that French patriotic sentiment in the early-modern era was a collective mentality which was related in varying degrees to all these factors and was significant in that it gave a sense of common identity to the inhabitants of the relatively disparate cities, towns, and provinces that constituted the realm of France. Of the various contributory influences, however, there is no doubt that the monarchy occupied a position of primary importance. French patriotism was a product of centuries of common historical experience, chiefly under the leadership of the crown, and continued to be so molded during the early-modern period. Indeed, the policies, purposes, and values of the monarchy provided by far the most important ideological bonds that ultimately united the severely fragmented elements of French society whose immediate concerns were more often those of family, social order, city, and province. And because so much of the power and prestige of the monarchy stemmed from tradition, and because an awareness of tradition depended upon a sense of history, it would seem appropriate to examine the works of early-modern historians when tracing the evolution of French patriotism during the Age of Absolutism.

During the late nineteenth and early twentieth centuries, when French liberalism and nationalism were in full vigor, French writers differed sharply concerning the contributions of the seventeenth century to the growth of patriotic sentiment. In fact, many liberals found it impossible to believe that absolutism and patriotism could coincide at all. Thus Alphonse Aulard wrote that under Louis XIV the *patrie* was absorbed by the king, and insisted that this rendered patriotism impossible because there could be no *patrie* without liberty.[1] The very able Henri Hauser even went so far as to assert that in the seventeenth century "the idea of nationality was eclipsed by the idea of the state"[2] and that the concept of the *patrie* "resulted from the dissociation of the idea of the king from the idea of the nation."[3] And in another context, Paul Hazard maintained that the writers of the Age of Absolutism "had not yet analyzed the content of the word *patrie*. They did not even have a clear concept of what the nation might be."[4] Such statements could have been made only if their authors believed the modern, libertarian concept of nationhood to be prerequisite to any true patriotism.

On the other hand, the same period witnessed the appearance of a very different viewpoint, notably in the writings of such authors as Taine and Renan in the nineteenth century and Johannet in the twentieth.[5] These scholars maintained that French patriotism had grown slowly but surely over the centuries and that before the Revolution the monarchy was its chief source, inspiration, and focal point. Such factors as territory, language, religion, and race may have contributed to the matrix, but these were merely *conditioning* elements whereas the monarchy was the molder, the dynamic force. It was the monarchy that built the realm by assembling its disparate territories and merging them into a single whole. Only the monarchy was capable of controlling the dissident elements in the complex social structure and directing them toward higher ends. Only the monarchy provided leadership for the common good, defended the realm against all enemies, and enjoyed centuries of glorious tradition. And only the monarchy among governmental agencies was the object of quasi-religious reverence. Only the monarchy, therefore, could have been the focal point of the spirit of patriotism, for without the monarchy neither nation nor patriotic sentiment could have existed. The interpretation obviously has some merit, but it ignores major differences in the

---

[1] *Le Patriotisme français de la Renaissance à la Révolution* (Paris, 1916), pp. 23-30.

[2] *Le Principe des nationalités: Ses Origines historiques* (Paris, 1916), p. 19.

[3] *La Modernité au XVIe siècle* (Paris, 1930), p. 77.

[4] *La Crise de la conscience européenne* (Paris, 1935), Vol. II, p. 218.

[5] Hippolyte A. Taine, *L'Ancien régime* (Paris, 1896), pp. 14-16. Ernest Renan, *Qu'est-ce qu'une nation?* (Conférence faite en Sorbonne, le 11 mars, 1870), *Œuvres complètes* (Paris, 1947), Vol. I, pp. 887-906, and *La Réforme intellectuelle et morale de la France* (1871), *ibid.*, Vol. I, pp. 323-407. René Johannet, *Le Principe des nationalités* (Paris, 1923).

relationship between the crown and French patriotism in the sixteenth, seventeenth, and eighteenth centuries.

In fact, a survey of the relationship between the French monarchy and patriotic sentiment demonstrates that the latter fluctuated significantly according to the fortunes, policies, and repute of the monarchy itself. During the sixteenth century, French patriotism assumed the form of a broadly based idealization of many elements of the life of the nation, the monarchy included. But in the seventeenth century, as part of the massive swing toward absolutism, this sentiment was more and more centered in the crown, even the person of the king. With the triumph of absolutism, both in theory and in fact, it was in the nature of things that the sovereign should symbolize the nation and become the focal point of patriotic sentiment. In the last years of Louis XIV's reign, however, a revulsion began to be expressed toward the equation of patriotism with loyalty to the Bourbon dynasty, and the way was opened for the much more comprehensive views of the Enlightenment which grounded patriotism in the life of the people and eventually led to the massive, virile nationalism of the French Revolution. In this essay, I propose to trace the rise and fall of this crown-centered version of French patriotism during the Age of Absolutism, chiefly as it was reflected in the writings of contemporary historians.

During the sixteenth century, French writers became increasingly conscious of the fact that life in the realm of France was acquiring a distinct set of characteristics, and their pride in things French grew accordingly. This sentiment found a solid factual basis in the relatively advanced organization of the French state. Its territorial foundation was firmly established, and its legal and institutional structure provided France with a functioning constitution, that is, a body of laws and institutions which determined the rights, privileges, and status of all segments of the population, their relations with the crown, and the monarch's rightful sphere of competence. The elements of this governmental system were outlined and praised by such disparate authors as Claude de Seyssel, Charles de Grassaille, and a large school of jurists who wrote during the second half of the century. Equally significant was the fact that the French wing of the Roman Catholic Church, the greatest international corporation in Europe, was institutionally identified with the realm through massive application of the principles of Gallicanism. The French state system was therefore acquiring a degree of maturity, and because many phases of French life were structured by customs, laws, and institutions that had developed over centuries of time, French patriotism acquired a strongly traditionalist orientation.

In parallel fashion, the heroic traditions of the French monarchy re-

ceived new emphasis following the successful termination of the wars of
the fifteenth century and the inspired work of Jeanne d'Arc, and the
experiences of the sixteenth century served merely to confirm the necessity of monarchical rule and to exalt its accompanying ideology. Furthermore, France as an element in the European community of states acquired a new significance for her more patriotic writers who revelled in
praising her qualities and characteristics—her natural resources, products, climate, favorable geographical position, and above all her people—
as uniquely favored among the states of Europe. And the whole was
capped with praise for the higher phases of French civilization when
such writers as Joachim Du Bellay and Pierre Ronsard celebrated the
glories of France in verse and had much to do with establishing the
tradition of French literature in the vernacular—an important cultural
addition to French patriotic awareness. Increasingly, distinctive and superior qualities were associated with things French, and life in the *patrie*
was accordingly prized by a growing number of loyal subjects of the
crown.

The very existence of this patriotic awareness, however, was jeopard-
ized during the latter part of the century by the chaos and disruption of
the Wars of Religion. Indeed, the nature of the struggle was such that the
monarchy and even the independence of the realm hung in the balance.
This threat to the very survival of the *patrie* called forth one of the most
massive outbursts of patriotic writing in the early-modern period. Its
authors, who were chiefly jurists, administrators, and historians, including
many with expertise in all three areas, looked increasingly to the French
past, studied the legal and institutional development of the French state,
and further expanded burgeoning French patriotism. Though their writings necessarily expressed their professional orientation, they may be
regarded as speaking for a large body of opinion.

This very extensive literature assumed a variety of forms and was
chiefly inspired by a desire to study and defend, even to glorify, the
traditions and greatness of the French nation and its monarchy. When
threatened with the loss of all that the *patrie* stood for, French writers
instinctively began to appreciate its wealth of significance in their lives
and found new meanings and values in its history, development, and
ideals. Before the outbreak of civil war, political writers had been content
to describe the French governmental system as it stood, but during the
second half of the century historical-mindedness sharply increased. The
result was extensive study of the French monarchy in its historical setting, combined with idealization of all that it represented in the life of
the realm. Such dissimilar authors as Charondas Le Caron, René Chop-
pin, Guy Coquille, Louis Le Roy, Pierre de Belloy, and Jean Bodin pro-

duced a wide variety of works in which they analyzed and defended the monarchical establishment as indispensable to the life of the *patrie*. All found the key to French greatness in the leadership of the monarchy, and all supported their views with extensive use of historical materials.

At the same time, a new and vital element was added to French patriotism by the revival of interest in the civic virtue of the ancient Roman Stoics. The best example of this is to be found in the works of the jurist and philosopher, Guillaume Du Vair. A supporter of the *politiques*, Du Vair extensively urged his countrymen to remain loyal to the monarchy and to exert all efforts to preserve civil society during the height of the power of the Catholic League. In his *Traité de la constance et consolation ès calamitez publiques*, he lamented the disasters that the League had inflicted upon Paris, his native city, the capital of the most beautiful realm on earth and the common temple of all France. He expressed his beliefs through the mouth of the dying de Thou, who exhorted his countrymen to remember that they were French, to go down with their weapons in hand, and to sacrifice all for the defense of the state and the preservation of the *patrie*. This ancient brand of civic virtue continued to be a potent element of French patriotism throughout the early-modern period.

The professional historians among this group of writers were especially active in searching out the traditions and achievements that contributed to the renown of France, and they extended their patriotism to the broader aspects of the life of the nation even while focusing on the monarchy. The Du Tillet brothers compiled immense collections of data about the events during various reigns, the kings' titles, honors, marriages, acquisitions, laws, and all manner of things concerning the *police* of the realm. The viewpoint of many was well expressed by the royal historiographer, Du Haillan, in his *Histoire de France*, which he dedicated to Henry III:

> History is necessary to all sorts of men, to the young, the old, the lowly, to princes and to subjects. . . . It is a faithful and bold counsellor of princes . . . and accurately indicates their duties, clearly showing them the faults of their predecessors. . . . It shows the subjects their duties toward their prince, renders private persons worthy of empires, and incites great courage for large and small enterprises by promises of glory and praise (which are the accompaniments of death for those who die honorably). . . . Now, Sire, if ever there was a written history filled with beautiful teachings proper to all conditions of persons, both princes and private individuals (and I do not discount the Greeks and the Romans), the history of France is that which has the most, for either the love of my rulers and my *patrie* must deceive me, [or] all that might be desired, beheld and sought as examples of religion,

devotion, justice, prudence, modesty, clemency, valiance, boldness, good
faith, and all other virtues are to be found in the kings, your predecessors,
in their ministers, both lay and ecclesiastical, and in their constructions,
laws, regulations, rules, ordinances, edicts and other actions.[6]

Du Haillan continued with a long recital of the contributions of various
French kings to the building of France.

An even broader concept of French patriotism was presented by
Etienne Pasquier whose very influential *Recherches de France* covered
the entire range of French history. Topical in arrangement, the work
discusses an incredible variety of elements of the life of the nation, what
he called the "beautiful histories" that constitute the "annals of France."
Pasquier placed great emphasis upon the contributions of the ancient
Gauls to French development, thereby taking his place in the growing
debate concerning the respective significance of the Gauls and the Franks
to French civilization. His fundamental approach to French history was
institutional, and he made this the basic framework within which he
analyzed innumerable components of the historical record. His considerable skepticism concerning many legends in the French past reflected a
strong dash of historical Pyrrhonism and a concern for adequate documentation which placed him among the most advanced historians of his
time. Pasquier's burning interest in the French past reflected an intense
patriotism, and he repeatedly expressed the fear that he was witnessing
the dissolution of the contributions of centuries to the growth of the
patrie. And like Du Ha;llan, Pasquier claimed that his work was en-
lightening to both the ruler and his subjects.

It is evident that sixteenth-century French historians held to a broadly
based concept of French patriotism. Though much of it was focused
upon and symbolized by the monarchy, a significant part of it was
grounded in values and experiences that were associated with the nation
at large. There even appeared momentarily a theory of contract between
the king and the nation, regulating the rights and duties of both parties
and providing for sanctions in case of offense by either. This was put
forward by important Huguenot writers and later by spokesmen for the
Catholic League, but the position rapidly declined during the reign of
Henry IV, which opened the Age of Absolutism.

The triumph of Henry IV and the crown-centered patriotism of the
politiques caused the monarch to become the focal point of French patriotism more than ever before. To illustrate the enormous, spontaneous
enthusiasm for the first Bourbon king of France, we might cite a great

---

[6] Bernard Girard Du Haillan, *Histoire de France* (Paris, 1576), Dedicatory epistle,
no pagination.

variety of works ranging from Pierre Pithou's "Harangue d'Aubray" in the *Satyre Menippée* to the *Question royale* of Jean Duvergier de Hauranne, later the famous Abbé de Saint-Cyran. But for our purposes, three outstanding historians will suffice: André Duchesne, Jacques Auguste de Thou, and Jérôme Bignon. Duchesne has been called the father of the history of France because of his many publications and innovations in the field, especially the very extensive documentation he provided. His works dealt chiefly with the history of France, many noble houses, aspects of ecclesiastical history, and bibliography. He amply demonstrated the nature and extent of his patriotism in two companion volumes which he published in the year 1609: *Les Antiquitez et recherches de la grandeur et maiesté des Roys de France* and *Les Antiquitez et recherches des villes, chasteaux, et places plus remarquables de toute la France*. The first is typical of the extravagant praise of monarchy prevalent in the period; emphasis is given to the superior nobility of the French kings, their precedence over all others, and their religious qualities, valor, power, justice, clemency, and majesty—all of which is presented in superlatives. The second, on the other hand, extends this idealization to the realm at large. After making the customary statements concerning the favors that God had bestowed upon France—fertile soil, favorable climate, central position in Europe, and a large, energetic population—he turns to an examination of her cities. Beginning with Paris, Duchesne lauds the capital as the most honored city in the world, describes the attributes of her three divisions (the *ville, cité, université*), praises the great beauty of her many churches, details her bridges, gates, royal palaces, noble residences, courts, etc., and then moves on to Chartres, Blois, and the many other centers of note. Duchesne's loyalty and enthusiasm for his *patrie*, which he defines in the broadest terms, are evident throughout, as is his pride in all that he associates with life in his divinely favored France.

Equally important, though different, was Jacques Auguste de Thou, an outstanding jurist, leader of the *politique* faction, and personal friend of both Henry III and Henry IV. His *Historia sui temporis* is a monument of historical scholarship and expresses well the growing view of the French monarchy. In his dedication of the work to Henry IV, de Thou took occasion to express his thoughts concerning the monarchy and the *patrie*:

> It is a maxim that I have received through hereditary tradition, not only from my father who was thoroughly upright and very attached to the old religion, but also from my grandfather and great-grandfather, that after that which I owe to God, nothing should be more dear and sacred to me than the love and respect owed to my *patrie*, and that I should cause all other considerations to yield to this. I have brought this sentiment into the

administration of affairs, being persuaded, according to the thoughts of the ancients, that the *patrie* is a second divinity, that its laws come from God, and that those who violate them, with whatever specious pretext of religion they may cover themselves, are sacrilegious and parracide.[7]

And de Thou urged Henry IV, to whom he said, "we owe our lives, our *patrie* and our goods,"[8] to continue his enlightened rule by maintaining the peace he had won and by enforcing the law, the true guarantee of the liberty of his subjects.

Even more famous during his lifetime was the celebrated jurist, Jérôme Bignon, who was also historian, administrator, and councilor of state, a man generally learned in all fields. His book, *De l'Excellence des Roys, et du Royaume de France*, published in 1610, was an answer to an earlier tract by Diego Valdez, who claimed precedence for the Spanish kings over all others. In his dedicatory epistle to Henry IV, Bignon stated his theme as follows:

I have sought to show the truth of the matter, not only to cause the French to understand what they are, their advantages and how much they should esteem and revere their kings, true creatures of heaven, the dearest children of God and the first-born of his Church, but also to show foreign peoples, who recognize Your Majesty for the greatest and worthiest of all who hold scepters, that it [your precedence] is as much by right of your crown as by your own virtue and valor. For this purpose, I have described the riches and the horn of plenty of this flourishing realm, indicated its treasures, and shown all its features. I have touched upon the praiseworthy qualities and perfection of its people, their valiance and warlike virtue, and how they have carried their victorious arms to all corners of the habitable earth; their understanding and skill in the arts and sciences, capable of anything. [I have also placed] in evidence the prerogatives of your crown, its antiquity and nobility, its indubitable possession of first rank through so many centuries, with witnesses and recognitions of all peoples. For the same reason, I have treated the kings, your predecessors, described many fine expeditions, courageous acts and heroic, divine virtues, and shown that none has been greater nor equal in justice, piety, and arms. Among these worthy souls, Sire, Your Majesty is given special attention not only for having retained first rank by your invincible arms but also for raising it higher than any of your predecessors. France, formerly conqueror of the world, has seen herself thrown into an abyss of miseries, her beauty tarnished by the malignity of foreigners and some of her children parricides. You have raised her from her fall, by superhuman strength drawn her back from the precipice on which she was outstretched, and placed her before the eyes of

[7] Jacques Auguste de Thou, *Histoire universelle* (French translation) (The Hague, 1733), Vol. I, p. lvi.
[8] *Ibid.*, p. lvii.

the world which sees her now triumphant because of you. She recognizes you as a new founder, true father and pious king. It is through you, Sire, that we live and enjoy our comforts. It is to you that we owe our peace, our liberty, and our lives.[9]

Such a statement literally breathes the spirit of spontaneous patriotism that was not only centered in the crown during Henry IV's reign but also comprehended the nation at large. Bignon devoted the first book of his treatise to France (her physical assets, riches, products, great cities, and the like); the second to the French people (the valor of both the Franks and the Gauls, and French accomplishments in letters, sciences, and the arts); and the third and fourth books to the prerogatives and achievements of all three races of French kings. Belief in the precedence of the kings of France over all other rulers was essential to the crown-centered patriotism of the period and paralleled the conviction that France was superior to the other states of Europe. Bignon believed that the surest means of establishing the pre-eminence of France's first Bourbon king was to stress not only his many crucial achievements in rebuilding France but also the greatness and glories of the realm that he ruled. This union of loyalties to king and nation was the principal characteristic of French patriotism in this key moment of its evolution.

The predominance of this crown-centered but broadly conceived patriotism was briefly challenged by the weakness of the regency of Marie de Medici, which laid bare the extensive social fragmentation and intense factionalism that continued to prevail beneath the surface and sharply qualified any all-embracing loyalty to the monarchy and the *patrie*. For the moment, loyalty to family, clientele, social estate, and province seemed to take precedence over loyalty to the monarchy. Cardinal Richelieu subsequently attempted to remedy the situation with his massive program of state-building, which sought both to discipline major elements of French society and to render loyalty to the crown the supreme loyalty of all Frenchmen regardless of their status, privileges, or competing interests. So extensive were his efforts in state-building that the great majority of dynamic developments in the period stemmed from royal policy—a fact that further identified the fortunes of the monarchy and the *patrie*. Though Richelieu's policies largely stemmed from his personal initiatives, they had Louis XIII's approval and were therefore *ipso facto* just and beneficial to the state, according to the proponents of absolutism. Richelieu did not hesitate to equate opposition to his policies with *lèse-majesté* and, in fact, made wide and unprecedented use of this charge against his opponents and critics. His constant theme was that the nobles,

[9] Dedicatory epistle, no pagination.

dévots, and others who opposed his efforts were *mal affectionnés à la France.* Obedience, he and his apologists maintained, was owed by all Frenchmen both as subjects of the crown and as good Christians, since both religion and political allegiance decreed unquestioning subordination to the divinely appointed ruler of Christian France. Such was his version of crown-centered patriotism. Opposition remained latent and powerful, as was later demonstrated in the Fronde, but the critics looked backward in time to a partly imaginary concept of limited monarchy and contributed nothing to the growth of French patriotism.

Beginning with Cardinal Richelieu's ministry and extending throughout the remainder of the century, French historical literature rapidly acquired certain characteristics that were appropriate to the Age of Absolutism. Not unexpectedly, the governing authorities made concerted efforts to create an official history of France centered upon the achievements of her kings. As Robert Flint wrote some eighty years ago, "the muse of history was gradually enticed and constrained to become a lady of the court."[10] For this purpose, governmental archives were assembled and made available to historians who wrote under official patronage and produced crown-centered works. These writings should not be regarded as mere specious propaganda in the guise of history. Instead they were straightforward and significant expositions of the predominant political conceptions of this thoroughly ideological age. Though the monarchical ideal owed much to previous centuries, it continued to crystallize in this highly self-conscious period of French history along lines that were thought to possess universal validity.

The absolutists and rationalists had much in common with the classicists of the period, since all believed they had discovered a conceptual framework that not only accorded with the natural order of things but also reflected and emphasized the highest elements of human nature, and they were correspondingly insistent in promulgating the respective virtues and necessity of their ideals. Likewise the elitism of these positions is readily apparent and clearly reflects the thoroughly aristocratic mentality of the age. Partly for these reasons, French patriotism during the Age of Absolutism never developed the virulent emotional qualities and hatreds that were so characteristic of nineteenth-century nationalism. Even during the wars of the seventeenth century, the governing aristocracies of Europe and their spokesmen maintained their fundamental respect for each other. During Cardinal Richelieu's ministry, two of his ablest supporters among the *literati,* Guez de Balzac and François de La Mothe le

---

[10] *Historical Philosophy in France and French Belgium and Switzerland* (New York, 1894), p. 203.

Vayer, wrote that though the Spanish were perennial aggressors and the natural enemies of France, they had many admirable virtues and should be given their due.[11] And later, during the wars of Louis XIV, French policies were defended on the basis of their essential justice and necessity to the defense of French interests, that is, universal principles rather than any animosity between peoples. The element of racism in French patriotism appeared only in discussions of the relative merits and significance of the Franks and the Gauls, but this debate centered upon the roles of both generic groups in various periods of French history and their respective contributions to French civilization. It was this reasoned, elitist, cultural patriotism that was set forth in French historical writing during the Age of Absolutism.

On the other hand, the ideological characteristics of the period go far to explain the major weakness of seventeenth-century historical writing, namely, the almost complete separation of historical erudition from history as literature. The great desire for authority and fixed canons in all fields of learning, plus the broad ideological pressures of the *grand siècle*, caused the relativism and Pyrrhonism of the most advanced sixteenth-century historians to be rejected. Instead, history was now valued as a vehicle of orthodoxy, a source of moral teaching and lessons by example. For this purpose historical accuracy was unnecessary and might even be detrimental. It should be noted that historical scholarship continued to advance in the seventeenth century, especially in the works by members of religious orders. Most notable were the Benedictines of the Congregation of St. Maur who produced a phenomenal number of publications, but these were devoted chiefly to religious and ecclesiastical history, local history, and the techniques of research, and they had little influence upon the broader histories of France. Many lay historians limited their efforts to collecting and editing documents, thus avoiding all ideologically sensitive issues. There was also no lack of analyses of the requirements of good history. Studies on this theme were published by Jean de Silhon, La Mothe le Vayer, the Abbé de Saint-Réal, and the Jesuit Father Rapin, among others, but their works contain little more than the usual exhortations concerning accuracy, matters of style, the study of personalities, historical judgments, and the like, and had little practical influence. The great majority of French historians who wrote on the history of the monarchy preferred to compose works that possessed certain literary

---

[11] Guez de Balzac, *Le Prince* (Paris, 1631), chap. 19. La Mothe le Vayer, *Discours de la contrariété d'humeurs qui se trouve entre certaines nations, et singulièrement entre la française et l'espagnole, traduit de l'Italien de Fabricio Campolini, Veronais* (Paris, 1636). This is not a translation from the Italian but La Mothe le Vayer's own work.

qualities and that would attract a wide audience, while making little use of the best available erudition. The result was a series of histories that were far from notable for their scholarship and accuracy but retain a certain value as expressions of contemporary opinion.

All these developments made their appearance during Cardinal Richelieu's ministry. As part of his campaign to influence public opinion, he gathered about himself and subsidized a remarkable group of historians, secretaries, and archivists. The latter included the highly regarded Pierre Dupuy and Théodore Godefroy, who devoted years to compiling and cataloguing documents and records of the French monarchy. Richelieu used these extensively to support his claims to border territories, notably Lorraine. His secretaries were charged with the composition of an official history of his ministry, and their efforts eventually produced the lengthy compilation that is known as Richelieu's *Mémoires*. Among the several historians of the group, by far the most important was Scipion Dupleix, who used documents that were made available to him by the Cardinal and presented the official view of the French past. As royal historiographer, Dupleix was admirably fitted for this task, since he was a militant Catholic and proponent of absolutism. His voluminous works, which he regularly submitted to Richelieu for approval before publication, cover the entire history of the French monarchy from Pharamond onward, and are full of detail and commentary. Nowhere is patriotism as such discussed, but his message is clear, to wit, that France owed all to her kings. His early works are replete with elaborate expositions of the divine right of kings, equal to anything written later by Bossuet. After recounting each reign, Dupleix reviews its contributions and successes, always from the standpoint of effective rule, and he makes it clear that one of his favorites was Louis XI. In his very important *Histoire de Louis le Juste*, which Richelieu undoubtedly read and approved, Dupleix lists the King's greatest accomplishments as (1) defeating the Huguenots, ensuring their obedience, and destroying the factions of great nobles, (2) extending the frontiers of the realm fort he first time since Charlemagne, and (3) rendering royal authority absolutely sovereign, thereby assuring peace in the state and reducing high and low to obedience. Though Dupleix attributed these achievements to the King, he made it clear that they were inspired by Richelieu, to whom he devoted the most extravagant praise, even claiming that his policies were divinely inspired and *ipso facto* just. The equation between patriotism and loyalty to the crown was complete.

The fact that some French historians preserved their spirit of independence even while receiving official patronage is illustrated by the career of François Eudes de Mézeray, whose works were considerably more successful than those of Dupleix. Mézeray fully subscribed to the view that history should come alive as good literature, even at the expense of factual accuracy, and he readily made use of such devices as placing fictitious speeches in the mouths of major historical figures after the manner of Livy and repeating legends that the sixteenth-century historians had destroyed. His *Histoire de France depuis Pharamond* and his *Abrégé chronologique* cover the whole of French history to the death of Henry IV, and their success during Mazarin's ministry brought him an appointment as royal historiographer with the usual pension. Mézeray's works retained their popularity for more than a century and were, in fact, the most widely read general histories of France composed during the Age of Absolutism. The reasons for this are not far to seek. Graced by a highly readable style, they also contain many pithy comments concerning men and events, and Mézeray did not hesitate to question the actions of men in high places when their policies seemed contrary to the general good. There was, however, no question of Mézeray's loyalty to the crown, and his great pride in the achievements of his countrymen is evident throughout his writings. He consistently condemned all civil wars and rebellions, especially those of the sixteenth century, and he never tired of glorying in the renown of French arms in Europe and the Near East and their many victories over their neighbors, especially the Spanish. His loyalism and his patriotism were therefore entirely sound. On the other hand, his spirit of independence was manifest in his readiness to criticize many abuses by the royal administration, such as the inequities of the *taille*, the *gabelle*, and venality of office, and he repeatedly deplored the misery of the peasantry. He may even have published several Mazarinades during the Fronde under a pseudonym, de Sandricourt. In any case, his criticisms of the royal administration eventually came to the attention of Colbert who informed him that he had not been made a royal historiographer in order to examine long-established practices. Mézeray yielded to pressure and prepared a second edition of his *Abrégé chronologique* under the supervision of one of Colbert's agents, but Colbert remained dissatisfied and had Mézeray's pension suppressed. Though his loyalty to the monarchy and his patriotism were unquestioned, his criticism of abuses was sufficient to arouse the wrath of the authorities in this ideological age.

With the beginning of Louis XIV's personal reign in 1661, crown-, or rather, king-centered patriotism truly came into its own. Because of well-known foreign and domestic developments, royal absolutism was at least tacitly accepted by the entire population. It was a period when Jacques Bossuet, speaking symbolically, could write: "All the state is in the person of the prince. In him is the power; in him is the will of all the people; to him alone it belongs to cause all to conduce to the public good. The service that is owed the prince must be conjoined with that which is owed the state, as things inseparable."[12] Louis XIV and a large majority of his contemporaries justified this equation of service to the king and the state by insisting upon the identity of the interests of both, for, as Louis XIV himself wrote, ". . . when the state is one's concern, one works for oneself. The good of the one gives rise to the glory of the other."[13] Thus, loyalties to the king and the *patrie* were quite fused. This king-centered patriotism continued to be predominant throughout the reign and was questioned only in its final years.

Because Louis XIV and his ministers fully believed that France under the Sun King stood as the heir to the ages, they upheld the tradition-oriented patriotism of their time and the parallel assumption that a knowledge of the past enlightened men's understanding of the present. Louis XIV also believed that an acquaintance with great events and the actions of illustrious men in earlier periods would inspire him to similar heroic deeds,[14] and he was carefully nurtured in the tradition of the greatness of his grandfather, Henry IV, concerning whom his preceptor, Hardouin de Péréfixe, Bishop of Rodez, wrote a biography for this express purpose.[15] Because of the strong traditionalism of the age and the vogue of historical scholarship in the culture of the period, the royal administration looked with favor upon historical study and extensively subsidized many experts in the field. Nevertheless, the ideological pressures of the Age of Absolutism militated against extensive inquiry into the political aspects of the French past—precisely the area of historians' greatest interest and concern. Analysis of earlier events and official policies opened the door to judgment of kings and ministers by all and sundry, and risked the dissemination of unconventional views among the subjects. So strong were official canons in this thoroughly ideological age that the governing authorities were reluctant to encourage the examination of anything related to the mysteries of state and even in earlier periods, as Mézeray learned to his chagrin. Scholarly inquiry, however, was relatively safe if devoted to limited subjects in remote periods, and this type of historical research continued to progress throughout the period. But it is noteworthy that no effort was made to utilize its findings in the writing of a general history of France until very late in the reign. Absolutism in action was conducive to scholarship but deterred the free expression of scholarly opinion.

[12] *Politique tirée de l'Ecriture sainte, Œuvres* (Paris, 1828), Vol. XVI, p. 246.
[13] *Mémoires de Louis XIV*, ed. C. Dreyss (Paris, 1860), Vol. II, p. 520.
[14] *Ibid.*, p. 96.
[15] *Histoire du Roy Henry le Grand* (Paris, 1661).

This dichotomy in official attitudes during the reign of Louis XIV is clearly reflected in the relations between the governing authorities and historical study. In fact, leading figures in the royal administration seemed torn between a desire to use history to glorify the king and his state and a reluctance to do so because of the nature and requirements of the discipline. In the early discussions between Colbert and Chapelain regarding various projects that might be undertaken for the glorification of the king—projects which later led to the creation of many officially sponsored academies—Chapelain approved the use of panegyrics, paintings, equestrian statues, triumphal arches, tapestries, etc., but rejected history because an expert historian must explain the ruler's motives and have access to official archives. This would be impossible during the life of the reigning prince without revealing state secrets. And Chapelain expressed doubt that any living historian could be found with the requisite knowledge of national interests, political ideology, war, chronology, geography, and the customs of nations. Slightly later, when tentative plans were formulated for a general academy of letters, arts, and sciences, historical study was included but was quickly dropped because it would touch upon too many sensitive issues. True, a number of ranking historians received *gratifications* during Colbert's ministry. These included Denis Godefroy for his editions of earlier works and studies of the royal prerogatives; the Valois brothers for their editions of the ancient classics and documents of the first two races of French kings; Le Laboreur and Sainte-Marthe for their studies of geneology and heraldry; Baluze as Colbert's librarian and collector of manuscripts; and, temporarily, Mézeray. Boileau and Racine were commissioned to write an official history of the reign, but their efforts proved abortive. The *Académie des Inscriptions et Médailles* pursued certain types of historical research, but its main publication late in the reign was the sumptuous *Histoire métallique* of Louis XIV, a pictorial tribute to the king's glory. When Torcy secured approval of the creation of an *Académie politique* in the Louvre in 1711, one of its purposes was to investigate the mass of documents in official French archives and to compose a history of the Sun King's long and glorious reign, but this objective was never fulfilled. These various activities indicate a continuing interest in historical scholarship, French traditions, and the greatness of her monarch, but made only limited contributions to knowledge of the French past and reflected rather than augmented the prevailing king-centered patriotism.

Almost all the histories of any part of the French national tradition that were produced during the first generation of Louis XIV's personal reign were thoroughly uncritical, laudatory accounts, unworthy of extensive examination. At most, they may be valued as reiterations of the prevailing ideology of French greatness and destiny. Probably the ablest was the *Histoire de Louis XIV, depuis la mort du Cardinal Mazarin en 1661 jusqu'à la paix de Nimègue en 1667*,[16] by Paul Pellisson, the King's secretary and one of the compilers of his so-called *Mémoires*. Pellisson's writings faithfully mirror the official position on a host of considerations, but his history is more sober and less extravagant in praising the monarch than many other writings of the period, including some of his own. Throughout his very factual narrative, his message is clear: that in the short space of seventeen years France had risen from dependence upon foreign allies to successful termination of a war against all her neighbors. Thus, he says, if France continues at this pinnacle of greatness, its origins and growth will be shown by his history; whereas if she proves unable to maintain her preponderance, a comparison of the events in his narrative with later events will indicate the causes of her decline and appropriate remedies. Again appears the prevailing sentiment that France under the Sun King had benefited from the work of earlier rulers but had now risen to unprecedented heights of greatness and glory. France was not only the heir to the ages but superior to them. The brand of patriotism that is manifest in such works is evident.

No comprehensive history of France was produced during Louis XIV's personal reign until the publication of Father Daniel's three-volume *Histoire de France* in 1713. The work covers the whole of French history to 1610 and is a landmark in French historical science for several reasons. Most important is the fact that it was one of the first in which the author sought to build his narrative upon massive historical erudition. A member of the Jesuit order, Father Daniel fully benefited from the extensive scholarship in ecclesiastical circles to which he added his own insights. In a lengthy preface, he explains that truth, the major objective of the historian, may be achieved only by reliance upon proven sources, and he lists those that he used, notably the publications of Duchesne and other *érudits* but, more importantly, the many manuscript collections to which he had access. In addition, he continues, the historian must adopt a certain skeptical attitude when developing his interpretations: "In this respect, that which is called historical Pyrrhonism may be permitted."[17] Daniel's break with the uncritical methods of Dupleix, Mézeray, and many others is patent. He severely criticized Mézeray's repetition of known fables and use of fictitious speeches, and he even insisted that the historian must maintain his detachment when recounting events in which he was emotionally involved, such as wars for religious causes and mat-

---

[16] This work was not published until 1749.
[17] *Histoire de France* (Paris, 1755), Vol. I, Preface, p. lv.

ters affecting his *patrie*. He was explicit, however, concerning the historian's proper choice of materials, and in this he clearly reflected the bias of his own age:

> The history of a realm or a nation has for its object the prince and the state; this is the focal point to which all should lead and be related, and individuals should have no place in it except insofar as they are related to the one or the other.[18]

The result was a sober, well-documented, and not very colorful narrative which traces the growth of the French state by examining the policies and contributions of her kings. Within this framework, Daniel found ample opportunity to exhibit his enthusiasm for monarchy and its great work in the building of the *patrie*.

Father Daniel's history is also notable for the great praise he lavished upon what he and many of his contemporaries regarded as one of the most significant achievements of Louis XIV's enlightened rule, namely, French contributions to European civilization. The founding of many new academies for the arts and sciences under royal sponsorship, plus extensive patronage of scholars and artists both in France and abroad, lent credence to this view. This pride in French cultural attainments at a time when French canons in letters and the arts were influential far beyond her borders was surely a vital contribution of the period to French patriotic sentiment. One of the best contemporary expositions of its appears not in the body of Daniel's history but in its dedicatory epistle to Louis XIV. After praising the King's conquests, wise government, extirpation of heresy, and the brilliance of his court, Daniel continues:

> I need not mention the many public works and royal residences so superbly built, so delicately ornamented, so richly furnished; so many cities, some fortified, others constructed on the coast or on the frontiers. You alone, I dare say . . . with the most exact truth, you alone have done more in this way than all your predecessors together since the foundation of the monarchy. . . . It is equally well known, Sire, that during no reign of your predecessors, and I also dare say of no other king or emperor, has one seen the fine arts brought to such a high point of perfection as in yours. Painting, sculpture and architecture have rediscovered, by means of your support, that pure, simple and noble style of learned antiquity, and antiquity itself would find much to admire in the endless productions of the several arts, the thousand marvels that France has produced in our time, which their inventiveness and skill never achieved.
>
> All the sciences from the least to the greatest have been brought to so high a point that decadence is henceforth more to be feared than perfection is to

[18] *Ibid.*, p. xcvi.

be hoped for. There remains nothing to be desired in France in the composition of works of the mind and those in which the sciences are treated. Purity of language, subtlety of touch, delicacy and solidity of thought, naturalness in style, order, method, clarity—all this is present and felt, is praised and applauded according to its merits, wherever it appears.

Poetry, eloquence in the pulpit and at the bar never reached greater heights. In medicine, anatomy, chemistry, physics, astronomy and mathematics, discoveries have been made that were unforeseen in earlier centuries. To conclude with an area in which your reign has been most outstanding, has military art on land and sea ever been brought to such a high point of perfection? . . .

I said at the beginning, Sire, that it was not a panegyric that I present to you, but mere reflections on the reigns of your predecessors and on your own. I believe that I have fully justified one [reflection] that contains all the others, to wit, that among the reigns which furnish the most beautiful materials for the history of France, there is none in which are to be found as many unusual and extraordinary things that render a reign memorable and worthy of admiration by posterity as in yours. But from this historical reflection there follows another; it is that so many marvelous things united in a single reign necessarily presume an assemblage in the prince of virtues and royal qualities, of which it would be difficult to cite many examples.[19]

It is hardly necessary to add that Father Daniel anticipated in a most remarkable way Voltaire's later treatment of the period as an age of cultural climax in his *Siècle de Louis XIV*.

During the second generation of Louis XIV's personal reign, the Jesuits had important reasons for continuing to praise the king, but the increasingly disastrous course of events in both foreign and domestic affairs gave rise to widespread criticism of royal policies by a large number of informed, responsible observers. The major reasons for this changed view of absolutism in action were undoubtedly the chronic warfare of the period and the resultant sacrifices that were required of the French people. The War of the Spanish Succession brought the dissident movement to a head, with important consequences for the evolution of French patriotism. Not only was this war the longest, costliest, and most calamitous of the reign, but for the first time the King's objectives were extensively questioned. The origin of the war was patently dynastic, and a growing number of high-ranking Frenchmen came to believe that the possible advantages of union of France and Spain under the Bourbons would be of no benefit to France proper. For the first time in the reign, the absolutistic maxims that the good of the king was that of the nation and that royal policies were *ipso facto* just were extensively challenged,

[19] *Ibid.*, pp. xlviii-li.

because national interest and the power and prestige of the Bourbon dynasty seemed clearly to diverge and not to justify the requisite sacrifices by the French nation. The all-important consequence was that many concerned, patriotic Frenchmen found it increasingly difficult to adhere to the unquestioning, king-centered patriotism that had predominated in France since 1661.

Many instances can be cited. In 1700, the great Vauban wrote that the territorial ambitions of France should be limited by the Alps, the Pyrenees, Switzerland, and the two seas; in 1706 he composed a peace plan, calling upon Louis XIV to renounce the entire Spanish heritage except for certain border territories to the north and east, which would signify that the King was acting in the interests of France rather than those of his grandson. Vauban's cousin, Boisguillebert, presented himself in his very critical *Factum de la France*, of 1707, as the advocate of the French people against misguided official policies. Archbishop Fénelon's extensive denunciations of Louis XIV's foreign policy are too well known to bear repeating. And from different standpoints, Saint-Simon and Boulainvilliers sought a variety of social and institutional changes for the purpose of easing France's plight. The patriotism of all these men was thoroughly intact. They had no quarrel with monarchy as such, but they did not hesitate to denounce royal policies which they found increasingly detrimental to the French nation.

The most important French historian to take this stand was Michel Levassor, a French Huguenot who wrote from the haven of exile in Holland and England. The purpose of his ten-volume *Histoire du règne de Louis XIII*, which was published in Amsterdam between 1700 and 1711, was to show the origins in his own day of French tyranny over Europe, and he treated Louis XIII and Richelieu accordingly. In his preface, he also made clear his attitude toward Louis XIV. Levassor vehemently claimed to be a loyal French patriot who loved his country. However, he continued:

Because I am of a nation, should I wish that it become the master of all Europe? Should I approve the inordinate ambition of the prince who governs it? Should I praise my compatriots for working to forge the chains with which they are crushed? . . . By a strange reversal of language and reason, in France a man is well disposed toward the state if he evinces I know not what ridiculous zeal for the king's power. Does this mean that the king alone is the entire state? The two are very different. The king is the person who is responsible for preserving the people and ensuring that they are as happy as each man's position permits. . . . To love the state and the *patrie* is to wish all advantages for it with such fervor that one is willing to sacrifice his life to gain them for it. . . . In this sense it is pleasant and upright to die for one's *patrie*. But to love what is called in France the power and glory of the king is to work for the establishment of tyranny. . . . What is understood by the word 'tyranny'? The government of those who seek only their own advantage. . . . Let those who are born for slavery call me a seditious writer if they wish. It is thus that they now speak of those who still love liberty in a land where it is completely extinguished. I am not troubled by it.[20]

No such statement was openly published in France before 1715, and the few French histories that did appear continued to praise the Sun King. There is evidence, however, that during the later years of the reign there was a rapidly developing crisis of confidence in contemporary history. Growing rationalism and skepticism, as in the works of Pierre Bayle, whetted appetites for objective truth, and this in turn increased dissatisfaction with the divorce of erudition from history as literature and with official pressures for conformity. The Abbé Du Bos, though willing to write propaganda tracts for the royal administration, was also developing views that required the fusion of historical erudition and narrative. Father Daniel's *Histoire de France*, which was published in 1713, was hailed by the expert Jean Le Clerc as the first of its kind because of its scholarship, and it is noteworthy that Daniel's discussion of his sources and methodology represented a marked advance over all similar treatments of these matters in the seventeenth century. Also in 1713, Lenglet du Fresnoy published his lengthy *Méthode pour étudier l'histoire*, in which he examined all elements of the discipline, asserted that there were no good histories of Louis XIII or Louis XIV, and made extensive suggestions for combining historical scholarship and exposition. In 1714, Archbishop Fénelon wrote a long letter to the French Academy concerning its various activities, stressed the need of good history, and elaborated upon its characteristics and requirements, emphasizing accuracy and objectivity. Dissatisfaction with the genre and the uses to which it had been put is evident.

Official pressures for conformity were as strong as before, however, as is indicated by the fate of Nicholas Fréret, who, upon admission to the *Académie des Inscriptions* in 1714, had the temerity to challenge publicly the accepted view of the origin of the Franks. Instead of presenting the Franks as a distinct Germanic race who conquered the Gauls and allowed them to retain all governmental rights and therefore their freedom (as indicated by their name, *franc*), Fréret argued that the Franks were not a separate race but a mere league of tribes that had been formed in southern Germany in the third century A.D. He also asserted that the word "*franc*" did not originally mean "free" but was closer to the Latin

---

[20] Preface, no pagination.

"*ferox*" or proud. For this indiscretion, Fréret spent four months in the Bastille early in 1715.

In view of this, it is not surprising that historians greeted the establishment of the regency immediately after the death of Louis XIV with an outburst of enthusiasm for liberty. To cite but one example, the jurist-historian Henri Philippe de Limiers, in his *Histoire du règne de Louis XIV* which was published in Amsterdam in 1717, wrote that it had been impossible to write accurate history of either Louis XIII or Louis XIV before the latter disappeared from the scene. He was of the opinion that the Regent would permit the truth to be published, provided that it was presented without malignity or artifice. De Limiers may have exaggerated the beneficence of the new regime, but his statement indicates much concerning the changed attitude of writers toward the ideology and practices of absolutism.

Meanwhile the shift of emphasis within French patriotism was gathering momentum. Within three months after Louis XIV's death, the procureur general, Henri-François Daguesseau, gave his famous oration on the love of one's country before the assembled Parlement of Paris. After duly praising the deceased and asserting that love of country should bind king and people together, he posed this question:

> But can it not be said that this love, almost natural to men, this virtue that we instinctively know and praise through reason, and should even follow because of interest, . . . is like a foreign plant in monarchies, does not grow easily, and whose precious fruit is enjoyed only in republics?[21]

After recalling the merits of Roman civic virtue, Daguesseau emphasized the risks to patriotism in monarchies:

> Unburdened of the care and deprived of the honor of government, they [the people] regard the fate of the state as [that of] a vessel which drifts according to the desires of its master and is preserved or perishes only for him. If his navigation is successful, we blindly rely upon the pilot who guides us. If an unforeseen storm awakens us, it excites in us only impotent desires and reckless complaints which often serve merely to trouble him who holds the tiller. . . . As zeal for the public good is extinguished in our hearts, so desire for our personal interests is aroused. It becomes our law, our sovereign, our *patrie*. We know no citizens but those whose favors we desire and whose enmity we fear. The rest are only a foreign and almost an enemy nation. . . . Where, then, do we find our *patrie*? Personal interest betrays it; indolence neglects it; vain philosophy condemns it. What a strange spectacle for a man of public conscience! A great realm and no *patrie*; a numerous people and almost no citizens. . . .

[21] Henri-François Daguesseau, *Œuvres* (Paris, 1759), Vol. I, p. 208.

A magnanimous spirit easily divests itself of personal interests. But there must at least be the pleasant and virtuous expectation of procuring the public good, which completely absorbs him and animates, sustains, and fortifies him for the honorable but laborious service of his *patrie*.

What consolation he finds, therefore, when because of singular good fortune or rather superior wisdom, he sees develop before his eyes a new order of government, almost a new *patrie*, which seems a certain omen of public felicity! Then love of the *patrie* is kindled in all hearts; the bonds of society are strengthened; the citizens find a *patrie* and the *patrie* its citizens. Everyone begins to understand that his personal good depends upon the public good, and what is even more comforting, the mind that governs us is not less convinced that the welfare of the sovereign depends upon the welfare of the people.[22]

Daguesseau, like de Limiers, concluded by praising the Regent's policies and objectives.

Though Daguesseau did not say so explicitly, his message was that the day had arrived when the ruler should place the interests of his subjects above his own. Only within this relationship could there be a true *patrie* of responsible, upright citizens. This position evolved in due course to the predominant stance of the Enlightenment: that the *patrie* was an association of free men who enjoyed the benefits of organized society under a government whose sole purpose was to increase their happiness and well-being. In point of fact, Daguesseau was ahead of his time in taking this position, but it was merely logical progression from his subjects-centered patriotism to that of the Revolution.

In sum, then, French patriotism during the Age of Absolutism underwent a series of significant changes. Throughout the early-modern period it followed the general evolution of French political ideology. The broadly conceived patriotism of the late sixteenth century developed into a king-centered view under Louis XIV, only to undergo reorientation late in the reign away from the exclusive role of the sovereign and once more toward the needs and interests of the nation. The historians in whose works these trends are visible reflected more than contributed to this evolution, partly because of the limitations of the genre and partly because of the circumstances under which much history was written. Initially, the growth of crown-centered patriotism during the Wars of Religion reached its climax under Henry IV, and in his reign there occurred the most genuine, spontaneous outburst of patriotic writings of the entire Age of Absolutism. For a brief moment, king and nation together were the objects of enthusiasm, loyalty, and pride, and the works in which these sentiments were expressed were the more authentic because a large majority were unsolicited. Under Richelieu and Louis XIV, however,

[22] *Ibid.*, pp. 208-13.

official history became more and more the order of the day. France had previously had royal historiographers, but never had there been such a concerted effort to make use of French history to the advantage of the crown. Because of the strong orientation of the French government and society toward tradition, historians were regularly called upon to contribute their talents to the support of the regime, and they duly reinterpreted the French past in the light of the greatness of the current monarch. Their works may have reflected the crown-centered patriotism of the time, but they suffered from the limitations of official sponsorship in an ideological age and failed to incorporate the contributions of the most advanced historical erudition. The histories that were published under Richelieu's aegis may have influenced opinion in his favor, at least by their number, but even this limited success was denied Louis XIV because of the failure of his regime to produce many such works. On the other hand, pride in French cultural achievements was undoubtedly strong during Louis XIV's reign, but this rarely appeared in historical treatises because most of them were limited to narrating the rise of French political and military preponderance in Europe.

In the final decades of Louis XIV's reign, French patriotism once more underwent an important metamorphosis when many otherwise loyal observers began to question royal policies because of the apparent divergence of the interests of the Bourbon dynasty from those of the nation. This was but the first step in the gradual elimination of the king from the concept of the *patrie*. With the disappearance of Louis XIV and effective absolutism, the thinkers of the Enlightenment placed primary emphasis upon the people and developed the idea that the *patrie* was a community of free citizens who enjoyed maximum liberty and happiness and whose government should be devoted to that end. In time, the monarchy was associated with despotism and was ruled out of the *patrie*, which was seen simply as a nation of patriots. Thus we finally reach the view, expressed by Professors Aulard and Hauser, that the concept of the *patrie* "resulted from the dissociation of the idea of the king from the idea of the nation," and that there could be no *patrie* without liberty. Actually, we know that France had been built by her kings and that they had therefore contributed mightily to the growth of French patriotism. But with the entry of France into the modern era, this was forgotten as the nation and its spokesmen moved beyond the spectrum of the Age of Absolutism.

SUGGESTED READING

Aulard, Alphonse. *Le Patriotisme français de la Renaissance à la Révolution.* Paris, 1916.
Barzun, Jacques. *The French Race.* New York, 1932.

Delavaud, Louis. "Quelques Collaborateurs de Richelieu," *Rapports et notices sur l'édition des Mémoires du Cardinal de Richelieu*. Paris, 1907-14. Vol. II, pp. 45-308.

Dupont-Ferrier, Gustave. "Le Sens des mots 'patria' et 'patrie' en France au moyen âge et jusqu'au début du XVIIe siècle," *Revue historique*, Vol. CLXXXVIII (1940), pp. 89-104.

Evans, Wilfred H. *L'Historien Mézeray et la conception de l'histoire en France au XVIIe siècle*. Paris, 1930.

Flint, Robert. *Historical Philosophy in France and French Belgium and Switzerland*. New York, 1894.

Godechot, Jacques. "Nation, patrie, nationalisme et patriotisme en France au XVIIIe siècle," *Annales historiques de la Révolution française*, Vol. XLIII (1971), pp. 481-501.

Hauser, Henri. *Le Principe des nationalités: Ses Origines historiques*. Paris, 1916.

Huppert, George. *The Idea of Perfect History: Historical Erudition and Historical Philosophy in Renaissance France*. Urbana, Illinois, 1970.

Johannet, René. *Le Principe des nationalités*. Rev. ed. Paris, 1923.

Kelley, Donald R. *Foundations of Modern Historical Scholarship: Language, Law, and History in the French Renaissance*. New York, 1970.

Klaits, Joseph A. *Diplomacy and Public Opinion: Louis XIV, Colbert de Torcy and French War Propaganda, 1700-1713*. Unpublished thesis, University of Minnesota, 1970.

Kohn, Hans. *The Idea of Nationalism*. New York, 1944.

Leclercq, Henri. *Mabillon*. 2 vols. Paris, 1953-57.

Lestocquoy, Jean. *Histoire du patriotisme en France*. Paris, 1968.

Lombard, Alfred. *L'Abbé Du Bos*. Paris, 1913.

Marcou, François L. *Etude sur la vie et les œuvres de Pellisson*. Paris, 1859.

Monnier, Francis. *Le Chancelier D'Aguesseau*. Paris, 1860.

Monod, Gabriel. "Du Progrès des études historiques en France depuis le XVIe siècle," *Revue historique*, Vol. I (1876), pp. 5-38.

Renan, Ernest. "Qu'est-ce qu'une nation?" *Œuvres complètes*. Paris, 1947. Vol. I, pp. 887-906.

Shafer, Boyd C. *Nationalism: Myth and Reality*. New York, 1955.

Tapié, Victor L. "Comment les français du XVIIe siècle voyaient la patrie," *XVIIe siècle*, Nos. 25-26 (1955), pp. 37-58.

Yardeni, Myriam. *La Conscience nationale en France pendant les guerres de religion (1559-1598)*. Louvain-Paris, 1971.

CHAPTER III

GERMANY

L E O N A R D   K R I E G E R

If we give our topic an interrogatory form and ask in general—was German life between Reformation and Romanticism really characterized in any appreciable measure by a distinctive historiography, a rooted political culture, and an articulate consciousness of nationality, whether these factors be considered jointly or distributively?—our common knowledge dictates that we reply, simply, no. Surely we must say, on this general level of question and answer, that we have the right factors but for the wrong period; the combination of historiography, political culture, and national consciousness fits nineteenth-century Germany so neatly as to give the appearance of having been modeled on it. In nineteenth-century Germany, after all, an explicitly labeled "historical school" of law, economics, and politics was connected with an equally indicative "political school" of historians primarily through a common, active national consciousness. This was a Germany whose historical facts precisely match our historiographical concepts and make the relations among our three factors a matter not of imputed logic but of actual process.

But our negations go beyond this notice of prematurity. Were the problem merely one of temporal misplacement, then we could simply look for the early-modern origins of the modern syndrome, because revolutionary watershed or no, as historians we do not believe in creation *ex-nihilo*. The fact is, however, that *mutatis mutandis* an analogous relationship of historiography, political culture, and national consciousness can also be found in medieval Germany. The Holy Roman Empire under its Saxon, Salian, and Hohenstaufen dynasties was regarded by its chroniclers as a German-based political order; it was popularly celebrated for its German base in the political lays of Walter von der Vogelweide and the Minnesingers; and authentic historians like Otto of Freising and Alexander von Roes identified imperial history with German history. The

judgment must be relative, of course, for we all know how our historiographical, political, and national categories must be qualified in their
application to medieval Europe, but when they have been so qualified for
the Romano-Christian culture as a whole, they apply to Germany as well
as anywhere else. Thus, the special weakness of these categories in early-
modern Germany assumes the provocative character of a hiatus rather
than the pacifying character of simple immaturity.

When we survey early-modern Germany for evidence of the missing
categories—that is, when we look in those places where, by projection
forward from the medieval past, backward from the nineteenth-century
future, or sideward from neighboring contemporary nations where these
categories are manifest—we should expect to find it. The facts seem simple and familiar enough to carry their own explanation and to blunt
further inquiry. In each of the three main stages of early-modern European historiography, German historians followed foreign models, served
extra- or even anti-historical purposes, and produced no work of real
international stature. During the sixteenth-century era of humanist historiography, Germans followed the Italian lead of Bruni for pragmatic
history and of Biondo for antiquarian history until Philip Melanchthon,
Luther's humanistically trained executor who has been called "the preceptor of Germany," promulgated the authoritative university curriculum
which reabsorbed history into theology, exalted church history over secular history, and subordinated empirical research to confessional polemic
in the motivation of historical writing. During the seventeenth-century
era of legal and constitutional historiography, Germans were in the tow
both of the French mode of critical conceptual analysis highlighted by
Bodin and of the empirical jurisprudence developed by the Dutch neo-
Stoics Justus Lipsius and Hugo Grotius. In German hands history sub-
served juristic concepts as their supporting material, whether these concepts stemmed from the fashionable natural law or the controversial
forms of the constitution. In the eighteenth-century Germans dutifully
traipsed after the French methods and standards set by Mabillon and the
Maurists, on the one hand, and by Voltaire and Montesquieu, on the
other, industriously working them into the ground or up to the heavens in
good Germanic style, concentrating on learned local studies or vapid
universal history. If we compare the historiographical resonance of Guicciardini, Bacon, Clarendon, Mabillon, Muratori, Vico, Montesquieu, Voltaire, Hume, Robertson, or Gibbon with historiographical personnages
such as Aventinus, Wimpheling, Sleidanus, Flacius Illyricus, Conring,
Pufendorf, Bünau, Mascov, Gatterer, Schlözer, Schlosser, and Spittler, to
name the best known (except for Leibniz, renowned, after all, for his
philosophy rather than his history), the point should be made, however
superficially. Only contrapuntally in the last third of the eighteenth

century—to complete this historiographical sketch from a teleological point of view—do the beginnings of the distinctive German attitude toward history appear which will merge into the political culture and national movement of the nineteenth century. Winckelmann's evocation of Greek art, F. A. Wolf's initiation of classical studies as a philologically based, historical discipline, Justus Möser's history of his native Osnabrück, and Herder's organic philosophy of history were the most visible marks of what recent research has shown to be a widespread historiographical movement toward the end of the early-modern period leading straight into the modern historicism of the romantic era.[1] But even these late eighteenth-century advances in historiography were not associated with parallel, unambiguous advances in a consciously political German culture. They tended rather to focus upon the aesthetic, the linguistic, the social, and the anthropological aspects of the human past and not on its politics. And despite the formal analogues of nationality in the concepts of the *Volk* and of the unifying and identifiable Volks-spirit upon which each of these historians lay such great store, it was not the national Volk that was ultimate: the Greek way was of universal validity; the German past funneled into particular Osnabruckian history; and the several culture-nations were so many manifestations of a single, versatile humanity. It is characteristic that Herder, who came closest to being a nationalist, was furthest from being an historian.

In these limits upon their national political culture, the budding historicists remained representative of early-modern Germany as a whole, where political culture and national consciousness remained not only separate from each other but underdeveloped in themselves by comparison with the western nations. The question of political culture requires little discussion, since the unpolitical character of the Germans, raised to explicit prominence by Thomas Mann and commonly applied as a running theme to all of German history, obviously holds *a fortiori* for the early-modern phase, when the empire was no longer a focus of actual politics, when the particular rulers were autocratizing their principalities by depoliticizing their societies, when politics was specifically distinguished—when it was acknowledged at all—from the ecclesiastical and legal concerns which made up the bulk of the public interest and was limited for all practical purposes to the narrow field of foreign policy. The fact that Protestant and Catholic confessions were becoming routine and law and government were becoming bureaucratic inhibited social participation even in the ecclesiastical and administrative cognates of

---

[1] See Andreas Kraus, *Vernunft und Geschichte: die Bedeutung der deutschen Akademien für die Entwicklung der Geschichtswissenschaft im späten 18. Jahrhundert* (Freiburg, 1963).

political culture. All this is well known enough, but what is perhaps not so well known is the consequence of the unpolitical culture for historiography. Unlike their fellow historians in other countries, the majority of German historians in the early-modern period were university professors, and the histories they wrote tended therefore to be either textbooks for their students or the historical justifications, advertisements, and genealogies composed for the princes who took their official historians from the professoriate. Quite aside from the effect of such insulation upon the quality of historical literature, the address of the textbooks to the future administrators who populated the authors' classes, of the white papers to governing-class audiences abroad, and of dynastic *res gestae* to posterity testifies to the segregated cultural impact as well as to the official origin of whatever political tinge German historiography might have.

We should be able to dispense with national consciousness as well in our general judgment of early-modern Germany, for the commonplace of fragmented Germany is surely as axiomatic as that of unpolitical Germans, and it is at least as tailor-made for the early-modern period. Indeed, the same factors that are adduced to explain the want of political culture are also adduced to explain the want of national consciousness: the impotent empire with its visionary supranational claims, the multiplicity of self-seeking sovereign princes and oligarchies, the divisive plurality of churches and conventicles, the persistence of localized economies, the centrifugal pull of powerful neighbors with more active political cultures and more integrated nationalities. The overlap of the political and national deficiencies found its rationale in the two compatible *personae* of each particular sovereign, thus establishing a direct ratio between the power the sovereign exercised over the politics of his own principality and the power he prevented the imperial organs from exercising over the nation as a whole. And once more a familiar general judgment on early-modern Germany has a special relevance for our special problem: the dialectical concepts of "cultural nations" and "political nations" have been devised precisely for this German situation, as hermeneutic aids to understand the kind of national consciousness—i.e., cultural—which was developed under the aegis of history in a German intellectual vanguard toward the end of the early-modern period, in contrast to the kind of national consciousness—i.e., political—which was not then developed in Germany and whose later development in the context of the prior cultural nationalism would establish the German version of a nineteenth-century political culture.[2]

[2] Friedrich Meinecke, *Cosmopolitanism and the National State*, trans. Robert B. Kimber (Princeton, 1970), pp. 10-19.

In short, by the standards of the modern categories which we have inherited from the nineteenth century—categories defining a historical sense as one which analyzes sources both sympathetically and critically to recreate the past in its own terms, a political culture as one which posits the state as a primary dimension of the human community and involves significant sectors of the society in its distinctive values and institutions, and a national consciousness as one which both registers the actual existence of the nation as a discrete association and attributes a unique value to it—by these standards early-modern Germany shows historiographical regression, political lethargy, and national semiconsciousness. Let us not misunderstand. History was written, territorial states were built, and the German empire persisted through the entire early-modern period, but because these activities did not approach the modern standards of historiography, political commitment, and national feeling they were not related to one another as the modern categories are.

If we shift our angle of approach from the ripened historicist *terminus ad quem*, whose origins we seek, to the intellectual structure of early-modern German historiography as such, we can talk about things more important than the degree to which it did or did not measure up to contemporary European standards, and more important than the imitative or adaptive nature of the process by which the eighteenth century prepared for the nineteenth-century schools of political and national historiography. If we understand that early-modern German historians were not only trying to live up to European standards of historiography and political culture but were also deliberately adjusting their history to distinctive German political and national conditions in which the past played a different role than it did elsewhere, then we can give a positive and substantive definition to the function of historiography in the early-modern version of German political culture and nationality. Since this descriptive definition has its own positive quality, moreover, we can consider it a historiographical model in its own right and use it to answer questions for which our more familiar models are inadequate. We find answers to the question of what sustained the Holy Roman Empire of the German nation in an increasingly practical age that found no practical use for it, to the question of what sustained loyalty to particular principalities over and above the traditional obeisance which was increasingly undermined and the practical services which were sporadically performed, and to the question of how the existence of the empire and loyalty to the principalities were reconciled. German historiography entered into all the answers and was formed by them.

We can also use the German model, if we regard its limitations for comparative analysis as positive qualities, to answer European questions. In the regular western European model, secular historical science, political culture, and national consciousness developed conjunctively, and our very notion of each bears connotations stemming from its genetic association with the others. The model is particularly useful, therefore, for tracing the synchronic process which has formed our interactive modern notions of history, of politics, and of the nation, and for answering questions about what is common to them. When we ask about Bacon's history, Bodin's politics, or Burke's national consciousness, for example, the regular model leads us to look in each case for the three-part continuum. The irregular German model, on the other hand, is useful for tracing the asynchronic process in those cases where history, politics, and nationality developed at different rates and, in principle, independently of one another. With it we can hope to answer questions, first, about the idiosyncracies of each category apart from the circular pursuit of mutual qualities and, ultimately, about the distinctive features each category brings to their mutual association when that conjunction occurs. With the aid of the German model, we hope particularly to answer in what follows the question of the distinctive function of the historical sense in the crystallization of an inchoate national political culture.

The fundamental structure of the German model was formed by the pervasion throughout public life and the persistence throughout the early-modern period of a condition which we may term unsatisfied duality. Within historiography, within the political realm, and within the attitudes toward German nationhood, attention and activity were divided between two poles, each of which was both real and valuable, each of which was limited by the other, each of which persisted despite this limitation, and each of which was ever reaching out for connections that would make it part of a larger unity. This situation existed until the late eighteenth century, which witnessed an asymmetrical denouement.

In the genus of early-modern historiography there were two sets of opposing species, neither of which was peculiar to Germany but both of which applied to Germany. One set was composed of contrasting historical methods. There was scholarly or learned history—to use the literal translation of the German *gelehrte Historie*—and there was discursive or pragmatic history—to use the literal translation of the German *pragmatische Geschichte*. As the German indicates and the translation does not, learned history was defined by the approach of the historian and pragmatic history by the nature of the historical process. Learned histories were documentary collections and monographic disquisitions whose leading motif was the historian's application of specialized critical techniques to his sources. Learned history flourished especially in the early sixteenth century under the impress of humanist editorial canons and in the eighteenth under the influence of Maurist diplomatics for the authentication of documents. Pragmatic history in its broadest sense referred to any work in which the past official acts and promulgations of governments were organized into a sequential narrative for the instruction of governmental officials. The discursive treatment which was always a necessary function of such material was extended in the eighteenth century, under the aegis of the Enlightenment, so that a meaningful and integrated pattern became an explicit requirement of pragmatic history, whatever its material. What was important about the distinction between learned and pragmatic history was the contemporary insistence upon the distinction, for until late in the eighteenth century, historians kept the two species separate. This had the effect of making the most sophisticated kind of history antiquarian and atomic and the most coherent kind of history presentist and relatively uncritical. The interest in the truth of the past for its own sake and the interest in the truth of the past for its meaning in the present are combined in our historical sense, but they constituted two different senses for history in the early-modern era.

The second set of opposing historiographical species was made up of divergent historical themes, which overlay the polarity of methods and intensified it. Early-modern historiography was addressed to two kinds of pastness—to origins and to continuous tradition. The concern with the real, definite, human origins of institutions, associated as it was with the criticism of legendary progenitors and with the exclusion of the biblical beginnings which had masked an indifference to temporal origins as such, was especially characteristic of early-modern historiography and, indeed, has been frequently equated with what was truly historical in it—that is, historical by our standards. The early-modern concern with tradition, on the other hand, carried over from medieval historiography; and because it stressed what was constant in tradition, it was obviously predicated upon the continuity of past and present. Consequently, this concern made not only for a kind of history opposed in principle to that in which the past is distinguished as the locus of origins. It also produced a kind of literature or jurisprudence which, in the judgment of many, is alien to the nature of history as such, because in their view, whether the past is seen as a projection of the present or whether the present is defined as an extension of the past, tradition, as validated custom, subordinates past and present alike to a continuity that abolishes the distinction between them and therewith the temporal dimension essential to history. But such a judgment remains a judgment in terms of our historical sense and not of early-modern man's. What he lacked was the notion of development which would ultimately make traditions an authentic historical object in our sense and integrate it with the history of origins. Nevertheless, his conception of a permanent institution in the form of an unchangeable tradition *was* historical in his sense and remained a persistent focus of his historiography. In his capacity as a citizen, he needed and invoked the historical past in order to validate institutions which lacked validity on contemporary grounds. In his capacity as a historian, he needed and invoked tradition because its very constancy provided him with the internal core of coherence through history required by the jettisoning of its theological framework.

It was, indeed, the history of tradition that became paradigmatic for coherent secular history and that thus supplies the key to the two meanings of pragmatic history in early-modern Germany. Because the governmental acts which constituted pragmatic history in its generic sense were conceived as the constituents of legal and political traditions binding past and present, pragmatic history could ultimately come to stand explicitly for coherent or integrated history. In a formal sense, the steady, rational principles of human nature which were the sinews of the historical process during the Enlightenment were historiographical extensions of the institutional traditions that had first made history seem an autonomous process during the centuries immediately preceding. Just as learned history and the critical study of origins collaborated to produce a syndromic historiography directed toward the ascertainment of discrete fact in the past, so did a pragmatic history organized by the clamps of invariant tradition—whether of long-lived institutions or of permanent human dispositions—produce an opposed syndromic historiography directed toward the elucidation of meaning from the concatenation of past and present facts.

If we think of politics as the autonomous category of collective human power-relations that was first segregated and defined in early-modern Europe, it is clear that the two sets of opposite foci into which the Germans partitioned the category made for alternative definitions of politics that were peculiar to them. The primary object of politics—the locus of sovereign authority—was either the empire or the particular principality. But this alternative meant something more, particularly in its relevance to historiography, than the familiar choice between unity and particularism, for both objects represented a very hybrid kind of politics, and their separation served to perpetuate the nonpolitical dimension which they did not share alongside the politics which they did share. The empire was not only the national government for Germany but also the international guardian of a Christian Europe it did not govern. The principality was not only a territorial government but a social and ecclesiastical corporation within the national community personified in the prince who was its head. The division of attention between these two centers of public life militated against the delimitation of a definite sphere of politics in either or in an intersection of both. Politics remained mixed with nonpolitics on both levels, with the result that political themes took refracted forms. The themes of domestic politics for the German historians of the era were either constitutional law or dynastic personality; the historical themes of foreign policy were global international relations as an offshoot of international law or dynastic legal claims. Law and personality, both national and dynastic, were prominent, to be sure, in the politics of all early-modern Europe; but in Germany either could become the historical cognate of politics itself, thus reducing the consideration of politics to the analysis of the legal means or personal agents of power rather than of its integral and fundamental relations to the community. German politics, historically considered, was either Romano-Germanic law in the guise of public tradition or the princely personality in the guise of dynastic chronicle, because the empire existed primarily as legal tradition and the principality as the personal union of assorted corporate bodies. The integrity of internal politics was obviously lost in this division and led to the projection of politics abroad, in the form of foreign policy segregated from the internal life of the community. Law, tradition, personality, and the primacy of foreign policy—could Max Weber have come from anywhere but Germany?

The axes of division within German national consciousness, like those within politics, meant not the absence of nationality but its refraction into alternative species which mixed nationality with ideals that transcended nationality. For national consciousness among the Germans, by the testimony of their historiography, goes back well into the Middle Ages and runs continuously through the early-modern period, despite the contemporary awareness of national impotence and the retrospective verdict of national indifference. What is important, then, is not the question of whether there was national consciousness but rather the question of what kinds of national consciousness could persist for so long without viable institutions to feed them—or, even more paradoxically, the question of what kinds of national consciousness could not merely persist but maintain life in institutions otherwise unviable. The two sets of national opposites were continuous with the division in the political objects of early-modern Germany. The national version of the political division between empire and principality was a subtle one. It can be best understood through an analysis of the formula, *Kaiser und Reich*. Literally a hyphenated composite to translate the corporate integration of head and members in the Romano-German imperium, the formula actually came to symbolize alternative foci of German nationality.

For the kaiser the symbolism is obvious, since he was also king of the Germans from the time of Emperor Otto the Great in the tenth century and since it was from the kaiser that the periodic surges for the political unification of Germany came, both in medieval and in early-modern times. But the national symbolism of the Reich apart from the kaiser was trickier. The Reich, as the organization of the German community led by the imperial princes and other imperial nobles and cities represented actually or virtually in the Reichstag, was, during the early-modern period, usually the overt arena for the conflict between the kaiser's centralizing projects and the particularizing resistance of the princes. In effect, this conflict tended to equate Reich either with kaisertum or with particularism and in either equation dismantled it as a national alternative to the kaiser. But however overtly true in terms of actual policies and events, this appearance distorts the reality of a languid Germany whose life was based more on the attitudes sustaining an ordered existence than on the actions that would change it. For the sake of argument, let us leave aside the subversion of the kaiser's claim to represent the nation by the Hapsburg kaisers' own dynastic, territorial, and confessional ambitions, since these ambitions did not affect the *kaiserliche* principle and in any event seemed to confirm rather than reverse the association of particularism with the Reich. Even so, we must take into account the steady, usually covert, current of opinion which recognized in the Reich, organized though it was into a collection of sovereign principalities, counties, baronages, and towns, a national institution distinct from the kaiser. What explains the persistence of this kind of national consciousness despite the obvious inviability of the Reich constitution was its investment not in any representative national organ, such as the Reichstag, but in the particular principalities themselves, which were viewed as authentic expressions of the national life. Though it is true that the Hohenzollerns, like Frederick the Great, were actually impelled by a blend of particular and European rather than by national incentives, it is also true that they were regarded as members of the long line of German princes and heroes. Occasionally the attitude surfaced, as in the national appeal and reception of Frederick's particularistic League of German Princes, but it was in German historiography that the Reich as the context of the German principalities would play an indispensable role. Far from eccentricity, as it may seem to our modern Atlantic eyes, the blending of national consciousness with what we think of as its opposite was standard for early-modern Germany. The blend of German nationality and princely particularism in the Reich was hardly more "monstrous" after all—to use a term partially responsible for our misunderstanding[3]—than the blend of German nationality and Romano-Christian universality in the kaiser.

[3] The label was popularized in Samuel Pufendorf's influential *De statu imperii Germanici* (Geneva, 1667). See below, pp. 86–87.

This distinction in the *objects* of national consciousness was connected with and can be partially clarified by a second set of alternatives: the distinction between the *Volk*, on the one hand, and the empire (that is, Kaiser-und-Reich), on the other, as the *sources* of German nationality. The national community of the *Volk* was constituted by common culture in general and by common language in particular, whereas the national community of the empire was constituted by common lordship, common law, and common political experience. The national community of the *Volk* was a structure whose nature was determined by its Germanic tribal origins and hence had unity in particularity built into its very ethnic essence. The national community of the empire was a structure determined by the changing composition of the territories it encompassed and subjected to its laws. The national community of the *Volk* went back to tribal origins in ancient times and the migrations of the early Middle Ages; the national community of the empire went back to the consolidations and reconsolidations of the great German medieval dynasties— Frankish, Saxon, Salian (that is, Franconian), Hohenstaufen (that is, Suabian), and Hapsburg. Consciousness both of *Volk* and empire was present in Germany from the beginning to the end of the early-modern era. Historians tended to choose one source or the other for their focus when they wrote German history—the *Volk* when they were concerned with common culture, particular principalities, or origins, and the empire when they were concerned with common political experience, universal principle, or continuing tradition. Whichever the focus, the alternate was omnipresent as assumption. Since the German empire always comprehended more or less than the German *Volk*—more in its morality and less in its actuality—the compatibility between focus and assumption was always in question. The gap between them was bridged by history.

Let us, then, survey the three main periods of early-modern German historiography to see what kinds of connections historians made, taking their stances at the opposite poles of their discipline, between the political and national objects which were the scrambled foci of their experience. Our aim is to see how historians made sense of this experience and how history, which we usually consider the record of human vagaries and discords made coherent only by the nonhistorical structures of humanity, came into the German case to be the unifying factor among the vagaries and discords of the German nonhistorical structures. Our concern is with secular historiography, though German ecclesiastical history runs throughout the era and its relationship to profane history, as its complement was called, is an interesting story in itself. The story of this secular historiography is a tale of three ages.

German historiography in the period of humanism—a period whose products were concentrated in the first third of the sixteenth century—was dominated by two sets of conditions: the joint passion for new knowledge, coherent style, and moral personality (both in writee and writer) absorbed from Italian humanism; and the new surge of national consciousness stemming primarily from resentment of Italian cultural and ecclesiastical dominion over Germany and secondarily from resentment of German political impotence *vis-a-vis* France. As a result, the German humanists treated the history of Germany as an autonomous intellectual genre. This consequence was distinctive in a negative sense because German history was the only history in which German historians made a significant contribution to European historiography. But there was also a positive sense in which German humanist history was distinctive. For the German humanists, the German nation was neither an exclusive, preeminent, nor unified focus: it was, precisely because of its multiple aspects, an organ linking the universal structure in which they still believed with the particularized existence in which they came to believe. History was the appropriate dimension for this approach to nationality in two ways: it was an essential constitutive element of the nation as well as the essential medium connecting the nation to values and realities above it and within it. Thus, history had a two-fold function for the nation: it was a prime ingredient of the German nation's being; and it was the vehicle of the German nation's connection with the cosmic framework of human destiny, on the one hand, and with free moral activity, on the other. History, in short, was involved in both the internal and external relations of the nation.

History is, of course, internally entailed in the formation of every national consciousness, but as signalized by the humanists, it played a special constitutive role for early-modern Germany, because in a sense the nation existed only through history. As the Hessian scholar Hessus Eobanus, albeit himself not a historian, acknowledged in typical humanist fashion:

> Other nations keep their identities. . . . Only the Germans are not spoken of. . . . Why? Because we lack not the deeds but the history of the deeds, and it is the history that gives identity. . . . When Germanic vigor flourished and before we were contaminated by our luxuries, then our ancestors performed memorable things; . . . but then too, since we lacked historians, our glory was drowned in the waters of the Lethe.[4]

Indeed, German secular history was triggered, not by a German, but by two Italians who wrote about Germany: by Tacitus, whose *Germania*

---

[4] Eobanus de Hesse's Preface to Ulrich von Hutten, *Arminius: Dialogue* (Paris, 1877), pp. 8-10.

was introduced to the Germans in the fifteenth century, and by Aeneas Sylvius, whose *Germania* showed the relevance of ancient tribal Germany to contemporary Germany, thereby initiating the conversion of German ethnology into German history. The way in which Aeneas Sylvius conceived this relevance, moreover, distinguished between the two kinds of German nation that had become the alternate cores of the two kinds of German national history. Against the Reichstag's politically based protests—*Gravamina*—of the German nation, Aeneas Sylvius invoked Tacitus to identify, at its origins, the linguistic and cultural Germany, which he purported to show still existed and flourished under the "translated" Roman Empire and within contemporary Roman Catholicism. German humanists responded with two lines of national history: one emulating Aeneas Sylvius' ancient tribal history and the other opposing his version of contemporary imperial history. The pattern was thus set, which would become familiar, of both appropriating and resisting foreign influence and of justifying both the emulation and the opposition in the name of the German nation. Both lines of humanist historiography mixed scholarly and patriotic motives, but in varying proportions.

If we take as our measure the deliberate production of a history of Germany, then it is to the pragmatic patriotic line that chronological priority must be accorded. As early as 1492, Jakob Wimpheling, the Alsatian humanist, had appointed himself spokesman for the emperor against the French; in 1501 he produced his own *Germania*, a pamphlet which mixed presumed proofs of Alsace's Germanic character since the days of Caesar with local advice to the Strassburgers on good city government; and in 1515 he would rebut Aeneas Sylvius' *Germania* with a polemic published under the awkward but revealing title: "Answers and Objections to Aeneas Sylvius for the Saving and the Honor of the Holy Roman Empire Out of Love for the Fatherland and for the German Nation."[5] Then, in 1505, Wimpheling published the Latin *Epitome of German History to the Present Time*, which is generally acknowledged to have been the first secular history of Germany. It was a work obviously affected by the humanist culture of the age, for it paid lip service to original sources; but it was in fact based upon recent Italian authorities, and its merits rest upon other than scholarly grounds. Wimpheling's primary interest was political and pragmatic—the galvanization of emperor and princes against the French, the Turks, and later the Italian ecclesiastics—and he supported his cause through a new use of history. He

---

[5] Enea Silvio Piccolomini, *Deutschland: Der Brieftraktat an Martin Mayer, und, Jakob Wimphelings 'Antworten und Einwendungen gegen Enea Silvio'*, ed. Adolf Schmidt (Cologne, 1962).

historicized the empire by viewing it through the personalities of the kaisers in medieval and modern history, and by invoking the cultural origins of the German *Volk* and its quinquepartite tribal organization to substantiate the German character of the emperor and princes. Wimpheling's *Epitome*, therefore, started with an introductory sketch of the five tribes into which the original Germanics were divided and then proceeded to the body of his history—the Holy Roman emperors from Charlemagne to the contemporary Maximilian, all shown to be ethnic Germans albeit with a European mission.[6]

This line of historiography rubbed off on and is illuminated by the poet-publicist-politician Ulrich von Hutten. He too called upon ancient tribal Germany to supply a national passion he felt to be deficient in his own day. His dialogue "Arminius" gave substance to the heretofore shadowy first-century war lord who successfully fought the Romans on behalf of tribal Germany. In the same work, Hutten recovered an historical figure and created a historical legend in Arminius, the "liberator of Germany," the "most German of the Germans" (*Germanissimus*), the Hermann of later poetic fame—and all this national awareness in 98 A.D.[7] The invocation of a presumed historical national reality to galvanize a present national potentiality into reality betrayed the fateful ambiguity of the patriotic humanist. Because he viewed politics through the personalities of the rulers, he invested the present German nation in the person of the kaiser. But where the Holy Roman Empire had become demonstrably German, legally through translation of the German imperium and actually through the shrinkage of its constituents, the Holy Roman emperor retained an indefinite wardenship over the world or at least over Christian Europe. Only through the invocation of cultural history, therefore, could the kaiser be recalled to his true role and his duties to the German kingdom.[8] In this line of humanist historiography, history was invoked primarily for its national political effect, and the crucial assumption was the personal basis of politics, for through it the cultural nature of early history could serve the political nature of late medieval and recent history.

The second main line of humanist historiography, whose outstanding figures were Conrad Celtis, Beatus Rhenanus, and Johannes Aventinus, concentrated on cultural history. Here the nation formed the main frame, but within it the pure love of learning bulked large, expanding on the

---

[6] Werner Goez, *Translatio Imperii* (Tübingen, 1958), p. 252.

[7] Hutten, *Arminius*, p. 48.

[8] Hajo Holborn, *Ulrich von Hutten and the German Reformation* (New Haven, 1937), p. 75.

Italian model and emphasizing historical origins. The historians of this school focused primarily on ancient tribal Germany to identify the linguistic, cultural, and ethnographic sources of the nationality, and they all aborted their own plans to use these origins as the basis for a general history of the nation both because their learned antiquarianism kept them entranced by the details of their discoveries in the early period and because they found the national culture dissipated by imperial politics—a facet of relative indifference to them—as it moved through the Middle Ages toward the present. Celtis, more a promoter of history than himself an historian, first proposed the seductive plan, borrowed from the Italian model of *Italia Illustrata*, of a *German Illustrata*—the prospectus of the great common enterprise, of an anthropological and geographical description of Germany in the context of its total historical development. German humanists would turn to this idea time and again and never carry it out. It was Celtis too who first directed scholarly attention to the study of ancient sources, which helps explain the frustration of the enterprise.

Rhenanus, the Erasmian who became the finest German historical scholar of the age, manifested in the successive stages of his career the different qualities and incentives that were intermingled in most representatives of this learned national history. He began as a classical theologian and gravitated toward history with his commentary on Tacitus' *Germania* in 1519 at a time when he had come to appreciate the new German humanist culture. He turned to national history itself—i.e., when he attempted to organize a *Germania Illustrata*—in 1525 after a period of religious travail which saw him choose Erasmus' way over Luther's. Finally, in 1531, he published his *chef d'oeuvre*, the *Three Books of German History* (*Rerum Germanicorum*). In this work he described Roman Germany dispassionately and, from critically evaluated sources and personally observed remains, traced the tribal movements through the empires of the Allemans, the Franks, and the Saxons, ending with the establishment of the German kingdom under Otto I in the tenth century—in all, not a German history, as Rhenanus himself acknowledged, but the beginning of a German history.[9] One of the basic characteristics of his historical scholarship—the categorical distinction between ancient and recent Germany—surely contributed to his actual failure to move from one to the other.

His friend Aventinus contributed what was probably the most successful production of the school in his *Bavarian Chronicle*, which was fin-

[9] Paul Joachimsen, *Geschichtsauffassung und Geschichtschreibung in Deutschland unter dem Einfluss des Humanismus* (Berlin, 1910), p. 137.

ished in its original Latin version in 1521, very freely translated into German by Aventinus himself by 1533, and which was appreciated by Germans well into the nineteenth century. He strikingly reveals the tenets of the cultural national school when his history departs from what it claims and seems to be. The chronicle was officially a dynastic history commissioned by the Bavarian duke, but it actually moved to and fro among the histories of the world, of the Germans, and of the Bavarians, ever drawn to the national level as its central thread and impressing its readership as "a German, rather than a Bavarian, chronicle."[10] Ostensibly a chronicle of Bavarian history which would trace the movement from the German tribal pattern to the politics of the Bavarian state until the present, it actually dwelt primarily upon the popular culture of the ancient German and Bavarian tribes, shaded off into a *pro forma* medieval narration, whose traditional chronicle format expressed the author's indifference to the recorded political events (leavened only by his genealogical interests in the ruling Bavarian families), and ended abruptly in the fourteenth century, when modern Bavarian politics began. Incidentally, even his projected *Germania Illustrata*, or *Chronicle of All Germany* as he called it, to which he repeatedly and apologetically referred his reader for more on the politics of the high and late Middle Ages, never got beyond the ancient period; and even this, characteristically, he devoted to a cultural synthesis.[11]

In the method as well as in the substance of his history, Aventinus demonstrated the role of the nation in reconciling incompatibilities. Though it was purported to be a work of learned history, the *Bavarian Chronicle* mixed outrageous legends with carefully researched facts in its representation of Germanic origins; it ensconced its empirical results in a cosmic framework still compounded of Biblical history, Daniel's Four Empires, Divine Providence, and classical cycles; and particularly in the German version, the narrative presentation of a past national life was interspersed with gloomy moral judgments, which imposed a suprahistorical classification upon events and intimated that the course of history was one of universal decline toward the present.

Through the restrictions placed on humanistic learned history, we can see what was *common* to the pragmatic and learned historians of the humanistic era with regard to the respective emphases on authorities vs. sources, on actions vs. origins, and on politics vs. culture, by which they were distinguished. In German humanist historiography, the nation was

---

[10] Quoted in Gerald Strauss, *Historian in an Age of Crisis: The Life and Work of Johannes Aventinus* (Cambridge, Massachusetts, 1963), p. 117.

[11] *Ibid.*, p. 227.

the central strand amid the several layers of consideration that extended from humanity, Christendom, or Europe in general through principalities, provinces, cities, and noble individuals; and history was the medium through which the new interest in the natural forms of human activity could be loosely collected within the familiar providential, cyclical, and ethical structures of meaning without requiring mutual accountability. Hence in all humanist historiography, historical and national consciousness referred to each other and complemented each other in their mediate and therefore limited function. National consciousness implicated history because the nation, as the unity of its particularist components, existed in the tribal or the imperial past; history referred to the German nation because, whether through the political bond of empire or the cultural bond among the tribes, the nation provided the schema for combining or juxtaposing the mass of new research with the stock of old traditions. So it was that national consciousness could drive even Wimpheling, the anticlerical patriot, and Hutten, the activist politician, to search for new truths about the reality of the nation in the past and to respect the scholarship that uncovered them; while even the comparatively rigorous standards of scholarship in a Celtis or an Aventinus did not preclude the invocation of national legend to fill the gaps between their critically researched materials and to give it some measure of plastic coherence. But be it noted, to conclude this survey of the humanist era, that these junctures of historical and national consciousness presumed notions of history and of the nation which in their *external* relations trailed off, mediators that they were, imperceptibly into ideas and commitments neither historical nor national, and which, in their *internal* relations, postulated a division into two kinds of history, correlated with two kinds of nation, learned with tribes and pragmatic with empire, under the assumption of a personalized conception of politics.

The second period of early-modern German historiography, running from the middle of the seventeenth century into the early eighteenth, was overtly dominated by imperial legal history and the jurists who wrote it—a preoccupation which, coinciding as it did with the demise of the German empire as an effective law-making institution, seemed merely an extension of the German habit of giving historical explanations for the deficient aspects of their nation. But these obvious descriptive categories obscure the real historiographical meaning of the period. If we consider the three outstanding exemplars of the genre—Hermann Conring because he initiated the history of German law, Samuel Pufendorf because he was the most popular and therewith the most representative figure of the genre, and Gottfried Wilhelm Leibniz because he ended the era and prepared the way for the next by combining law and history as two independent variables—if we consider these examplars, then the two really important historiographical achievements of the age emerge. First, though the leading historians of the era were indeed trained as jurists, were employed in the law faculties of the universities or as legal counselors in the state governments, and were prominently concerned with German law, their historical investment in the law was neither an original nor a specialized commitment to law as such. Rather, it was a consequence of a more general interest: they were concerned about German politics, and positive legal relations were the only political mode of expression for national institutions to which the fundamental principles of political power did not apply (as they did not apply to the relations either between the empire and Europe or between the principalities and the empire); history, moreover, was the only medium in which the law acquired political significance. The derivative nature of the law is reflected in the intellectual character of the personalities involved. To the Germans, they were not jurists, primarily, but *Polyhistoren*—academic jacks-of-all-trades for whom, implicitly, history was the common medium. Conring was a physician who had exhibited a humanist love of scholarship and had received training in Aristotelian philosophy before he addressed himself to the study of law; his professorship of politics (*Politices*) in the law faculty of Helmstedt University reflected his lifelong involvement with the practice of public policy. Pufendorf's first publications were in the field of classical philology, and his juristic vocation, both as writer and professor, was simply the centerpiece of a career that extended to philosophy, theology, and professional history. Leibniz, finally, took his degree in jurisprudence, but he refused a professorship in the field, preferring to spend his life bouncing to and fro among philosophy, mathematics, genealogy, ethnology, linguistics, political brain-trusting, academic consulting, history, and, of course, the law. All had varied theoretical interests; all were also interested in political theory—taken from Aristotle, from Bodin, and from Grotius—but found it inapplicable to Germany; all were committed to the practical politics of restoring Germany to a place in the European system of powers; and all turned to the law and its history as the means of identifying the empire which was to be resurrected.

But more important in the long run than the legal cognate of imperial politics was the second achievement of the period: the agency of German nationality was transferred from the empire to the principality through the medium of history. What was conflict between empire and principality in contemporary politics became the harmony of principle and realization in legal history. The activities of the particular principalities were justified by national values in the present, and the existence of the imperial constitution was justified by its role in preserving these national values from the past for realization by the principalities. It was the neatest trick of a seventeenth century renowned for legerdemain. Let us see how it worked.

In Conring we find, precisely reflected, the problem of the age—that is, the focus of attention on the national law of the empire at the very moment the political impotence of the empire became inescapably apparent. Conring was a political realist who, writing toward the end of the Thirty Years' War, both understood and accepted its implications for the triumph of the independent principalities in Germany but who remained nationally conscious, nostalgically and functionally, all the same. In his *On the Origin of German Law* (*De Origine Juris Germanici*) of 1643, he showed that there had been no translation of the Roman to the German medieval empire both because the Romans had no universal jurisdiction to transfer and because the German emperors did not validate the Roman law for the new empire. This epoch-making demonstration confirmed the German character of the Holy Roman Empire and its laws over and above its universal Roman tradition, and the consciousness here displayed was more than one of national origins. At the conclusion of the *De Origine* itself he called for "new . . . German laws," and he insisted on another occasion that "Germany will live forever," explicitly referring "today's German misery" to a future "German glory."[12] But when, on the other hand, he considered the German law itself, in his *De Germanorum Imperio Romano* of 1643 and his *De finibus Imperii Romano-Germanici* of 1654, he acknowledged that in fact without the unifying distortion of the Roman tradition the actuality of the German law showed not the integrity but the limitations upon the rights and powers of the empire by the autonomous principalities, and he went beyond this acknowledgment to recommend an even greater extension of the power of the princes. The answer to the conundrum is, of course, that Conring saw the empire as a national institution vested not so much in the emperor as in the princes, and he favored the consolidation of princely authority for the explicit purpose of strengthening the empire. He accused the Hapsburg emperors of serving antinational interests, and he implied that this was a characteristic not simply of the Hapsburgs but of all emperors when he later recommended the election of Louis XIV as German emperor to pursue the purely international interests of the empire in a pacified order of Europe. The associated princes, on the other hand, embodied the na-

[12] Erik Wolf, "Idee und Wirklichkeit des Reiches im deutschen Rechtsdenken des 16. und 17. Jahrhunderts," *Reich und Recht in der deutschen Philosophie*, ed. Karl *Larenz* (Berlin, 1943), pp. 111-13.

tional dimension of the empire, and the national basis of their particular political powers stemmed from the living tradition of the actual German law. Despite its dramatic impact, Conring's demonstration of Germanic legal origins had an essentially negative function by excluding the anachronistic centralizing features of the German empire as unnational. He directed the positive content of his national consciousness toward the subsequent history of the German law, which he considered to be a continuing tradition, by throwing a national mantle over princely politics. Imperial law, presented as pragmatic history, was the form of national politics which was compatible with the interest-politics of the particular states.

Conring was essentially a politician who invested history in the law to supply a national context for the reason of state, but the role of history in the transmission, however crucial, remained implicit. But in Pufendorf, who was jurist and historian successively, and a German patriot and Prussian official optionally, the relationships involved in the legal conception of German nationality and in the historiographical conveyance of it to particularist politics become explicit—all the more visible, indeed, since Pufendorf's failure to integrate these factors left them juxtaposed, contiguous, and still identifiable. In the *De Statu Imperii Germanici* and the treatises on irregular commonwealths which he wrote in the 1660s during his juristic phase, Pufendorf demonstrated that the German constitution was incomprehensible—"monstrous"—in terms of political categories, and that only through the history of legal facts could its political irregularity be understood. For these facts showed a historical drift from a national monarchy under the emperor's sovereignty to a present near-confederation of princes complicated by the remnants of the emperor's pre-eminence and knowable only through the peculiar present constellation of historically rooted legal relations. The German empire could become a regular political body only as a pure confederation, a state-system composed of "several states that are so connected as to seem to constitute one body but whose members retain sovereignty." Thus the German empire, whose legal history had produced the present internal power-position of the princes, was now to become an international polity through the political will of the princes.[13] Hence the subsequent division of his writing. When he wrote his general history of European empires and states, the German empire, treated as a unit, was his only entry for central Europe *vis-à-vis* the other powers. When he went to Berlin to write the contemporary history of the Brandenburg electors, it was, he

[13] Leonard Krieger, *The Politics of Discretion: Pufendorf and the Acceptance of Natural Law* (Chicago, 1965), pp. 156-64, 178-86.

said, because "I can be more useful to my Fatherland in Berlin,"[14] and he carried over to this particularist political history the same documentary emphasis his century had invested in the pragmatic history of imperial law. Both in content and in method, history became for him the vehicle for transmitting national tradition into particularist politics.

With Leibniz we come to a fascinating problem. Aside from three collections of documents and some inconsequential brief occasional pieces, the only history he wrote was an unfinished work in chronicle form that was published long after his death. What we do have and what we know of his contacts with Maurists, Bollandists, and Muratori correctly identify him as an importer of the new scientific historical methods into Germany. His indebtedness to other sources raises the question of whether his historiography would be discussed at all, beyond this mention, had he not been such a great philosopher and had his philosophy of individual monadic development not had the delayed historiographical impact that it did.[15] The answer brooks two alternative formulations, and both demean Leibniz' history: either his history was not connected with his philosophy and has been raised into false prominence by its fortuitous identity with the philosophy, or his history was connected with his philosophy and is important only for its subliminal impact upon that philosophy.

Certainly, what Leibniz had to say directly about history as such seems to support the judgments of its inessentiality to him and of his inessentiality to it, whatever the formulation, for his propositions on the value of history were utterly banal. He summarized them under the familiar rubrics of "entertainment" (*delectatio*), "usefulness" (*utilitas*), and "truth" (*veritas*). The entertainment in history he found through the usual "pleasure of viewing the unusual aspect of things" and "pleasure of knowing origins." His serious justification of history lay in his judgment of it as "that source from which we receive . . . a great part of our useful truths." He prescribed, therefore, that men "draw from history what is most useful in it," i.e., "the useful lessons furnished us by examples." Utility, in turn, included the whole range of ill-assorted meanings that historians have always lumped together in it: history "is useful for the origins and rights of states and illustrious families"; "history would be most useful if it would only maintain in men their desire for glory, which is the strong-

---

[14] *Ibid.*, p. 275.

[15] For the distinction between the historiographical insignificance of Leibniz's history and the long-range historiographical significance of his philosophy, see Lewis W. Spitz, "The Significance of Leibniz for Historiography," *Journal of the History of Ideas*, Vol. XIII (1952), pp. 333-48.

est motive for fine deeds"—especially in "sovereigns"; but history also has the more exalted use of "teaching prudence and virtue by examples and then showing vice in a way that produces aversion to it." Yet, all these uses notwithstanding, in another context "history has no other usefulness —entertainment aside—than to demonstrate the truth of the Christian religion, because this cannot be done otherwise than by history." While the different species of usefulness were incompatible with each other, even less compatible with the concept of usefulness as a whole was Leibniz' avowal of history's dedication to truth at any cost. "The soul of history in its entirety is truth. . . . History without truth is a body without life. . . . The truth must be told whether it is opportune or inopportune for the occasion, . . . and for the rest the care of it must be left to God, who will know how to preserve it." Such expressions of traditional historiographical piety, be it noted, were advanced not only in casual independence of one another but without reference to Leibniz' own more sophisticated philosophical position that the truth of contingent, *a posteriori*, particular facts, which includes the truth of history, is merely "hypothetical," "probable," "morally certain" (that is, relative); and it has, moreover, only a limited, "mercenary" usefulness.[16]

Leibniz' utterances about history, which were uncharacteristically sententious, were thus not only different in quality from his philosophical thinking but seem to follow from his explicit distinction between the imperfect realm of singular hypothetical facts that history features and the perfect necessity of the general demonstrable reasoning that science and philosophy feature. When we add to these factors his uncertainty about the relations between the two realms (he vacillated between attributions of inferiority and complementarity to the factual realm in general and to historical erudition in particular *vis-à-vis* the rational realm of true science and philosophy) and his consistent aversion to any synthesis or generalization within history itself, the independence of Leibniz' history from his philosophy appears to be confirmed. Alternatively, however, the monad's internal law of development proffers a real temptation to think of Leibniz' dynamic metaphysics as the philosophical translation of his historical orientation. But in fact both these alternatives turn out to be wrong. Leibniz' historical interests and activities went far beyond his writings; they have an autonomous pattern that differs from the substance of his philosophy; and they have a historiographical importance that is indirectly connected with his philosophy through the common mold of the mind behind both.

[16] Quotations from Louis Davillé, *Leibniz Historien* (Paris, 1909), pp. 284, 337-40, 360-67, 508, 547-48, 628.

Leibniz was an omnivorous consumer of ideas and impressions, traditional and novel, particular and general, scientific and aesthetic, consistent and anomalous; and in this all-embracing maw of a mind, the
comparison between the processing of the historical material on the one
side and of the scientific-philosophical material on the other invites
mechanical analogy. When dealing with the sciences and philosophy, he
operated like an intellectual cement mixer, ingesting heterogeneous ingredients and emitting a smooth current of solid product, homogenized
by pre-established harmony in accordance with the law of continuity.
And thus in science and philosophy he, along with Locke and Newton,
synthesized the sundry strands of seventeenth-century thought into forms
immediately usable by the eighteenth. But in history the case was different. Here the mind of Leibniz was a veritable vacuum cleaner, picking
up everything and emitting very little save a warm, aerated stream of
talk, correspondence, and projects. The difference can be found in his
ideas, not in his publications, since, as is well known, his continual shifting among his innumerable interests, his repeated sorties into academic
administration, and his frequent voyages as self-appointed consultant for
international or ecclesiastical relations or as the book- and manuscript-
hunting librarian, which after all was his vocation, meant that Leibniz
published little of anything in his lifetime. But when his intellectual
legacy was probated, there was found to be a categorical difference
between the processed continuum of closely knit philosophical and scientific doctrine, on the one hand, and the broad range of historical ideas
and materials, on the other, which were brought into mutual contact but
left unconnected—a collection conveniently incorporating the available
historiographical elements and representing a first indication of the desire
to connect them, but whose synthesis awaited a future generation.

Leibniz' failure to develop an intellectual system for history was a
failure not of will but of capacity. He worked on his *Annals* off and on for
some thirty-five years, but by the time of his death in 1716, he had only
reached the year 1005, and even that was accomplished because of ducal
pressures. The reason for the protraction and the truncation was not only
his inability to reconcile the incompatible elements, a problem he never
admitted, but the constant extension of the scope, the constantly nagging
uncertainty, and the consequent difficulty of controlling the materials,
which were problems he openly recognized. Leibniz was not aware of the
underlying reasons for his difficulty: he was continuously exposed to
every kind and level of history; not only did this accessibility to the most
varied materials attract him to an ever-expanding orbit of research, but
even more importantly, they bore within themselves different principles
of cohesion which his particularized conception of history did not permit

him to reconcile. This had the effect of chronically irritating what he called his "perfectionist disease."[17] Thus, on the one hand, Leibniz was a fanatic for the new learned history, with its antiquarian emphasis upon the certain truth of discrete facts for their own sakes, with its focus upon origins, with its invocation of ancillary methods and fields such as diplomatics, genealogy, epigraphy, archeology, and, above all, linguistics, and with its preferred object of national culture. But, on the other hand, he also never lost his juristic concerns. They passed over into the pragmatic ingredients of his history, committing him to history as the medium of the universalistic, nationalistic, and pluralistic traditions of the empire—to all of which he subscribed.

As in his philosophy, Leibniz' thinking about ethnography and jurisprudence followed a pattern of "unity amid multiplicity," of "the coincidence of opposites." In both of these structural foundations of his history, German nationality was the concrete universal which was the middle step between such universals as humanity, Europe, or Christendom, and the concrete existences of the several individual nations and states. He studied the linguistic origins of all the nations of Europe, but he concentrated on the German because he found German cultural origins essential to the understanding of the origins of his particular principality, Brunswick, and because he found German linguistic culture a necessary vehicle for the moral education of the citizens in the contemporary empire.[18] The empire itself was for him a continuing series of unities amid multiplicity. "The Empire is the chief member [*Haupt-Glied*], Germany the middle of Europe," he wrote around 1670, and he proceeded to work out both sides of this Janus-faced German empire in his characteristic mode. For Europe, Leibniz proposed that the emperor should function as head arbitrator, thereby establishing harmony amid the diversity of nations to deter the common enemies of peace, of Europe, and of Christendom. For the empire, he developed a truly dialectical juristic argument, in a legal treatise of 1677, which transcended his century's running conflict between the kaiser and the Reich, i.e., the assembled princes. He maintained that every German principality was a reflection of the empire, that every prince represents the emperor—in Leibniz' revealingly Germanized Latin terminology, that the *Fuerstenerius* (the princely principle) is also necessarily *Caesarinus* (that is, has the quality of the emperor)—and that the empire is thus a "new kind of civil person" with a divided sovereignty compatible with the sovereignty of its members.[19] In essence, Leibniz'

[17] *Ibid.*, p. 316.
[18] Gottfried Wilhelm Leibniz, *Politische Schriften* (Frankfurt a/M., 1966), Vol. I, p. 142.
[19] Wolf, "Idee und Wirklichkeit," *Reich und Recht*, ed. Larenz, pp. 156-57.

legal solution for the problem of an impotent and divided Germany was to rationalize the national tradition in both its external and internal relations: he confirmed the universal tradition of the empire by assigning its modern, international function to the emperor; and he confirmed the empire's sanction of internal authority by assigning it to the German-oriented princes.

The crucial point, for us, about Leibniz' ethnographic and juristic structures is that, in principle, they were not present realities but models drawn from past existence whose realization required action in the present. The elements of the two structures—that is, of the national linguistic culture and of the bipartite empire—were present in contemporary existence but without the life that unified them. History was necessary to demonstrate that the structures were living processes. Leibniz' history does bear these structures. Indeed, they constitute the assumptions behind his historiography. But in his history the elements of European culture and the elements of the German empire were related to each other only externally and for brief periods. Ultimately he was driven to distraction, as a historian, by the centrifugal pulls of these materials. The connections he sought to make are revealed in his documentary collections: two volumes of diplomatic documents, the first concerned with all of Europe in late medieval and early-modern times, and the second primarily with documents concerning the German empire; an edition of medieval German historians; and a parallel edition of medieval Brunswickian historians. These collections were completed and published because juxtaposition was all that was required.

But his *Annals* were a different story. Starting from his commission by the Duke to write a history of the House of Brunswick, Leibniz was led by genealogical, ethnological, and constitutional questions to a long search for all kinds of German and European materials, since narrative coherence demanded an ever larger context, particularly of antecedents, and the construction of a certain, positive truth more integrable than was required for the critical edition of documents. Characteristically, his unifying framework for the concatenation of Europe, nation, and particular principalities was the empire. The empire thus became a synthetic methodological principle for him. He believed his *Annals* were necessary to tie together the sundry Italian and German connections, personal and legal, of the original and medieval House of Brunswick. Hence there was real meaning in the apparently ambiguous title, the *Brunswickian Annals of the Western Empire* (*Annales imperii occidentis brunsvicenses*). Indeed, from an original consequence of his particular study, imperial history became an autonomous concern, as his working title, *Annals of the Western Empire Bound Up With* (*innexi*) *the Annals of Brunswick*, implies.

By then he was simply asserting that "I have not been able to do the History of the House without doing that of the Empire."[20]

The fact was that, trying to do both, he did not do much of either. The unfinished work was long on the origins of everything—of the European peoples, of German language, tribes, and culture, and of the Brunswickian dynasty. It was not published until the middle of the nineteenth century, and while the many-sided correspondence and personal contacts that Leibniz built up around it undoubtedly helped to disseminate the standards and approaches characteristic of the new learned history, we shall do better to think of Leibniz as a representative rather than an influential historian. He reflected the full range of historiographical possibilities open to the eighteenth century. To pragmatic legal history with its emphasis on the influence of the national constitutional tradition on the particular state, he added the universal imperial tradition, which had been submerged, and the learned history of national cultural origins, which had been revitalized by the new passion for the sources and the critical techniques of treating them. These elements were combined in various ways to form the main lines of eighteenth-century German historiography.

The two outstanding features of the third and final era of early-modern German historiography, comprising the generation before the French Revolution, undoubtedly were (1) the overt division in German historical literature into two main lines, radically different and often opposed and (2) the beginnings of what would grow into a distinctive German historicism. Let us see what the division meant and what it had to do with early historicism.

The apparent basis of the historiographical dichotomy in eighteenth-century Germany was methodological. Recent historians, like their predecessors, were divided into two schools. On one side, there were the devotees of learned history, enthralled with the opportunities given by the new methods to discover new truth in the form of certainly ascertained facts, and on the other, were the devotees of pragmatic history, now buttressed generally by the Enlightenment's faith in the integration of history through rational principle and particularly by the models of Voltaire and Montesquieu. The distinction is undeniable, for certainly the spate of documentary publications and intensive monographs was informed by an antiquarian enthusiasm quite at variance with the edificatory histories-in-the-large written to instruct men about the principles of human nature.

But actually, however preponderant these emphases in the respective

---

[20] Quoted in Davillé, *Leibniz Historien*, pp. 238, 327.

schools, this distinction was not the primary one. It was bridged for one thing by the fact that in both schools most of the authors who wrote history now wrote it not as humanists or as jurists but as historians, usually by university profession but at least by avocation. It was bridged, secondly, by the important, if subordinate, presence in each school of the approach dominating the other school. The learned historians frequently likened their historical facts to the truths of phenomena scientifically processed by mathematics, and perhaps more than learned historians elsewhere the Germans connected their facts with notions of legal continuity and of pragmatic cause-and-effect.[21] The pragmatic school, correspondingly, adopted new methods of empirical science. Most prominent was A. L. von Schlözer, the rationalist historian who pioneered in the use of statistics for history and at times even defined each in terms of the other: "History is a developing statistics, and statistics is a static (*feststehende*) history."[22] The new statistics and the new economics were used by German pragmatic historians, to write international economic history. And even the well-known secularizer of world history, Johann Christian Gatterer, who gave the ultimate definition of the pragmatic in history as "the universal nexus of things" and of the pragmatic historian as one who "makes general maxims for himself about how events are wont to arise," was also a follower of Maurist learned standards, and his history was a compilation of global tables of juxtaposed facts.[23]

The primary distinction between the two schools was not in the method but in the object of history. During the eighteenth century the empire practically disappeared as an object of history, and the two lines of history in that century were formed by the separation of the two components which the imperial legal tradition had tenuously and ambiguously held in historical relation. The object of one school became international history, that is, of Europe and the world, and the object of the other became the particular principalities. The pragmatic approach was especially appropriate to the new international history—or secularized universal history, if you will—because this history was viewed primarily in terms of its movement into modern international politics and international law. The learned approach was especially appropriate to the history of the principalities when these principalities were considered in terms of genealogical and legal origins and when they were seen in the context of the tribal national culture, whose precedent guaranteed the

[21] Kraus, *Vernunft und Geschichte*, pp. 429, 446, 549-51.

[22] Heinrich Ritter von Srbik, *Geist und Geschichte vom deutschen Humanismus bis zur Gegenwart* (Munich, 1950), Vol. I, p. 124.

[23] Kraus, *Vernunft und Geschichte*, p. 36; Eduard Fueter, *Geschichte der neueirn Historiographie* (3rd ed.; Munich, 1936), p. 375.

national character of the principality. Thus humanity was the prime object of a historiography largely pragmatic and foreign-political, but with an infusion of scientific empiricism. The principality was the prime object of a historiography largely learned and particularistic, but with an infusion of legal pragmatism; and it was linked with the nation through the connection of legal and tribal cultural origins in the historical beginnings of the principality. It was because of the emphasis on the linkage of the tribal nation and the particular principality at its origin that learned history in eighteenth-century Germany concentrated so heavily on the Middle Ages. Nationality thus remained cultural, tribal, original or legal, particularist, and continuous. Characteristically, even in the rare case of a pragmatist appealing to nationality, such as the Prussian manager of the Berlin academy, Hertzberg, it was the ancient tribal Germany that supplied nationality to the modern principality. In a lecture, which incidentally was delivered in French, Hertzberg said, ". . . northern Germany, or Teutony between the Rhine and the Vistula, the area principally of the present Prussian monarchy, is the original fatherland of the heroic nations who in the famous migration of peoples destroyed the Roman Empire and founded and peopled the principal monarchies of Europe."[24]

Historicism was initiated in Germany when the blend of learned and pragmatic approaches to history was balanced enough to link national cultural origins with the particularist legal present through the notion of national political development. The mechanics of the juncture were most visible in Justus Möser, by the general consensus of posterity the only eighteenth-century German historian comparable in stature to the French and British masters. Möser had the learned historians' appreciation for the variegation of original historical facts but also the pragmatists' taste for the centrality of law and their need for thematic unity in history. He focused these different historical tendencies upon a single integral agency: "the common landed-property-owners," who must be considered "the authentic constituents of the nation" and whose history "supplied not only the unity, the direction, and the power of an epic . . . but also the origin, the development, and the several proportions of the national character amid all its changes."[25] These propertied commoners, in their undifferentiated community, formed the original German tribal nation, and it was their legal differentiation first into the free and equal estates of nobles and commons (edlen und gemeinen) and then into oppressed

[24] Heinz Gollwitzer, Europabild und Europagedanke: Beiträge zur deutschen Geistesgeschichte des 18. und 19. Jahrhunderts (Munich, 1951), p. 76.
[25] Justus Möser, Sämtliche Werke ed. Paul Göttsching (Hamburg, 1964), Vol. XII, Part 1, p. 34.

subjects of empire and principalities, deprived of honor, property rights, and freedom, that constituted the genuine history of Germany. Emperor and princes alike, in this conception, did not form the "body" (Körper) of the nation but were mere "accidents" that happened to it. Thus the emperor and particular princes were servants of the people who had removed themselves despotically from the nation and whose history was therefore not the history of the nation. "My ideal," Möser wrote, "is the history of the nobles and commons. To them I give a general [the emperor] with the power of appointing his officers [the imperial princes]. Thus I keep sovereignty in the people and exclude the Emperors' and princely parties [*Cäsarinos und Fürstnerios*], who have hitherto squabbled over things which belong not to either of them but to the people."

With this "exciting new theory," as he called it, Möser claimed that he had simultaneously "revolutionized all previous systems of Imperial and particularist history [*Reichs—und Landesgeschichte*] and limited Imperial and princely rights [*die kaiserlichen und landesherrlichen Rechte*] on the basis of entirely new principles." He believed that, through historical and legal focus on the "common landed-property-owners," he had found the historiographical, political, and national unity hitherto lacking in Germany.[26] With "the history of the people [*Volks*] and its form of government" as his subject, cultural history would be joined to political history—"the history of religion, of jurisprudence, of philosophy, and of the fine arts is indivisible from the history of states"[27]—and legal history to both. In this way, German history would be seen for what it really was: the continuous, "epic" passage of the common landed property-owners from the original cultural integrity of the ancient German tribal community, through the successive stages of its organic differentiation into the estates of nobles and commons and its abrupt "denouement" in an imperially imposed inorganic "dissolution" under "territorial sovereignty and despotism," into its current postscriptural reintegration under the aegis of "state-citizenship"—all measured by the touchstone of the changing public and private law bearing upon the liberties and rights of the property-owners.[28]

But Möser's expectations were not quite matched by his actual achievement. Though he looked forward to the integrated national history of the nineteenth-century future, his achievement epitomized the centrifugal qualities of the fissiparous early-modern historiographical past. Indeed, he climaxed and confirmed all three of the leading attri-

[26] *Ibid.*, Vol. XII, Part 1, pp. 15, 17.
[27] *Ibid.*, Vol. XII, Part 1, p. 43.
[28] *Ibid.*, Vol. XII, Part I, p. 19, 34.

butes which we have been following in this historiography. First, for
Möser, like historians before him, political relations were reduced to legal
categories through the medium of history. His total historical performance rests on this point of view, as "the rediscovery of the fundamental
levels of the distinctive German *Volk* and its integration into the system
of public law." Second, for him, German nationality was invested in the
particular states of contemporary Germany: the "fortunate particularism"
which he celebrated was a judgment which reflected precisely the exclusive national agency that he assigned to the several territories.[29] These
particular territories were so many articulations of the German nation for
Möser because he identified them with their "people"—landowners and
estates of landowners—and not with their princes. He was nationally
optimistic about German particularism because he saw the territorial
estates recovering the rights to property and of self-government which
linked them with the ancient German tribal past and which would reas-
sert their legitimate authority over the territorial leaders, who were originally their representatives and whose divisive princely sovereignty was an
outgrowth of the illicit powers invested in them by the medieval emperors.
"I prove," he wrote summarily, "that a count or a duke was originally
nothing but a representative of the commons in the national diet [*Reichstag*] . . . , [and] that our particular territorial estates [*Landstände*] are
in effect the old national estates [*Reichstände*]."[30] Hence his method for
developing a newfangled "history of Germany" turned out to be simply a
preface for what was in fact a history of the ecclesiastical principality of
Osnabrück. The limitation can be attributed more to Möser's essential
convictions that the fourth and final stage of German history was characterized by "the perfection of particularism" and that "the illumination
of one's province" was particularly revealing of the rich variety of the
national life than to his acknowledgment of the practical challenge which
the scope of a truly national history laid down to some future "German
Livy."[31]

But it was in his third representative function that Möser transmitted
the characteristic of early-modern German historiography which would
prove most influential in the subsequent history of Germany: the primal
association of German nationality with the original culture of the ancient
German tribes. It was this theme, indeed, on which the varied tendencies
of his historiography converged, which endowed them with the only
consistency they had, and which gave his work the appearance of whole-

[29] *Ibid.*, Vol. XII, Part 1, p. 39; Vol. XII, Part 2, pp. 16-17, 22.
[30] *Ibid.*, Vol. XII, Part 1, pp. 15-16.
[31] *Ibid.*, Vol. XII, Part 1, pp. 39-45.

ness despite its incompletion in historical time and its localization in territorial space. He combined classical humanism and barbarian patriotism by attributing Roman attributes of citizenship to the presumed civil rights and duties of the tribal Germans; he combined cultural origins and legal tradition by applying philological criticism to legal sources; and he combined his irrational love of the individual and the organic with his insistence on systematic plan, pattern, and utility, taken straight out of the pragmatic Enlightenment, by making the original integrity of the variegated tribal communities the constant theme of German history and the recurrent end of writing German history. Hence Möser's preoccupation with cultural origins, like his focus on the national microcosm in Osnabrück, was based on essential rather than practical grounds: they conformed to the fundamental direction which German history gave to German historiography in the early-modern period.

The distinctiveness of the German historiography follows logically from our survey. Where the regular model of western Europe shows a divided historiography ultimately synthesized by a unified political object and a common national consciousness, the German model shows a historical synthesis which would ultimately homogenize a split national consciousness and provide cultural support for mass politics. Certainly it is not too much to see in the historical constitution of the legitimate bases of German politics a built-in conservative tendency which would carry down to our own time. But is it too much to draw a lesson from the fact that scientific historians were the first to build into the German national consciousness the original German tribal culture which would become the outstanding authentic conviction in the Nazis' appeal?

CHAPTER IV

ENGLAND

JOHN POCOCK

The perception of history in its relation to national consciousness is a
subject that raises awkward questions of definition when we are dealing
with a prehistoricist, early-modern society in which the various forms of
historical writing and understanding were differently, and perhaps less,
organized than they are today. To me it seems that, at least in respect of
early-modern England, this is not a matter that can be most conveniently
treated in terms of historiography, if by that word we mean the writing
of histories. It is not identical (to say the same thing in other words)
with what has been called the Historical Revolution in England,[1] the
rapid development between 1550 and 1700 of Englishmen's ability to
write histories which embraced new materials and displayed new techniques of narrative, criticism, and control. Such a rapid development did
indeed occur, and it is a part of the subject at hand; but the point I want
to emphasize is that the writing of histories, especially in a culture where
the genre was dominated by the chronicle and by humanist-classical
methods, is not necessarily identical with the articulation and employment
of images of the nation or national structure as it was seen to exist in time.
Expressions of national consciousness, when they did occur, were not
confined to histories; they were present in other literary forms as well.
Likewise, the articulation of historical awareness is not the same as the
writing of histories; though the latter may well serve as a valuable source
of evidence, direct and indirect, about the former. Since we are concerned in this essay with history as a form of political culture and a
branch of national consciousness, it seems to follow that we should turn
our attention to those modes of awareness in which the nation and its

---

[1] F. Smith Fussner, *The Historical Revolution: English Historical Writing and
Thought, 1580-1640* (London: Routledge and Kegan Paul, 1962). See also F. J.
Levy, *Tudor Historical Thought* (San Marino: The Huntington Library, 1967).

politics were seen as existing in time, and that we should study them in their origin and function as well as in their content. This will define our subject—to employ the jargon I recommend for such purposes—in terms not so much of historiography as of the time dimension of political thought.

I am proposing, then, that we should study time dimensions—images of pasts and their continuities with presents—first and histories second, the latter coming in as they arise. But time dimensions and pasts of what? The more I have worked in this field, the more I have been impressed by the diversity of answers that can be given to this question. I am responsible for a good deal of rather undigested theory suggesting that in a complex, scribal, and institutionalized society there may be as many pasts as there are institutionalized activities capable of preserving and transmitting a memory and, further, that these pasts and their transmission will vary according to the structure of the institutions of which they are the time dimensions.[2] Early-modern England will bear this out if it be true—as I think it is: this was a society in which, for example, a cleric, a lawyer, and a herald might remember very different historical pasts and remember them for different reasons. But the position is further complicated when one introduces the concepts of "nation," "national consciousness," and "national past." "Nation" is a symbolic entity under which are grouped a diversity of social institutions and activities, many of which possess pasts of their own, and yet, at the same time, "nation" attracts to itself myths and symbolic stories suggestive of a common past which may or may not be related to the institutional pasts. The difference between "national epos" and "institutional past" is therefore important but not absolute, since some institutional pasts will play a more visible part in composing the epos than others.

What then was "England" and what past did it possess? Put in another way, when did those inhabitants of the island of Britain who were neither Celtic-speaking nor subjects of the northern line of kings develop a common awareness of "England" as an identity including them all and of a national epos which was part of its definition? I have a fairly strong sense that I do not know, that not many people do know, and that those who ought to know and perhaps do are medievalists. Nevertheless, it would be valuable to know more about the national perspective of the patriotic

[2] "The Origins of Study of the Past: a comparative approach," in *Comparative Studies in Society and History*, Vol. IV, no. 2 (1962), pp. 209-46; and "Time, Institutions and Action: An essay on traditions and their understandings," *Politics and Experience: Essays presented to Michael Oakeshott*, ed. P. King and B. C. Parekh (Cambridge: Cambridge University Press, 1968), pp. 209-38, reprinted in J. G. A. Pocock, *Politics, Language and Time* (New York: Atheneum, 1971), pp. 233-72.

mythographers of Elizabethan and Jacobean literature—for example, when and why they thought it desirable to write "England," when "Britain," and when "Albion." I mention this matter because, however glibly we talk about "British history" and ourselves as "British historians," it remains true that, since the heroic but premodern labors of William Camden, considered today one of the giants of his period, no worthwhile "history of Britain" has in fact been written.[3] Francis Bacon indeed proposed to James VI and I that because the two crowns were now united, a converging history of the two realms ought to be put together;[4] but Bacon was proposing more than was ever performed. The characteristic that has dominated "British" historiography ever since has been neatly summarized by Daniel Defoe in the lines:

> The silent nations undistinguished fall
> And Englishman's the common name for all.[5]

The ethnocentricity and conceptual imperialism of English national consciousness do mean, however, that it forms a self-sufficient and thereby a more intelligible field of study. What follows in this essay is, therefore, focused upon England and is based less on the study of the national epos than on that of the national and historical consciousnesses (the plural is deliberate) emerging from what I have termed the time dimension of political thought. Such consciousnesses, or modes of consciousness, I want next to suggest, occur in two forms or may be looked at from two angles. The first is the more strictly institutional: organized modes of behavior, subsocieties, or institutions preserve images of their continuous activity and existence in a past which is constituted by the image itself, and these are preserved in order to legitimize the continued existence and activity of the institution in the present. The result is that the mode of legitimation and the mode of continuity are largely, if not wholly, created by extrapolation from the activity of the institution in question. In Tudor England, the church, the law, the crown itself, and on a lesser scale of importance, the college of heralds can be detected as possessing such institutionalized and self-legitimizing pasts; and it can be noted both that the modes of consciousness thus generated entered into

---

[3] Such a history would presumably depict the concurrent existence and interactions of the diverse peoples and cultures which have from time to time inhabited the Atlantic archipelago adjacent to northwest Europe and have established offshoot cultures at various points further beyond seas. It would be too serious a matter to be left to the English.

[4] F. J. Levy (ed.), *The History of the Reign of King Henry VII, by Francis Bacon* (Indianapolis: Bobbs Merrill, 1972), Appendix, p. 255.

[5] *The True-Born Englishman: A Satyr* (London, 1701), lines 364-65.

the national epos and colored it—as well as being colored by it and by each other—and that all (including the national epos) remained to a high degree institutionally self-sufficient and distinct from one another.

The second kind of time dimension is less institutionalized and it may help to think of it as occurring in the present rather than in the perfect tense. It can be located by identifying the modes of political action which are held to be available to the members of a political society, by asking what public realm or theater of action these modes presuppose, and by determining what dimension in time it is necessary that these structures of behavior possess. Should a society have institutionalized all its modes of action to a comparable degree, the time dimensions identified by this second kind of inquiry will of course be identical with those located by the first. But it is also possible that we shall find conceptions of action that were marginal or external to the institutionalized structure or, as performed by the individual actor, that existed prior to any institution; and when this happens we shall be in the interesting position of having located conceptualizations of history in terms of structures of contingent action. In the period with which we are concerned, there were two extreme and limiting cases: first, action by the antinomian saint, justified by direct personal contact with the sacred in acting against, or without reference to, the whole structure of secular institutions; second, action by the Machiavellian or Hobbesian individual, finding no pre-existent structure of institutional sanctions and driven to rely upon the capacity for political action itself—Machiavellian *virtù* or Hobbesian "institution"—to legitimize what was being done. Each of these entailed a time dimension, and these in turn, as might be expected, differed widely.

In what is to follow I intend adopting the second of these broad schemes of categorization as an explanatory and analytical device. There are several reasons why it seems expedient to do this. In the first place, since it permits proceeding from the less to the more institutionalized, the second scheme can be handled in such a way as includes the first. Englishmen of the sixteenth and seventeenth centuries were capable of extraordinarily radical action while remaining highly conservative and even traditionalist in their modes of perception and behavior; the procedure I propose to adopt permits us to see in relation to each other the time dimensions apparent to both halves of their strangely divided minds.

In the second place, I shall have the opportunity of recommending, and employing, a model which seems to span the extremes of both the schemes of categorization I have outlined. It does so by affirming that the early-modern, or post-medieval, mind was initially able to deal with history as the structure of contingent time. That is, they could perceive the sequence of particular secular events only by subsuming these under one of three general concepts: usage, which gave rise to time as the dimension of institutionalized tradition or custom; grace, in which time appeared as the dimension of providence, prophecy, or eschatology; and fortune, in which it became the dimension of the altogether contingent.[6] Political action might thus be seen as undertaken by the individual as institutionalized and custom-maintaining animal, as sanctified individual justified by grace, or as delegitimized animal adventuring in a sublunary sphere of contingency and action. Each of these modes of perception entailed its corresponding theater of action, with a dimension in time, and none of the three was, either in principle or in practice, hermetically sealed against the other two. The individual's action in time was multidimensional, and consequently so was time itself. This of course has to do with the mixture—at times the dichotomy—of radicalism and conservatism that was apparent in English political self-perception and behavior.

In the third place, the approach I recommend has the advantage that it enables us to deal directly with the problem of English civic consciousness. This has been usefully defined in a recent work by Donald W. Hanson[7] as the individual's awareness of himself as a political and public actor as well as his cognizance of the existence of a public realm capable of serving as the theater of his actions. But Hanson goes on to develop the argument that such a consciousness was not really possible until the civil wars of the 1640s, because until the traditional constitution collapsed, English thought was enslaved to a way of thinking to which he gives the name "double majesty." This presented government in terms either of authority descending from the king or of privilege and liberty ascending from the people, and the two were conceptually incompatible to the point where the individual could find no means of conceptualizing himself as civic actor. When the double order disintegrated and he was forced to account for his own actions, there occurred a trauma in some ways resembling Hans Baron's revolution of *vita activa* and *vivere civile* against the hierarchical values of the high Middle Ages;[8] English civic consciousness was demedievalized and appeared.

Hanson's thesis is in some respects useful. The duality of descending

[6] For other statements of this model, see *Politics, Language and Time*, pp. 81-85; and "Custom and Grace, Form and Matter: An approach to Machiavelli's concept of innovation," *Machiavelli and the Nature of Political Thought*, ed. M. Fleisher (New York: Atheneum, 1971), pp. 156-59.

[7] *From Kingdom to Commonwealth: The development of Civic Consciousness in English political Thought* (Cambridge, Massachusetts: Harvard University Press, 1970).

[8] Hans Baron, *The Crisis of the Early Italian Renaissance*, (rev. ed.; Princeton: Princeton University Press, 1966).

authority and ascending liberty did inhibit thought in ways he describes, and the intellectual responses of the First Civil War and Rump-Commonwealth periods are in large part those of individuals forced to assert themselves by that duality's collapse. But the model-building in which I have so far been engaged will, I think, convey my sense that civic consciousness, as he defines it, can occur in many forms which "double majesty" might not effectively preclude. It is possible that the archetypical Tudor Englishman saw England as a structure of authority rather than a theater of action and that he viewed its continuity through time as the transmission of that authority rather than of any mode of civic action by the individual. We must remain alert to this possibility. But a good deal of evidence and a wealth of recent interpretations show that the early-modern period was one in which the individual's consciousness of himself as social being and political actor—as humanist counselor or as Puritan saint, as radical soldier or as Whig proprietor, as classical citizen or as parliamentary representative—was on the increase and entailed changes in the structure of political thought. I think it can also be shown that an explosion of civic consciousness in various forms preceded the Civil War and helped occasion it, instead of occurring, as Hanson would suggest, merely as its consequence. Even if Hobbesian man be thought of as engaged in the privatization of his social life under the sword of the mortal god's authority, Hobbes's language is that of a conscious reactionary, engaged in trying to reverse a swing toward political activism which he thought had gone too far. We may therefore take the risk of emphasizing, throughout at least the Elizabethan and Jacobean periods, those forms of social and historical awareness which were founded on the individual's perception of his role, while remaining alert to those which were founded on the transmission through time of systems of authority. The inclusion, in the model I outlined earlier, of custom and use as one mode of responding to the contingent may help to bridge the gap between the two; for the individual as inheritor and bequeather of custom was, I shall suggest, more than a simply "traditional" animal—in Chinese terms, he was a creator as well as a transmitter.

But most of us would say that English humanists were the first within our period consciously to see themselves as secular political beings outside the citadel of supreme power. The problems of definition and interpretation with which they confront us are far from having been overcome. Arthur B. Ferguson's *The Articulate Citizen and the English Renaissance*[9] is to me the most stimulating treatment of these matters, because he treats English civic humanism—I know that using the term is begging

---

[9] Durham, North Carolina: Duke University Press, 1965.

the question—in terms of an evolution of the idea of the counselor. Through Thomas Starkey, Thomas More, and Thomas Smith, he traces the developing image of the distinctive skills, functions, and moral responsibilities which the counselor exercises in advising his prince, until the fomer has become a political being—and something like a citizen— in his own right, and the realm itself a community of counsel in a secular as well as a moral sense. Even though Ferguson detects by the time of Smith the beginnings of an awareness that the realm has grown and improved itself in secular time, he does not suggest that the lineage of thinkers whom he studies produced a historical image of England, or a mode of writing English history, distinctively their own. A critic, desirous of emphasizing the other side of the model Ferguson presents, might suggest that the moral aspects of counsel remained, after all, uppermost in the majority of minds and ensured that the humanist presentation of English history was reabsorbed by the literature of the rise and fall of princes, of the *Mirror for Magistrates* and the chronicle plays, which remained essentially moralist and Christian, dominated by images of fortune, providence, and the seven deadly sins, and linked in its turn to the nonhistorical presentation of the human universe as a "frame of order," of correspondence and degree, so well known to us all.[10] Such a critic might further link these phenomena with a tendency on the part of the humanist counselor to become a courtier and act in terms of an ethic derived from Castiglione, through Elyot, conveying no image whatever of public action in a public realm, or of history as the time dimension of these things.

We might indeed reply by pointing out that for every man who successfully became a courtier, several more retired in dudgeon to their estates, or to London or Saffron Walden, and began laying the foundations for an ideology of the alienated country.[11] So far, however, attempts to classify late-Tudor humanists on the basis of a court-country distinction have yielded little satisfaction; it may nevertheless be that these attempts have been wrongly conceived. To look at persons who may be considered "humanists" within the meaning of the relevant Act of a Historical Congress, and to categorize them as belonging to court or to country, may simply be to operate with the wrong sample. To the extent

[10] The most recent exposition of this theme is that of W. H. Greenleaf, *Order, Empiricism and Politics: Two traditions of English political thought, 1500-1700* (Oxford: Oxford University Press, 1964). Since this book was published, emphasis has tended to shift to the less hierarchical and more kinetic aspects of the Elizabethan-Jacobean political vision, and the time may be ripe for a reassessment.

[11] H. F. Kearney, *Scholars and Gentlemen: Universities and society in pre-industrial Britain, 1500-1700* (London: Faber, 1970), pp. 34-45.

—and we agree that it is a large one—to which humanism in England became the ideology of the counselor, would it not be well to remember that the great theater in which was played out the drama of counselors at loggerheads with the prince who sought their advice, and in which men sought influence and advancement first through counseling the prince and then by opposing him, was, or came to be, parliament fully as much as it was court?

In this great anti-court there took shape an ideology which is that of counselors exploring the ambivalences of their own position: the ideology of parliamentary privilege, of the Ancient Constitution, of the common law as a body of immemorial custom inclusive of all the institutions of the realm. From parliament and the Inns of Court, this ideology radiated through the whole body of the increasingly self-conscious parliamentary and country gentry; and of the lawyers and antiquarians who were active at every stage of its growth, surely it is safe to say that here we have the true country humanists of England. To describe them by that term does indeed pass over the question of how their home-grown brand of learning can be said to have descended from any of the movements in scholarship properly known as humanism, but there is reason to believe that question could be answered; while the advantages of saying that there was an English brand of legal humanism, to set beside that of the great scholars of Bourges and Paris, are not to be ignored. More broadly than this, we do speak of humanism in one sense as, the intellectual and scholarly expression of a conscious involvement in the documents and institutions of secular society and, in another, as the ideology of those whose personal activity in the government of monarchical realms was heightened through performance of the role of counselor to prince. The legal antiquarians, at all events, served as ideologists to a profession (the common law), to a political grouping (the House of Commons and its electorates), and to a social class (the country gentry); and their thought very powerfully affected the culture of all three.

The doctrine of the Ancient Constitution is the first magisterial expression of a time dimension in English political society with which my method of analysis has led me to deal, though I am not certain that it was necessarily the first to emerge in point of historical time; and I have yet to show that it was the time dimension of a mode of conscious political activity. It would be superficial to dismiss it as the mere conceptual extension into the past of the mode of activity of the parliamentary gentry, without pointing out that its seminal idea, drawn from the procedures and paradigms of the courts of common law, was custom and usage. It presented the English past as an immemorial continuity of custom, which was constantly adapted and no less constantly maintained, in a way which makes it one of the greatest articulations of traditionalism and the philosophy of tradition to be found in the history of civilized man—only classical Confucianism, I believe, ranks with or surpasses it. The conceptual sophistication of which it was capable, in hands like those of Selden or Hale, should remind us that traditionalism may be very much more than a mere inert acceptance of tradition. We are to some extent disposed to mistake it for such, by the habit which was till recently prevalent among social scientists of using the concept "traditional society" as the antithesis and prelude to "modernization"; but both philosophers of conservatism and historians of social thought can teach us better, by reminding us that conservation is an activity as well as a disposition and is not a mere posture of acceptance. The custom-bearing social individual was seen, by his seventeenth-century hypostatizers, as receiving, remembering, refining, and transmitting usages; he was capable of interpretation, criticism, rejection, and even fiction. This was a mode of public action; the realm as a structure of law, possessing a common custom, was its theater; and the immemorial past was its time dimension.

The explanation which I have elsewhere offered[12] for the existence of this mode of thought is structural: the common-law courts were an established part of freeholding society, and its assumptions were embedded in English social consciousness. Because society was assumed to be a fabric of law, law assumed to be custom, and custom assumed to be immemorial, it followed that there was nothing in the social structure which could not be affirmed to be immemorial. I still believe this explanation to be good as far as it goes, but it does not tell us why the doctrine of the Ancient Constitution is rather hard to find in the early sixteenth century and extremely prevalent at its close. What, in other words, is the developmental, as opposed to the structural, explanation of its coming into being? It is tempting to try to overcome this problem by demonstrating that the consciousness of the parliamentary gentry expanded as they moved into litigation and education, office and parliament. But there is another dimension of time consciousness and a new historical ideology, which grew up alongside legal antiquarianism and seems in several ways to have been interlaced with it, so that the two need to be looked at together. This is nothing other than the growth of a national apocalyptic; beside the Ancient Constitution it is necessary to set the Elect Nation.

In *The Revolution of the Saints*,[13] that brilliant study of seven years

[12] *The Ancient Constitution and the Feudal Law* (Cambridge: Cambridge University Press, 1957; New York: W. W. Norton and Co., 1967), chap. II, pp. 30-55.

[13] Michael Walzer, *The Revolution of the Saints: A study in the origins of radical politics* (Cambridge, Massachusetts: Harvard University Press, 1965).

ago, Michael Walzer depicted the Calvinist intellectual—Huguenot and Puritan—as the first alienated radical, the first man of modern times so deeply convinced of his loneliness before God and his separation from the institutions and traditions of society that he constructed for himself a theology and a discipline, indeed an activist program, conceived throughout in the only terms appropriate for individuals associating on the basis of their utter separateness from each other. It has always seemed to some historians, myself included, that Walzer offered a splendidly satisfying account of one side of the Puritan personality but that there were other aspects into which he did not penetrate. He deliberately refrained, for example, from extending his analysis to the separatists and sectarians of the Civil War and Commonwealth years, whose radicalism took a form different from the austere withdrawal he ascribed to the classical Calvinists; they staged a militant attempt to remodel the institutions of society, in which they were confronted by radical saints very like themselves, except in their determination to retain those institutions as far as possible. Nor did he investigate the millennialism characteristic of all factions, Anglican and Puritan, in those years and earlier, which was part of what made the English Independents as horrifyingly incomprehensible to Scottish, Dutch, and French Calvinists as they were to Lutherans and Catholics. Walzer's saints follow Calvin himself in a bleak refusal of specific millennial expectations, though as we shall see this was at no time characteristic of English Puritans. Now in the model I set out earlier in this lecture, apocalyptic is one of the modes of dealing with the contingent event; the latter is rendered intelligible by equation with one of the occurrences or persons foretold in canonical or uncanonical prophecy. That is, the secular is assimilated to the apocalyptic, a technique likely to be adopted only by minds so deeply committed to the secular that they are willing to invoke sacred history to explain it. Given the undeniable addiction of English Puritans to apocalyptic, did it follow that there was an aspect of their personalities as deeply involved in the secular order as the aspect studied by Walzer was divorced from it? Might this be the key to the division of revolutionary Independency into radicals and conservatives, which he abstained from exploring? Contemporary with and subsequent to the publication of *The Revolution of the Saints*, a number of works have appeared which are devoted to this question, and whatever this impact upon Walzer's argument, they have uncovered a new dimension of English historical thought in this period.

William Haller's *Foxe's Book of Martyrs and the Elect Nation*[14] is the key study in this regard. Foxe's history, he points out, is a product of the

[14] New York: Columbia University Press; London: Jonathan Cape, 1963.

Marian exile, and the exiles were not the alienated individuals depicted by Walzer any more than they were the upwardly mobile paranoiacs of Norman Cohn's *Pursuit of the Millennium.*[15] They were, on the contrary, learned and gifted members of a ruling clerisy, entertaining high hopes of legitimate power in a structure of authority which they accepted as wholly legitimate.[16] As Protestants, they repudiated the claims of the sacramental church to be the Body of Christ, i.e., the real presence in time of a communion which was otherwise in eternity. This disposed them to see the church as a community of faithful continuously expecting the fulfillment of a salvation prophesied for the end of time. But because of their belief that the false church had been justly legislated out of existence, in an England which "sundry old authentic histories and chronicles" revealed to have always been an "empire," they were as strongly disposed to believe in a high degree of identity between the true church and the justly legislating empire and nation. The latter must occupy a position, or play a role, in the struggle between true church and Antichrist which took up the time between Christ's ascension and his return and was the matter of apocalyptic prophecy; but the nation must do this as an institutional and historic structure possessing a past of its own, which might be not unlike the time dimension of institutional continuity —the Ancient Constitution. In his *Acts and Monuments*, therefore, Foxe developed a new structure for apocalyptic time, one in which England— the Elect Nation—with its history became the principal actor in the struggle against Antichrist; and Antichrist himself, ceasing to be the demonic impostor who should come just before the end of time with the false claim that Christ had already returned, was portrayed as the pope, with his equally false claim that Christ was always present in the sacraments and in the church as his body. History was pitted against the real presence as the true vehicle of Christian redemption, and England was shown as the embodiment of this truth throughout history, and in a certain sense the embodiment of history itself. Before Foxe his friend, John Bale, and after him his superior, Matthew Parker, labored to build up a new national epos, in which Joseph of Arimathea, Constantine, Wyclif, and Elizabeth were seen as asserters of England's independence of the pa-

[15] This work, first published in 1957, concerned itself with chiliasm as a phenomenon of a certain sort of medieval social radicalism. Since Cohn did much to pioneer the modern revival of interest in millenarism in all its branches, it is perhaps unfair that so many subsequent writers—Lamont and myself included—have felt moved to point out that millenarism, or the apocalyptic mode of thought, could be found in conservative contexts as well as radical; Professor Cohn did not seek to persuade us otherwise.

[16] Haller, *Foxe's Book* (London edition), p. 85.

pacy and of England's role as standard-bearer of the true church and as Elect Nation. Institutional continuity joined hands with apocalyptic uniqueness; and God revealed himself, as his manner was, first to his Englishmen.[17]

Of what mode of civic action may we say that this was the time dimension? It was not that of Walzerian saints, it would seem, but of God's Englishmen: inhabitants of a secular realm whose sovereign and imperial independence was not only the badge but, in a sense, the mode of its election. Several inferences may be drawn. In the first place, it is clear that Foxean apocalyptic was the consequence of involvement in, not alienation from, secular institutions; and we are reminded that apocalyptic, which sacralizes secular time, must always in an opposite sense secularize the sacred, by drawing the processes of salvation into that time which is known as *saeculum*. The apocalyptic and millennial tones which distinguish English Puritanism from adjacent forms of Calvinism are therefore, in some degree, the product of English secular and institutional nationalism; the ancient constitution did not make the nation elect, but obliged it to consider its election as that of a nation. In the second place, secular autonomy and the ability to govern itself in history were the mark of the nation's independence from Roman jurisdiction, its religious purity, and—in England—its elect role as the adversary of Antichrist. A kind of historicism thus made its appearance in the language of nationalist anti-Romanism, in which the sovereignty of national institutions was reinforced by the assertion that their uniqueness was the consequence of conditions peculiar to the nation in question and to its existence in secular time. In the case of France, Donald R. Kelley has traced the association between Gallicanism and the emergence of protohistoricist scholarship,[18] in which the very complex interaction of French institutions came by the time of Etienne Pasquier to be depicted as a process of national self-formation unrelated to conditions or authorities existing outside the realm. Nothing like this kind of sophistication could develop in England, owing to the grip which the common law and its presumption of immemoriality exercised over the English mind. However, it could be, and was, asserted that the national institutions, being nothing more than custom, emerged strictly from the experience of the English people and evinced the uniqueness of their genius and their capacity to evolve institutions perfectly satisfactory to themselves, "like a silkworm which spin-

---

[17] Levy, *Tudor Historical Thought*, pp. 76-123.

[18] Donald R. Kelley, *Foundations of Modern Historical Scholarship: Language, law and history in the French Renaissance* (New York: Columbia University Press, 1970), pp. 151-82, 261-63, 296-99.

neth all her web out of herself only."[19] It is easy to see how this could enter into the context of Foxean apocalyptic and help to make uniqueness a further badge of election. England, like Israel and repeating its types, was a peculiar people. In Scotland, by way of comparison, the people was under as strong a compulsion to declare itself peculiar, but in the absence of a common law like that of England there could be no myth of the Ancient Constitution, just as, in the absence of a coordinating jurisdiction like that of the French *parlements*, there could be no equivalent of Gallican historiography. Does it not follow that there was no equivalent of Foxean apocalyptic either, no myth of the Scottish nation elect in its history?[20]

The interactions of the time dimensions of custom and of grace, of the Ancient Constitution and the Elect Nation, provide the clues to much that was to follow in the development of English historical self-imagery. As a form of legal humanism, the culture of the Ancient Constitution possessed something of the humanist capacity to generate, through strictly scholarly enquiry, its own methods of self-criticism. The Jacobean legal antiquaries, setting out with an orthodox enthusiasm to probe into the past of immemorial custom and religious nationalism, had before the Civil War begun evolving, through means that involved study of the laws and languages of adjacent Europe and correspondence with their Continental fellows and colleagues, a perception of the English past that included a massive introduction of feudal institutions which had developed elsewhere, followed by the slow working of these institutions either out of or into the main-stream of English custom. The implications of this, whose story has been told elsewhere,[21] were of course revolutionary, and may be compared with those of the perception by Florentine classical humanists, that medieval *volgare* culture was autonomous, the product of its own conditions, and not to be reduced under classical norms.[22] But while the effect of realizing that English history was not autonomous, but partly European, might in the long run be to render it more unique, the immediate effect was to challenge its capacity to legitimate existing institutions. A perception of the past based on the autonomy of historical criticism must be in part relativist. The pasts uncovered by historical

[19] Sir John Davies, writing about 1614; quoted in Pocock, *The Ancient Constitution and the Feudal Law*, pp. 32-4.

[20] Such are the findings of Arthur H. Williamson of Washington University in a doctoral dissertation now in preparation: "Antichrist's Role in Scotland: The Imagery of Evil and the Search for a National Past."

[21] Pocock, *Ancient Constitution*, chaps. IV and V.

[22] Baron, *Crisis*, chap. 15.

criticism had existed for their own sake, not to legitimate the practices of succeeding ages, and it could follow that at no moment in its history had government been wholly legitimate. These pasts might have to be understood by means that did not involve or aim at legitimation, and the national consciousness might have to take on a new dimension of self-criticism. This leads us to an interesting question, the answers to which have not yet been fully settled and which probably lie somewhere within the life-span of Sir Robert Cotton: To what extent did the appearance of a past which included an element of unlegitimated feudalism coincide with the emergence, in the soured minds of Jacobean courtiers, of Tacitean and Machiavellian modes of understanding politics,[23] whose time dimension would certainly not be one of uninterrupted legitimacy? It would seem that Raleigh and Bacon pioneered the idea that the first Tudors transformed the structure of English politics by destroying the military power of the nobility and by bringing themselves face to face with the commons in parliament—a view which combined some understanding of what may be termed feudalism with elements of what may be termed Machiavellism.

A change in past-awareness of this order—one, that is, produced by a relatively autonomous movement in critical scholarship—is difficult to relate to changes in the national consciousness. The crisis in relations between the two dominant modes of past-awareness we have so far detected—between the Ancient Constitution and the Elect Nation—has been located, through the studies of William M. Lamont,[24] about the year 1641. He identifies it with the increasing tendency of radical Puritans to move from the apocalyptic of John Foxe toward that of Thomas Brightman and, specifically, with their assertion that the Church of England, as by law established, was merely the "church in Laodice" (denounced as lukewarm in the third chapter of *Revelations*) and that the "church in Philadelphia," which had kept the faith even though it had but little power, lay elsewhere, in Scotland or New England, or in the future.[25] Philadelphia, the saving remnant, is a symbol that recurs through the centuries in heterodox apocalyptic; it is found in Joachite and Fraticelli prophecies of the fourteenth century,[26] and one wonders whether Wil-

[23] Levy, *Tudor Historical Thought*, pp. 250-74; Introduction to *Henry VII*, pp. 40-53.

[24] *Marginal Prynne, 1600-1669* (London: Routledge and Kegan Paul, 1963); *Godly Rule: Politics and religion, 1603-60* (London: Macmillan, 1969).

[25] *Marginal Prynne*, pp. 59-64; *Godly Rule*, pp. 49-52.

[26] Marjorie Reeves, *The Influence of Prophecy in the Later Middle Ages* (Oxford: Oxford University Press, 1969), pp. 225, 245-47, 412-14; John N. Stephens, "Heresy in Medieval and Renaissance Florence," *Past and Present*, Vol. 54 (1972), p. 47.

liam Penn may have had more than brotherly love in mind. But the decision to reject the Anglican Church as Laodicean—which occurred only as a result of Laudian pressures—had profound consequences for minds like those of God's Englishmen. The Church was by law established, and to reject it implied rejection of the law. It sustained the supremacy of one whom the whole thrust of Foxean thought identified as the Godly Prince—of one who was obdurately upholding the Church in its Laodicean, or Antichristian, form. If the prince were not godly after all, who or what in the Elect Nation was? Moreover, the offence of the Laudian bishops, and of all who supported them, was to claim for themselves a *jure divino* authority, which detracted from the secular and apocalyptic sovereignty of the Elect Nation.[27] If the prince upheld them —later, if parliament upheld the *jure divino* claims of a presbyterian clergy—then the authority of the Elect Nation was apostate; it was denying itself. But the authority of law, of prince, of parliament, each of which was rejected in its turn, possessed a past—was part of the past of the Ancient Constitution; and with each act of rejection came the necessity to repudiate a past and to rewrite it, because the structure of apocalyptic time remained intact.

We have reached a crucial point in our exploration of the relations of custom and grace, and of the time dimensions dependent upon them, for now we can see that a kind of historical antinomianism was possible, and that antinomianism itself, like apocalyptic, might be as much an indicator of involvement in the secular as of alienation from it. If antinomianism is the moment at which the spirit breaks free from the law, and the law is seen as existing in the *saeculum*, then an antecedent period of dependence on the law is a logical corollary. We have argued that English apocalyptic arose because Englishmen were so deeply involved in their laws and traditions that they imported them into their notions of the sacred and rewrote their accounts of sacred time in order to accommodate their time dimension. The Philadelphian moment—so to call it—was one at which the authority of existing institutions, which had been seen as protecting or embodying the freedom of the spirit, was no longer considered adequate; that spirit began reconstructing the institutions and, in order to do so, drew on an authority of its own, which might be seen as independent of secular and even of prophetic time. But with few exceptions, both temporal structures retained a certain authority over even the most antinomian spirit, whose freedom was seen as attained in a context of prophesied salvation—that is, in a millennium of some kind which was now at hand. To the very large extent that it was seen in a

[27] Lamont, *Marginal Prynne*, pp. 14-23 and *passim*.

context of reborn and respiritualized social institutions, these, having continuity and duration in time, could only with great difficulty be reconstructed in ways that did not involve the reconstruction—not merely the repudiation—of their time dimensions. There is consequently a relationship between the millennium, which many Puritan radicals expected or declared to have arrived, and the pre-Norman or pre-papal golden age, to which many of them looked back. *The Agreement of the People*, it might be said, is the antinomianism of the Ancient Constitution.

However, the time perspective of sectarian radicalism, even in its most rationalistic Leveller forms, was too heavily spiritualistic and millennial, on the one hand, and too heavily legalistic and traditionalistic, on the other, to produce much in the way of a radical restatement of English history. We can imagine that, had such a thing appeared, it would have taken the form of a highly English version of *Ketzergeschichte*, that presentation of religious history in which truth is recurrently declared by "Philadelphian" dissenters from a perennially corrupt establishment.[28] The *Ketzergeschichte* of the Elect Nation would have presented English history in terms of repeated attempts to restore a lost birthright and rescue the free spirit from perennial apostasy; but as far as is known at present, nothing much in this genre ever appeared. The fundamental restatement of English history produced by the Civil War and Interregnum came out of a different area of tension.

In 1642, on the eve of the Civil War, there had appeared *The King's Answer to the Nineteen Propositions of Parliament*, a highly important if misconceived document[29] in which the English constitution was presented as a balance of monarchy, aristocracy, and democracy that was sure to collapse in anarchy if the Commons pressed on with their innovative demands. Its authors were appealing to a tradition of thought of which we have so far said nothing: a classical and humanist tradition which depicted civic society as a balance of virtues in a polis or republic, a balance which must either remain perfectly stable or become corrupt and only with great difficulty be restored. Derived from Aristotle through Polybius, Machiavelli, and other Italian writers, the key ideas composing its time structure were virtue, balance, corruption, and fortune; and that of which it was the time dimension was the republic of equal citizens, the structure of purely civic action, something not to be found in England and as yet scarcely to be imagined there. Its rhetorical value in 1642 lay

---

[28] See the study of Gottfried Arnold in Friedrich Meinecke, *Historism* (English translation of *Die Entstehung des Historismus* [London: Routledge and Kegan Paul, 1972]), pp. 30-37.

[29] Counne C. Weston, *English Constitutional Theory and the House of Lords* (London: Routledge and Kegan Paul, 1965).

in its presentation of the sharing of power among kings, lords, and commons—itself none too familiar a concept—as a balance, which if disturbed could lead only to anarchy. The monarchy thus presented itself as the preserver of balance and of order.

By 1649, therefore, apologists for the regicide were declaring that monarchy in England had always been a source of disputed succession and civil war; but, far more important, by that time there existed—as the author of the most dramatic single declaration in the history of English political consciousness—an army prepared to announce itself a body of freeman and not of mercenaries, which had taken up the sword because the individuals composing it were dedicated, through law and conscience, to a religious and political settlement of the kingdom. The sword, in brief, was the sign and vehicle of their conscious capacity for civic action, and the classical republican tradition was a literature of the foundation of civic capacity on the individual's right and willingness to bear arms.

Links can consequently be drawn[30] between the *Answer to the Nineteen Propositions* of 1642 and that belated apologia for the democracy of the army, Harrington's *Oceana* of 1656. Harrington, drawing on the tradition of feudal interpretation which he derived from Bacon and Selden, argued that, from the Anglo-Saxon settlements to the Tudors, England had been ruled by an unstable nobility on whom the people had been feudal dependents and who had existed in a relation of permanent imbalance with the monarchy. All talk of an ancient constitution or a balance of the three estates was therefore absurd; England had never known political stability. But the Tudors had undermined the nobility by abolishing military dependences and, in so doing, had undermined the power of the monarchy itself. All that now existed was a democracy of armed freeholders, who had the opportunity to restore the republic of classical antiquity and make it better balanced than king, lords, and commons had ever been. Harrington had established in the present the image of the Englishman as classical citizen—armed, personally autonomous, and therefore publicly virtuous and capable of entering into civic relations— and had endowed his commonwealth with an appropriate time dimension: a cycle of creation, corruption, rebirth, and escape from the cycle into timeless order. The patterns of civic humanism had entered the English political consciousness.[31]

---

[30]J. G. A. Pocock, "James Harrington and the Good Old Cause: A study of the ideological context of his writings," *Journal of British Studies*, Vol. X, no. I (1970), pp. 30-48.

[31] Pocock, *Ancient Constitution*, pp. 124-47.

Though Harrington's attempt to provide a blueprint for rule by a democracy in arms swiftly failed, it had a long future before it. The restoration of king and parliament in 1660 affected English historical awareness in a number of ways. In the first place it brought about an exclusion from serious debate of everything known as "enthusiasm," and with it nearly all that apocalyptic and potentially antinomian consciousness of England's role in sacred history which had been so powerful for the last one hundred years. The Elect Nation being dethroned, the Ancient Constitution survived; and the balance of the constitution among king, lords, and commons, as laid down in the *Answer to the Nineteen Propositions*, could be spoken of in terms of immemorial usage as well as of timeless equilibrium. As the Exclusionist movement gathered intensity from about 1675, therefore, two lines of argument were prominent. One was a renewed insistence by the House of Commons of its antiquity and autonomy, which brought down upon itself, in the so-called "Brady controversy" of the early 1680s, the wrath of a formidable group of scholars which mobilized feudal learning to prove that neither parliament nor common law could claim to be older than the thirteenth century.[32] The other, also Exclusionist in its provenance, was a neo-Harringtonian attempt to demonstrate that since the royal authority had been restored without the support of a feudal nobility, it was now resorting to patronage, parliamentary corruption, and the development of a professional army to assert itself against the independence of property. In this scenario, however, the House of Lords figured on the side of property and virtue; the ideology of the Ancient Constitution remained intact; and the commonwealth of freeholders, independent because they retained the sword in their own hands, was located not in a Harringtonian millennium but in a heavily defeudalized Gothic past.[33] To stress feudal history against the Ancient Constitution was, for the moment, a Tory device.

In the reign of William III, however, parties and their ideologies changed roles. As Tory dislike of the regime of 1688 blended with the attitudes of a country party, the latter's hatred of political management and standing armies merged into hatred of the new devices of public credit and finance on which these things seemed to rest. The financial revolution that began in the 1690s—the foundation of the Bank of England and the national debt—marks a turning point in English historical perception: it brings the first conscious and secular revolt against modernity. A world in which creditors could live off the interest paid them by a state that used their loans to maintain soldiers, bureaucrats, and excise-

[32] *Ibid.*, pp. 182-228.
[33] Pocock, *Politics, Language and Time*, pp. 104-47.

men was dressed in the colors of classical corruption. The citizen was selling to the government part of his capacity to act as a naturally political animal, part of the virtue which made him a man; and eighteenth-century Englishmen, on both sides of the Atlantic, lived in the dread of the progressive alienation of their civic and moral personality, which they called corruption and loss of virtue.[34] But civic virtue, it turned out, rested on a degree of personal autonomy almost unattainable in its Spartan or Roman austerity, and on a social and material foundation which was that of the Harringtonian freeman, assured of participation in his own government because he owned both land and arms. But that freeman had by now been relegated to a Gothic past, whither he had taken much of what now seemed essential to the Ancient Constitution; and it could not be denied that standing armies and public credit were based on technological and commercial innovations which could now be seen as entering the world at the end of the feudal era. The arms-bearing freeman was fighting the stream of history; only beyond the Atlantic or the Appalachians might he be reborn; westward the cause of virtue took its way.[35]

But something of immense significance—deeper in its implications than any theory of progress—had occurred when history was defined as a material development away from moral, civic, and even natural norms. If the world of Robert Walpole and John Law was to be justified by a theory of history, the rise of commerce and credit must be explained in terms of new ways of creating prosperity and new ways of creating moral and social norms. But what we might glibly refer to as a bourgeois ideology was indeed a revolutionary creation; it had to fight its way into existence against an established, pessimistic, but extremely vital way of defining both virtue and its material foundations.[36] All the hymns that were sung to the goddess Trade and her daemonic sister Credit could not alter the fact that England must be perceived as an agrarian society—unlike Holland, which Pieter De la Court in the 1670s had explicitly said came into being as the result of the revival of medieval commerce[37]—

[34] *Ibid.*, pp. 80-103.

[35] Bernard Bailyn, *The Ideological Origins of the American Revolution* (Cambridge, Massachusetts: Belknap Press, 1967); *The Origin of American Politics* (New York: Knopf, 1968); Gordon S. Wood, *The Creation of the American Republic* (Chapel Hill, North Carolina: University of North Carolina Press, 1969).

[36] J. G. A. Pocock, "Virtue and Commerce in the Eighteenth Century," *Journal of Interdisciplinary History*, Vol. III, no. 1 (1972), pp. 119-34.

[37] John DeWitt [i.e., Pieter De la Court], *The True Interest and Political Maxims of the Republic of Holland West Friesland* (London, 1702), pp. 46-51. I am indebted to John M. Wallace for help with this reference.

and the agrarian mode of depicting both values and history was over-
whelmingly Country in its dispositions. The Court Whig apologists of the
new mercantilist world therefore tended to adopt a pragmatic skepticism
toward a history that was not on their side. They assailed the "Country"
appeal to the Ancient Constitution and Gothic liberty by stressing the
feudal interpretation of the past; they borrowed arguments from the
radicals of the Commonwealth and the Brady school of the 1680s to show
that liberty was not ancient but modern; they scouted the appeal to
history and propounded a pragmatism of the moment; and no doubt
there are instances of their identifying this hardheaded willingness to do
what the moment called for with the commercial virtues of self-interest
and industriousness.[38] But for serious attempts at a commercial interpretation of history or any major presentation of English history as a dia-
lectic between land, commerce, and government, we do not look to the
history of national consciousness in England; we look to its history in
Scotland.[39] In the century between the revolutions, English historical
and political thought is perhaps best seen as expanding into a complex
grouping of Atlantic cultures, disrupted by the great civil war of the
American Revolution. Among the consequences of that disruption we
might place the revision of ideologies which went on in England during
the era of Burke and Bentham. The so-called Augustan period, however,
the half-century between Shaftesbury and Walpole, must remain a
watershed, marking the transition of political culture from a post-
medieval to an early-modern state.

[38] Isaac F. Kramnick, *Bolingbroke and His Circle: The politics of nostalgia in the
age of Walpole* (Cambridge, Massachusetts: Harvard University Press, 1968).

[39] There is more work on the efflorescence of Scottish social and historical thought
in preparation than has recently been completed. See, however, Duncan Forbes's
introductions to his editions of Adam Ferguson's *Essay on the History of Civil Society*
(Edinburgh: Edinburgh University Press, 1966) and David Hume's *History of Great
Britain* (New York: Penguin Classics, 1970); Giuseppe Giarrizzo, *Hume politico e
storico* (Turior: Einaudi, 1962); David M. Kettler, *The Social and Political Thought
of Adam Ferguson* (Columbus, Ohio: Ohio State University Press, 1965); W. C.
Lehmann, *John Millar of Glasgow* (Cambridge: Cambridge University Press, 1960).

CHAPTER V

RUSSIA

MICHAEL CHERNIAVSKY

The political culture and the emergence of national consciousness in early-modern Russia is a subject that spells danger—the danger of terminological and semantic snares, too easily resolved by anachronistic fallacies. What does "early modern" mean? What does "national consciousness" mean? And, to answer these questions, there is the danger of seeking some intellectual source which spelled out, at the right time, in the language of good cultural history, what it meant to be a Russian. While pointing to the problems of definition, I do not mean to deny the validity of these concepts nor that they took different shapes from culture to culture. To give some easy examples, the "douce France" of the *Chanson de Roland*, the panegyrics of the thirteenth-century poet Richier, and the "Kingdom of Sweet King Jesus" of Joan of Arc are all reflections of consciousness which certainly differed from the one that emerged from the slogans of the French Revolution—the one we really know how to recognize—and yet which seem to touch the same chord, as Geoffrey of Monmouth, Shakespeare, and much later, Kipling did in England.

There are similar and parallel glimpses and flashes of consciousness in early Russian society. But before dealing with them, I should first indicate the methodological framework for my analysis: that if, using the French example, "douce France" and "aux armes, citoyens" are both instances of consciousness but of different kinds or degrees of consciousness, we are really dealing with the issue of identity—both collective and, inevitably, individual. Clearly, at all times, men have identified themselves in one way or another. Hence, our problem is to determine the criteria for self-identity at a particular moment; how they change in time; whose identity is expressed; and at what point—in Russia, in this case—should the individual and collective self-identification be characterized as "national consciousness."

118

Let me briefly trace some strands of consciousness of identity in medieval Russia as presented in three literary works (and we do not have many more than these). "The Tale of Igor's Army," written about 1200, describes a campaign fought by Prince Igor of Pereiaslavl' against the Coumans which ends in his defeat and captivity. Igor leads his regiments against the enemy "for the Russian land"—*za zemliu russkoiu*; upon his defeat, there is an appeal to the powerful Russian princes of Kiev, Galicia, and Suzdal' for help—to revenge the wounds of Igor, to revenge the defeat, and to safeguard and honor the Russian land. The poet bemoans the princely strife that allowed the Coumans to ravage the Russian land; and when Prince Igor escapes, he proclaims "the joy of the Russian Land." What is the Russian land? It is a political entity, the patrimonial triangle of Kiev, Chernigov, and Pereiaslavl' (the early Russian equivalent of the Ile de France) but its appeal, its emotional power, extends beyond the political borders, to the northeast and the new center there (Suzdal') and, in another direction, all the way to Galicia in the Carpathian foothills. Its power and appeal are quite specific; it is defined by the princes: by those who are within it, identified as "Russian princes," and by those who are outside of the political boundaries but who, as princes, preserve their identity as "Russian princes." The poem is a princely epic and it describes an identity, the Russian land, which is possessed by a tribe—the descendants of Riurik, the princes of Rus', who are all one family.

"The Tale of the Destruction of the Russian Land," of the late thirteenth century, bewails the Mongol conquest of northeast Russia. The tale or, rather, the fragment that has survived begins lyrically: "Oh brightly bright and beautifully beautiful Russian Land!" The land is full of beauty in its nature—lakes, forests, rivers—and in its people—awesome princes, noble boiars, many great men; "with all this is full the Russian Land, oh, the orthodox Christian faith." This Russian land reaches all the way from the Hungarians and the Poles to the Arctic Ocean, and then all the way east to the Volga and Turkic peoples living there. "All this was subdued by the Christian God" and given to the great rulers of Russia who made the world tremble—"the Germans across the blue sea" and the Byzantine emperor in Constantinople. We can register the changes in the concept of Russian land as well as the continuity: it is still identified by its princes, but it is now extended to include the aristocracy and is used to measure and identify its rulers, the grand princes back to Vladimir Monomakh, the conquerors who, in effect, carried the Russian land with them on their campaigns. The Russian land provides another criterion in this tale—that of Orthodox Christianity. Its boundaries are essentially defined by a religious identity.

Again, I am summarizing when I jump, now, to the early fifteenth century and the "Zadonschchina" ["Beyond the Don"], the tale which describes the first Russian victory against the Tatars in 1380, on the field of Kulikovo, beyond the Don river. The Russians were led by Grand Prince Dimitrii Donskoi (the epithet came from the victory) of Moscow. He and his cousin, Prince Vladimir, are imbued with courage and the desire to fight "for the Russian Land and for the Christian faith." The battle will be a hard one, and the wives of the great nobles weep in anticipation for their husbands who will "lay their heads down . . . for the Russian Land, for the holy churches, for the Orthodox faith. . . ." But the great battle must be fought, and so the Russian princes gather "like eagles," and Grand Prince Dimitrii calls them "My beloved brothers, Russian princes, the single nest of the Grand Prince Ivan Danilovich." The "Zadonschchina" is a complex text, and I have obviously chosen those passages appropriate for our purposes, but hopefully without serious distortion. We have here a consciousness of the Russian land, more and more closely identified with Orthodoxy, with Christianity; one recognizes it by its churches, its faith. One fights and dies for it because it is the land of God. In other words, we see here the development of the same idea as one finds in medieval western Europe: the identification of one's land with that of God (the Holy Land, the Crusade) and hence the equation of death for the fatherland, the *patria*, with death for God or Christ. But the identity of the *patria* is quite specific still—it is, to a large degree, literally the *patria*, the patrimony of the Russian princes. One fights for the faith and for God while fighting for one's own property. This is not exclusively so, for the identification includes in many respects the aristocracy. In most of the redactions, we are given lists of the nobles who fought and fell at Kulikovo, and they died for the Russian land, for the Orthodox faith. The consciousness of the Russian land, the identity it could provide, was expanded to include a larger group of individuals. And the focus of that Russian land has shifted: it is now not Kiev or Suzdal', but Moscow. The Russian host is led by the Grand Prince, who is prince of Moscow, and it is Moscow which defines the identity of the Russian princes as a whole. Dimitrii calls them all eagles of the nest of Ivan Danilovich, i.e., Ivan I, the Moscovite prince who successfully claimed the title of grand prince of northeast Russia, the first of the dynasty of the grand princes of Moscow. Here, then, identification or consciousness was based on a combination of three concepts: the Russian land, Orthodox Christianity, and Moscow. In terms of this admittedly over-simplified analysis and comparison of significant sources, the circle of consciousness seems to have become both wider and narrower. It is wider in that identity was offered to more people and on more levels —

Moscow, Orthodoxy, as well as the Russian land. It is narrower in the sense that the identity was becoming more concrete, more specific, more and more defined by the political sway of Moscow. A glance at the general Russian context within which this kind of consciousness appeared may help us to understand it, if not explain it.

If we take the context to be fifteenth-century Muscovite Russia, some very obvious facts are relevant. First, *all* of Russia's neighbors were of a different religion from its own; they were pagans, Moslems, or Catholics —i.e., pagan, infidel, or heretical. In its world, Russia was the only Orthodox, the only truly Christian, state. And, after 1453 and the fall of Constantinople, it was the only Orthodox Christian state left in the world. Second, through most of the fifteenth century, Muscovite Russia was, in law at least and frequently in fact, a part of the Chinghizid empire, of the Tatar Golden Horde. At no time during the "Tatar Yoke" (1240–1480), did Russian princes ever challenge the legitimacy of the sovereign, the khan of the Golden Horde. Even in describing the battle of Kulikovo in 1380, the great Russian victory over the Tatars, the chronicles are most careful to point out that Grand Prince Dimitrii was not fighting his legitimate tsar, the khan, but that power in the Horde had been usurped by the Tatar emir, Mamai, who was not of the blood of Chinghiz. In effect, Grand Prince Dimitrii was fighting on the side of law and order and legitimacy. Hence, when Moscow was devastated and Tatar power reimposed by Khan Tokhtamysh, a few years after Kulikovo, the chronicles record no special dismay or indignation. Third, and this is the most difficult and complex fact, the fifteenth century was the period when northeast Russia was consolidated under Moscow and a centralized, or rather centralizing, monarchy emerged. Without tackling the problem of defining these equally dangerous terms, let me describe the context as one in which the consciousness of the identity of Moscow, Orthodoxy, and the Russian land was being matched, more and more, by the political reality of this identity. More than this, the political reality, at the end of the century, was a decisive shift in the balance of power: in 1480, Grand Prince Ivan III officially threw off the "Tatar Yoke," and by this time, the most powerful segment of the Golden Horde, the khanate of Kazan', was a vassal state of the Moscow grand prince.

What was the effect of this political reality, if not on the image of the Russian land, at least on the image of its ruler? Briefly, as I have tried to show elsewhere, it meant that, rather than throwing off the "Tatar Yoke" and liberating Russia, Ivan III became the khan himself, with the capital of the khanate now at Moscow. But the problem is more complex, both in the realm of consciousness and of political culture. After the victory of 1380, the tales of the battle and the *vitae* call Grand Prince Dimitrii "tsar"

—not in his office, so to say, but in his essence—because of his victory. And at the same time, they acknowledge the reality and legitimacy of the Tatar tsar, the khan of the Golden Horde. Let us try to untangle the strands in this apparent paradox.

The answer lies in the meaning, the consciousness, and the identity of the tsar. We begin with the fact that, as a Christian society, Russia shared the common Christian political conception: that, in the cosmic order of things, there was only one legitimate political entity, the Christian Roman Empire, of which all Christians were a part; and that there was only one legitimate sovereign of all men, the Christian Roman emperor— the tsar (caesar). Hence, there was, in Russia also, what we may call the usual Christian political dilemma: the ambivalence toward the emperor, whereby the people acknowledged him and yet rejected his authority and denied, unsurped, or claimed his status. The Russians also had, from the thirteenth century on, another, and equally universal, emperor competing for their consciousness and legitimation—the khan.

In theory, the two conceptions are mutually exclusive. The historiographic solution has been to overlook the khan, to assign him to the area of political reality rather than of consciousness, and then to describe the gradual process by which the Russian grand prince, after the fall of Constantinople particularly, took on the prerogatives and the self-image of the Christian Roman emperor. One can make a good case for this; after both eastern Rome and the Tatar power had fallen, we see the Byzantinization of the Moscovite court, ritual, coronation, and image of the ruler. The grand prince of Moscow and Russia became the Orthodox Sovereign—the only authority in the world, human in his nature, divine in his power. And Moscow became the Third Rome, replacing the first two, which fell from divine favor and lost their legitimacy; "and a fourth there shall not be."

But political culture is not rational political theory. Fortunately so, for there was an exceptional paucity of political theorizing in medieval Russia. In fact, one could argue that this paucity is most revealing of the political culture. We have here a Christian society which had available to it the many strands of the Christian Byzantine-imperial political theory and ritual. That an intellectual juridical tradition did not exist in medieval Russia is a different problem; the fact is that there were many paucities. We find, for instance, that though the grand prince was installed in some manner, the chronicles record no ceremony of any kind. There appears to have been no court ritual, no regalia; all this was quite suddenly created in the late fifteenth century. One might argue that these lacunae were owing to distance from Constantinople, to intellectual backwardness, to the lack of independence of the Russian state; yet enough awareness was manifested, enough ideas and objects appropriated by Moscow in these centuries, to make the argument rather weak.

We do find, however, that in the world empire of the Chinghizides, and in the world of the Turkic peoples in general, there is no tradition of political theory, no coronation ritual, no particular court ceremonial, and no regalia except for the battle banner of the khan. So, on one level, what I am suggesting here is repetitive: namely, the cultural validity of the image of the khan, at least in the eyes of the Russian grand prince and his court. And, on another level, I believe, this illustrates the essence of political culture (and all culture)—the existence of options for consciousness and the play with these options. Hence, the Russian grand prince as khan, as Roman emperor, as *the* Orthodox sovereign, and as descendant of the dynasty of Ivan I (a loyal subject of the khan) were concepts that existed simultaneously, not contradicting but reinforcing each other. Therefore, Ivan III was encouraged to resist the khan in 1480 by Archbishop Vassian of Rostov, who wrote to the Grand Prince claiming that he was the Orthodox tsar and that his allegiance to an infidel ruler was never legitimate. After his victory Ivan III minted coins where, in Arabic, his name, Iban, replaced that of his predecessor, Khan Akhmet.

As the playfulness increased, the options were extended in the early sixteenth century. Though the ruler of Moscow was still, officially, only a grand prince, the imperial Byzantine coronation rite, court offices, and court ritual made their appearance together with the imperial Mongol ambassadorial ceremonial. The ruler was only a grand prince, but his capital, Moscow, was an imperial, glorious, and reigning city; and he was served by Tatar princes who were of the blood of Chinghiz khan and were therefore correctly called tsars. He, too, was a tsar, however—not by coronation and not only because the Second Rome had fallen, but because imperial power devolved on his dynasty very much earlier, in the eleventh century, when his ancestor, Vladimir Monomakh, as victor over the Byzantine emperor, received the imperial crown—the symbol of the Christian Universal Empire. And this claim was not contradicted by the discovery that the Russian rulers descended, in a direct line, from Emperor Augustus, who granted to his brother, Prus, the lands in the north (Prussia) from whence came Riurik, the first ruler of Russia and the ancestor of all Russian princes.

Why all this playfulness? One may suggest that the wealth of options not only enriched political culture but made the image of the ruler and the consciousness of the Russian state in his eyes and in the eyes of those who partook of his identity—the aristocracy, the court, and the emerging gentry—less dependent on any one option or image, less bound than if there had been a single political cultural tradition. And the playfulness was not restricted to the realm of political culture: Italian architects building the palaces and churches of the Kremlin; Greek-Byzantine diplomats; Italian and German gunners, German doctors; Persian gardens, medicine, and astrologers; Hungarian fashions, homosexuality and the dandy were also options which made up consciousness.

Now, what did these options really add up to? What kind of consciousness did they both reveal and create? In 1547, the seventeen-year-old Ivan IV was crowned tsar. The rite was the Byzantine imperial one (with an interesting addition of gold coins poured over the tsar after the coronation), and the chronicles present him as the Orthodox tsar of all Russia, autocrat, and the only true Christian emperor. With great vigor the young tsar pursued the policy of his grandfather and his father in the west: the reconquest of all the patrimony of the Moscow rulers, of all Russia, from Kiev to the Baltic. And with equal vigor he tackled the problem posed by one of the two successor states of the Golden Horde, the khanate of Kazan' (the other was the khanate of Crimea). Kazan' had been a vassal state since the 1470s, but an unstable one, in which Muscovite puppet khans alternated with Crimean protégés in endless palace revolutions. In 1552 Ivan IV conquered Kazan'.

Before starting on the campaign against Kazan', the Tsar made what could be called a pilgrimage, visiting the old cities of northeast Russia and praying in their churches. There he received a letter from the metropolitan of all Russia, Makarios, blessing him for his task: ". . . may you stand firm, oh tsar . . . against your godless enemies, the Kazan' Tatars, apostates and traitors towards you, who always shed innocent Christian blood and defile and destroy the holy churches. . . . Because of all these calamities, that much more strongly should you fight for our holy and pure and most truthful Christian faith of the Greek Law, for in the whole universe, like the sun, shines the Orthodoxy in your imperial domain [which is also that] of your grandfather and your father."

Eventually Ivan got to Kazan' and the hard-fought siege began. Finally the city fell, and all the commanders, boiars and princes, greeted the Tsar: ". . . May you live long, oh sovereign, and reign over the Kazan' tsardom, given to you by God. You are, in truth, our intercessor before God against the godless infidels, by you our unfortunate Christians are made free for ever. . . . We continue to pray to God that he prolong your life and hurl all your enemies under your feet. . . ." Ivan replied with proper humility. And then, according to the account, Tsar Shig-Ali said to Ivan: "Live long, sovereign, having conquered for ever your enemies in your patrimony of Kazan'." Shig-Ali was a Chinghizide, Moscow's unsuccessful but legitimate candidate for the khanate, and if such a meeting took place, it is hard to imagine that he would have expressed such humility. In any event, the chronicle's comment after these greetings was: "And, before this, there were no tsars in the Russian Land."

Ivan then made a ceremonious entry into the city, an imperial *adventus*, accompanied by the acclamations of his army; and "with his own hands" he placed a cross in the city and ordered the building of a church dedicated to the Virgin, the protectress of the grand princes of the northeast since the twelfth century (and, before then, the special patroness of the imperial city, Constantinople). The return of the Tsar to Moscow was a triumphal procession through the towns of Russia. Outside of Moscow, he was met by the Metropolitan and the clergy. The Tsar made a speech, describing his victory and assigning it to God and to the prayers of his clergy. Afterward, the Metropolitan also spoke. He compared Ivan's victory to those of Constantine the Great and St. Vladimir of Russia, to the victory of Dimitrii Donskoi over the "barbarians," and to those of St. Alexander Nevsky over the Latins. He pointed out that Ivan, with the help of God, had conquered the imperial city, Kazan', and placed the cross over it. After the exchange of greetings, the Tsar changed his clothes, shedding his armor and putting on imperial raiment, the cross, the diadem, and the crown of Monomakh. He then proceeded to the cathedral church of Muscovy, the cathedral of the Dormition of the Virgin. The chronicle ends the account with the remark that, at this time, a throne for the Tsar was placed in the cathedral.

There is in all this the general mood of triumph; everything the young tsar tried turned out gloriously, from internal reforms to foreign conquests. So pervasive was this mood that Russian historiography was permanently affected by it: compare the shining and glorious years of the early reign of Ivan IV with the terror and disasters of the latter part of his reign, when he was known as Ivan the Terrible. But beyond this, the conquest of Kazan' spells out many things. It is the triumph of Orthodoxy, of Christianity over the infidels; the Tsar traveled from church to church on his way to Kazan', and on his way back, he sanctified the conquest personally with the cross and marked it with a church. It is the image of the Byzantine Christian emperor, received with ritual acclamations, acting out the rites of imperial ceremonial, and finally seated on his throne in the Russian equivalent of Hagia Sophia. The throne is most interesting; it is the *tsarskoe mesto*, the tsar's place, but it exists today, and it *is* a throne. Moreover, it is the earliest throne known to us in Russia. It has a baldachin and its high wooden sides are covered with carvings which depict the triumphs of the twelfth-century Vladimir Monomakh of Kiev, triumphs which culminate with the scene in which the Byzantine emperor hands over to the Russian prince the insignia of empire.

Therefore, we see on the one hand the stress on Orthodox Christianity. On the other hand, Ivan proudly proclaimed his religious tolerance, stating that everyone in his tsardom of Kazan' (and, later, Astrakhan') was free to practice his own religion as subject of the tsar. Over and over we are told that Kazan' is an imperial city (*tsarstvuishchii grad*), a reigning city, the twin of the other imperial and glorious city, Moscow. In fact, rather strikingly, it was Ivan's patrimony, the land of his fathers, which he next reconquered; this is why Ivan as tsar (or khan) gave the treasures of the city to his army and took for himself only the imperial standards and the cannon—the symbol and the reality of sovereignty, which are his by right. Finally, the conquest of Kazan' precipitated the true coronation of the Tsar: ". . . before this, there were no tsars in the Russian Land." In this light, the coronation of 1547 appears to have been only symbolic. The conquest of Kazan' made it real, through the consciousness of an empire as well as that of a tsar who is khan and basileus and possibly more by being both.

So far, we have seen a grandiose and exhuberant spelling out of the options which reinforced and focused on the consciousness of empire: tsar, imperial cities, an imperial society. But it is at this time that a new element appeared—what seems to have been a massive broadening of consciousness. The evidence is tricky but suggestive. First, there is Russian folklore, but the problem here is that popular tales and songs were not recorded until the eighteenth century, and we can only guess at their original wording, nuances, and even form. Yet I think folklore is an expression of historical popular consciousness, and if we accept this premise, the evidence is quite striking. For the whole of Russian history before Peter the Great, two moments seem to have lived (as late as the early twentieth century) in the consciousness of the masses of the Russian people: the age of St. Vladimir, expressed in the huge cycle of songs and tales about Vladimir the Beautiful Sun; and the age of Ivan the Terrible, particularly, the conquest of Kazan'. The social emphasis in the songs about Kazan' is clear; the heroes are the Tsar himself and the gunners (*pushkari*) of the Muscovite artillery stationed in Moscow, who were city dwellers and lower class, but who were central to the achievement, which was considered so important that the memory of the conquest of Kazan' lived on for centuries, while most of Russian history was neither known nor felt.

The other piece of evidence I offer is more solid, materially at least. Before the Kazan' campaign, the Tsar offered the usual sort of vow, i.e., to build a church as an offering to God if he were victorious. So, we read that in 1554–55, in fulfillment of that vow, the Tsar ordered the construction of a church, dedicated to the Trinity and to the Virgin, to be built by an architect named Barma and some associates. The Tsar attended the beginning of the construction with all his court and laid the first stone with his own hands. The architectural style of the church is revealing. I have already mentioned the great building program which began in the late fifteenth century, which reflects a cultural aspect of the centralizing monarchy. The walls of the Kremlin, its palaces, its great cathedrals were built to symbolize the growing imperial city. They were built by Italian architects, by Pskovian masters, by anonymous builders, and they are generally all of a style which I suggest is Renaissance. Let me give just two examples. The first is the cathedral of St. Michael the Archangel—the imperial cathedral and the burial place of the Russian grand princes and tsars of the Muscovite dynasty (see Figure 1). The second is the church I have mentioned already, the cathedral of the Dormition of the Virgin (see Figure 2). Even with the oriental domes on top of the basic structure, the style is identifiable: it is simple, severe, majestic; it is Italian Renaissance modified by the great tradition of Suzdal' and Vladimir or by Byzantine pastiches.

Now let us look at what Ivan built in 1554 in celebration of the conquest of Kazan'. This is the church "On the Ravine," which we know today as St. Basil's Cathedral (see Figure 3). At the very least, it is different. Others like it appeared later—for example, the church of St. John the Baptist in Diakovo, which was built later in the same year (see Figure 4)—but at the time it was different and new. To my knowledge, nothing like it was built before. And, interestingly enough, it has become virtually the picture-postcard symbol of Russia in modern, photographic times. Let me make my point very carefully and cautiously. St. Basil's Cathedral is a statement; it is a public statement, for unlike a text read by a few clerks, it was designed to be seen by the multitudes, seen and accepted and possibly understood. It is a deliberate statement, and it is explicitly associated with the conquest of Kazan'. It is exuberant, wildly playful, vital. What does this statement signify? On what we may call the "scientific" level, we do not know. To my knowledge again, no Russian of the time intellectualized about it or commented about it in any way; in fact, no one has discussed it up to now. To be sure, there are careful architectural studies, but I have not been able to see any connections between the kind of cupolas, the shapes of towers, the number of chapels, and the particular aspects of consciousness existing in mid-sixteenth-century Muscovy.

But on another, symbolic, level, we may be able to decipher the statement of St. Basil's. To put it most simply, I think the statement meant that "we" are different now from what "we" were, and *this*, is what "we" are. Well, what are "we"? What is Russia? Moscow? And implicitly, what

FIGURE 1. Cathedral of St. Michael the Archangel
(the Kremlin).

FIGURE 2. Cathedral of the Dormition of the Virgin (the Kremlin).

are the Russians? I submit that, essentially, they are the triad: Autocrat, Orthodoxy, Empire. That is, if someone asked himself the question, "What am I?" in a social, collective context, whether he was tsar, aristocrat, gentry, even peasant, his answer would be based on the consciousness of these three strands of political culture. These strands do not make up a national consciousness; but perhaps we can see them as the basic elements of a national subconsciousness, in the sense that they are the bricks out of which the structure of national consciousness was later built. Or rather, they are the chemicals—chemicals that can be put together in a compound, and that can interact with each other. But more, they are chemicals where the mix can be different, so that when one puts in more of one than of another, the results can be quite different.

If this metaphor is valid, to analyze the consciousness of self-identity we must register the balance of the mix. We must also analyze the tensions between kinds and expressions of consciousness, for even collective identities are not the same for different groups and individuals. Such identities are created and taken on in order to bolster the individual or collective ego, whether by enhancing and glorifying it or by protecting it. What this means is that some forms of consciousness—like a particular mix of chemicals—may be, exactly, a reaction to another consciousness in which the mix, or the emphasis, is different, different enough to produce a different consciousness.

Let us return to Russia after 1553, after the conquest of Kazan', to the second half of the long reign of Ivan the Terrible, in what may be a digression. As much as the first part of the reign represented glory, victory, brightness, so the last twenty-five years represented (in Russian historiography) gloom, despair, and disaster—in short, of madness. There was, of course, a reality behind this image: the terror that the Tsar instituted, the severe defeat in the Livonian war, and the exhaustion of resources. However, I think that more serious in consequence were the years of famine and of plague in the 1570s, events divorced from the policies of the Tsar. Still, in contemporary accounts and in modern studies there is reflected a particular consciousness of tragedy, of apocalyptic drama; possibly, this awareness was and is in response to a particular aspect of the political culture of those years—the enormous ideological escalation, on the part of Ivan certainly, and in the Russian setting as a whole. The events appear to be part of a cosmic drama; everything is measured on a cosmic scale; and Muscovite Russia is a cosmic stage. The political terror is absolute, the defeats catastrophic, the *terribilita* of the Tsar world-shaking, and the countryside depopulated.

The game with options and the exploitation of options continued reflecting the escalation in consciousness which was a consequence of the

FIGURE 3. St. Basil's Cathedral in Moscow. Photo courtesy of Harper & Row, Publishers, Inc.

FIGURE 4. St. John the Baptist in Diakovo.

mid-sixteenth-century synthesis. Certainly, Ivan pursued to the limit the Christian-Byzantine conception. He was the Orthodox ruler, ever in church, visiting monasteries, full of humility. He was acknowledged by the eastern patriarchs as the emperor, and he initiated the creation of Moscow as a patriarchate, the fifth one of the Orthodox world. He even burlesqued his role when he endowed his instruments of terror—the members of the institution called *oprichnina*—with monastic garb and ritual. With even greater intensity Ivan was conscious of the dynastic component of is image: tsar of all Russia, grand prince of Moscow, tsar of Kazan', tsar of Astrakhan', lord and sovereign of many lands. As the titles rolled off, the image of the Russian tsar grew in its uniqueness. Those around him—Chinghizides, descendants of Riurik and of Gedimin, the founder of the Lithuanian dynasty—were his servants (*kholopy*), and he appears as a shah-in-shah, the king of kings, the ultimate image of autocracy and cosmic monarchy. He, direct descendant of Augustus, is virtually blocked off from dealing with other monarchs in his diplomatic correspondence. At least so he reminds the kings of Sweden and of Poland—whence they hail, and who he is.

But other options of the political culture developed as well, of which there is a striking example from the 1560s. In 1564 the Tsar ordered frescoes to cover the walls of the Cathedral of St. Michael the Archangel. It was the necropolis of the Moscow dynasty (the St. Denis of Russia), and the walls and pillars, from the floor to the dome, are portraits of dead rulers—Muscovite, Russian, and "foreign." As I have tried to show else-where, the iconography is unique and I have been able to interpret it in only one way: that is, the pattern of the iconography—the princes por-trayed in the cathedral—add up to the image of an imperial family whose justification to rule a cosmic empire is simply the family itself. The only possible model I could find is that of the Chinghizides. In their world empire, the empire itself and the right to rule derived from one fact, being of the blood of Chinghiz, and no other justification was necessary. In that sense, Ivan of Russia was copying from a model which was legitimate and cosmic. And at the same time, he was replacing the Chinghizides with the Moscow dynasty, which was imperial, cosmic, and self-contained. An ironic twist to this dialectical consciousness of the Tatar-Mongol image came in 1575, when Ivan handed over his throne to a Tatar Chinghizid' prince in his service, Simeon Bekbulatovich. Simeon became the legal tsar of all Russia while Ivan, grand prince of Moscow, wrote particularly humble letters which conveyed his orders to the legal Chinghizide tsar. This comedy continued for some months.

All this has been interpreted by historians as anecdotal, in the sense of being the expressions of Ivan the Terrible as an individual—playfully mad, or simply mad—but this explanation will not quite do. Ivan's monstrous dynastic arrogance was reflected not only in the fury of Prince Andrew Kurbsky, who fled to Lithuania and from there accused his tsar of losing all sense of measure, of exceeding all limits set by morality, respect for others, and human and divine law. It was also reflected in the servitors of Ivan the Terrible, men such as Prince Bel'sky who called himself a serf (*kholop*) of the Tsar but who, as a descendant of Gedimin of Lithuania, addressed the Polish king, correctly, as "my brother." The implications of the frescoes of St. Michael did not pass unnoticed, notably when the Polish-Lithuanian envoys were negotiating with Russian diplomats in 1554 on various issues of the common frontier and objected to the comparatively new title of "tsar" claimed by the Moscow grand prince. The title, they argued, was not appropriate and could not be recognized by them, for "no Christian sovereign calls himself 'Christian caesar' but only infidel tsars do so." And finally, the twisted farce of the Tatar Tsar Simeon was, apparently, not a farce at all. At the end of the century, when the Riurikid Moscow dynasty ended with the death of Ivan's son, Tsar Theodore, Boris Godunov was elected to the throne. We find that the only man he feared as a competitor was Tsar Simeon, who by this time was very old, blind, and living in total obscurity; Godunov feared him enough to force Simeon to become a monk. Moreover, at the end of the great social crisis called the Time of Troubles (1605–13)—a time of civil war, foreign intervention, fleeting candidates to the throne, and pretenders—when the ruling circles of aristocracy and gentry gathered together to re-establish social order under a new dynasty, they seriously considered electing a Tatar Chinghizide prince to the Russian Orthodox throne before they chose Michael Romonov.

Let me use this rather contrived transition to the seventeenth century to explore the issue in more depth. To start, we can register the fact that the awareness of options within political culture was not limited to the autocrat; it also existed among the aristocracy and the gentry who seriously consider Tsar Simeon or another Chinghizide prince. But these groups went much further: during the Time of Troubles these men, proud of their lineage, offered their service to the pretender, the False Dimitrii, and when he was killed, to a second False Dimitrii. And not only did they consider a Tatar prince before they chose Michael Romonov, they also offered the crown of Monomakh, by formal petition, to Prince Vladislas, son of the king of Poland.

The traditional interpretation of this behavior has been that the ruling elite, lacking all patriotic feeling, pursued its own selfish interests, and that the restoration of the Russian state came through a "national" revival, whose strength was drawn from the lower classes of Russian society. Aside from its glaring anachronistic fallacy, this interpretation misses the point. If we accept the conception of the chemical building blocks of consciousness which emerged in the mid-sixteenth century, then the aristocracy *and* the gentry reveal, through their behavior, a particular balance of consciousness: their identity is most strongly expressed in the consciousness of *empire*, of the imperial society. This is the dominant strand of their consciousness and political culture. Next their identity is expressed in their consciousness of the autocrat, of the tsar, no matter who he may be as long as he rules their cosmic empire. Least of all, their identity is defined by Orthodoxy, which became a formal, rather than psychological, identification. The Tatar princes did choose to be baptized, and Vladislav of Poland *was* required, by treaty, to convert to Russian Orthodoxy.

I am arguing two things at this point. First, I am saying that consciousness in our context is social in nature; that the identities of different social groups are different; that, put most simply, collective identity is a class phenomenon. The Russian ruling class expressed its identity through the consciousness of empire, i.e., of being, collectively, the empire. Second, I am proposing that this "tilt" in the consciousness of identity in the ruling class was permanent and historically justified. The choice of identity was determined by the psychological and material benefits to be derived from such an identity; and certainly the Russian ruling class derived both psychological and material benefits from an imperial-autocratic consciousness, for it *was* the empire.

It is this tilted balance of consciousness that marked the period of early absolutism of the Romanov monarchy. And I believe it explains the particular play of cultural options in the seventeenth century. It can be conveyed, briefly, in symbolical terms: in the mid-fifteenth century, Grand Prince Basil II spoke Tatar at home; in the mid-seventeenth century, Tsar Alexis spoke Polish at home. One can find many good technological and political reasons for this shift. Clearly, in political terms, the "eastern" outlook was less and less meaningful and the western orientation which emerged signifies the process of "westernization." But this term alone should give us pause: it implies a shift, but an unbalanced one, for it does not follow a period of "easternization." And it certainly implies a cultural identity—nonwestern—which verges close to national consciousness.

Moreover, the process of westernization—that is, of more and more massive adoption of clothes, habits, army organization, technology, literature, and learning from lands to the west of Russia—began in a specific ideological setting: Namely, the apparent triumph of that aspect of consciousness called "Orthodoxy." Tsar Alexis was, in effect, the epitome of the Orthodox hieratic ruler. He was "The Most Gentle Tsar," a Byzantine title. He literally lived in his chapel where services ran all day and far into the night so that Orthodox priests from abroad collapsed in exhaustion, while the Tsar prayed and conducted his business and his courtiers and his young children stood endlessly on the cold stone floors. When he traveled, it was from monastery to monastery, where he served the monks with his own hands. On Palm Sunday, when the patriarch re-enacted the primal scene, riding into the city on a horse caparisoned as a donkey, the Tsar walked on foot, leading the pseudo-donkey by a long bridle.

All these expressions can be traced back to Ivan the Terrible and even further. But they appeared with particular intensity in the mid-seventeenth century. To repeat, the disappearance of the khan in the image of the tsar is easy enough to explain by political and technological reasons. The argument has been made that the style of Orthodoxy was an expression of a national reaction to the foreign interventions of the Time of Troubles. But this argument overlooks several factors. First, no "nation" had been identified at this point. Second, the cultural style of the court made "Orthodoxy" into a purely formal ritual. Third, the struggle in Alexis' reign, between tsar and patriarch, between the state and the church, and the complete triumph of the state indicate that, if anything, Orthodoxy was appropriated by the Tsar for different and "wrong" reasons.

More fruitfully, I think, we can explain the disappearance of the khan and the intensity of the image of the Orthodox tsar as indirectly related to each other, as phenomena of a single process. I would call that process secularization—the transfer of the criteria for human social values, and for many individual personal ones from heaven not only down to earth, but to a particular piece of earth defined by political boundaries, a state. And if this definition is at all valid, one has to take very seriously the process of secularization as the emergence of a new religion, of a different framework for religious values, the religion of the state.

Therefore, the strands of consciousness that we have been discussing were not drained of their power or "secularized" in the popular and wrong sense of the word, on the contrary, they were transcendentalized, imbued with a new religious content in the process of secularization. And if the consciousness of tsar and of empire was a religious one, it no longer required a historical justification, or in fact, any justification at all. Hence the idea of state, the image of autocrat, became *sui generis*, outside of history, metahistorical. The components of historical consciousness represented by the khan and even by the Byzantine basileus became less and less relevant politically and not necessary ideologically in the framework of the new religion. To put it another way, as the consciousness of tsar and empire moved from "becoming" to "being," the "becoming," which was the historical process and the past, became less interesting and less functional. The same logic applied to the issue of Orthodoxy. The consciousness of Orthodoxy as an identity lost its historicity and hence its autonomy within the new religion. Orthodoxy continued to function in the identity, but one within the new heaven, here on earth. The hieratic religiosity of the Most Gentle Tsar and of his polonized court had the same meaning as the Edict of Nantes issued by Henri IV and its revocation by Louis XIV. And Patriarch Nikon, fighting against the secular state and the autocrat, misunderstood the new nature of religious identity which Cardinals Richelieu and Mazarin understood very well.

In order to make my point, I have exaggerated of course. The new religion was not created so quickly and so consistently. The historical traditions buttressing consciousness continued to be evoked; the history of the empire and the glory of the dynasty continued to be recorded and Tsar Alexis would have insisted, correctly, that he was a genuinely pious and thoughtful Christian, whose faith was founded on events and judged by criteria outside of Russia and its history. The religion of the state, as all religions, is necessarily syncretistic—absorbing the past as much as replacing it—and its evolution was uneven; but its eventual triumph can be attested by all of us today.

Implicit in all the levels and aspects of consciousness and of political culture that have been discussed here, of course, is a social context. The image of the tsar held by the tsar and the ruling class and the image of empire held by tsar, aristocracy, and gentry are social statements, and so is the new religion, the idea of the secular, absolutist state. Hence, it is necessary to examine, however briefly, the social reality of the seventeenth-century Russian absolutist state. It was the consequence of the successful mobilization of social and economic resources by a state which we characterize as "absolute" because it produced the necessary apparatus for this successful mobilization. Very sketchily, the way in which Russia's available resources were utilized can be indicated by the regularization of the taxable town population in the interests of the state; by the virtual secularization of church property; and most dramatically, by the enserfment of the peasantry. Nothing new was invented by the absolutist monarchy, of course; yet there was a difference in quantity which becomes qualitative when compared to the medieval setting and possibilities. This difference was based on a huge increase in resources—demographic and economic—as well as on the existence of an expanded and perfected administration, which was made possible by the increased resources and which, in turn, exploited them to a far greater degree. And, implicit in the social context is social, class interest; some groups benefit in the absolutist state and most are exploited. Hence, in Russia, as elsewhere, the seventeenth century is marked by serious social tensions. In fact, every decade can be identified by major manifestations of popular discontent. This long chain of reasoning was designed to make two rather simple points: that consciousness is social as well as psychological in nature; and that the social tensions in seventeenth-century society were far greater than before.

Obviously there were social tensions and popular discontent in earlier centuries, as demonstrated by the peasant revolts and town uprisings. In Russia, particularly, we know virtually nothing of the ideology or programs of the dissidents. But the little we know allows us to make the generalization that the tensions and discontent assumed the forms of heresy and appeals to the sovereign. And, I submit, both of these forms are expressions of popular consciousness and hence of popular identity. This social protest was expressed through an Orthodox Christian identity. The argument was that collective identity had been distorted or lost and that the priests, nobles, and the wealthy were not truly Christian because they were exploiting the lower classes; therefore, one could justify the fight against them exactly by virtue of being an Orthodox Christian (these were heresies, of course, because the dissidents lost). The appeal to the ruler and the yearning for him was the evocation not of the khan, but of the Orthodox, Christ-like, saintly, and just prince (even tribal), who, in his person, confirmed and reinforced popular Christian identity.

All this is very obvious and well known but let us return to St. Basil's Cathedral for a moment. I have argued that we know what it expressed of the consciousness of Tsar Ivan the Terrible: that this is what *"we"* are, i.e., Orthodoxy, tsar, empire. And I am arguing that the cathedral, public and popular in its function, accepted and revered, was also an expression of popular consciousness or was, at the very least, understood by it. But given the nature of the vague popular consciousness I have described, this hypothesis permits two important conclusions. First, the identity of Orthodoxy, Tsar, and Empire was shared by the masses and circumscribed their consciousness, which is perhaps an elaborate illustration of the fact that the rules of the game of consciousness, of political culture, are usually set by those who possess the political power in a society. But second, while self-identity was made up of the same chemical blocks, the mix or the balance was a different one, and the tilt was toward Orthodoxy.

The weight of all these conclusions is too heavy even for St. Basil's. Let me make the case for the nature of popular consciousness and identity during the century and a half after the cathedral was built. There is a striking example of it early in the seventeenth century, after the social crisis of the Time of Troubles; this was the consciousness of "Holy Russia." Given the origin and the usage of this epithet, it is an expression of popular consciousness. As I have tried to show elsewhere, it was antistate and antitsar in its thrust, but I should modify this interpretation. "Holy Russia" did not exclude the tsar or the empire-state, rather, it subsumed them under "Holy Russia," i.e., it absorbed them into a conception of a Christian Orthodox society in which the "holy" was justified by the social justice granted to the oppressed, whose consciousness was expressed in the epithet. Tsar, empire, and Orthodoxy were aspects of popular identity when the synthesis of these chemicals was "Holy Russia"—a social statement.

Yet the antistate and antitsar nuance was there, and given the setting and history of this expression of consciousness, it reveals an important aspect of popular self-identity: namely, it was a reaction to the growing assertion and increasing weight of the other identity, that of tsar and empire and even Orthodoxy. I have tried to explain the assertion and the weightiness: the process of secularization was one of increasing moral and psychological autonomy for the self-identity of the autocrat and the ruling class. Hence, though the terms remained the same—tsar, empire, Orthodoxy—their content was determined less and less by any criteria outside of the secular state, the heaven on earth. And within this new heaven, self-definition coincided with political power. The weight of tsar and empire, not limited by any other consciousness in effect, became so great that it required a popular consciousness as extreme as "Holy Russia" so that popular self-identity would not be excluded psychologically, from the identity of the autocratic, imperial, absolutist state.

I am arguing that the social structure and policy of the absolutist state brought out and generated an increasing tension between the self-identity of the tsar and the ruling class and popular self-identity. Both identities continued to be expressed in the same terms. But the psychological autonomy and ideological purpose of the secular state—salvation here, on earth—meant that it offered identity, more and more, to those who could gain salvation here—the ruling class, the active "citizens" of this new heaven—and excluded, more and more from its identity those who, sharing the consciousness of tsar, empire and Orthodoxy, had no role in defining this consciousness. Popular consciousness was a reaction to this process, expressing itself through the traditional categories but shifting the balance, and trying to hold on to those historical and mythological aspects of tsar and Orthodoxy which would provide the masses with a valid identity.

The Church Schism of the seventeenth century makes the whole problem clear, I believe. In briefest summary, it started over the issue of changes and reforms in church ritual and practice. Very quickly it became a mass popular movement against the power and right of the state to change the forms of the faith, to legislate on all matters, to enserf the peasants. But the arguments were theological and ideological, not explicitly social, and enormously revealing of the popular consciousness. The immediate confrontation was with the church hierarchy, and the appeal against Patriarch Nikon and the bishops was to the Tsar. Over and over again, the leaders of the "Old Believers" (as they were called) appealed to Tsar Alexis to remain the Orthodox tsar, to keep the faith of his ancestors and of the Russian tsardom. Not by accident the most frequent evocation was of Ivan the Terrible, of that moment when there was a consensus of identity, when everyone agreed, or thought they agreed what tsar and Orthodoxy and empire meant. But the Tsar did not respond, and Archpriest Avaakum, spiritual father of the Old Believers, spelled out the issue: the tsar had no right to "possess the Church and to change dogma"; his task was only to protect the faithful, "not teach them how to hold the faith." In desperation, Avaakum wrote to the Tsar, "After all, we are not taking away from you your empire . . . but are defending our faith."

Avaakum's threat was to remove the "tsar" from the ingredients of identity, and his plea was for a popular identity which, he claimed, did not threaten the empire, the identity of the secular state. One more argument was left, and Avaakum used it in another letter to Tsar Alexis. Begging him to disregard the advice of the oriental patriarchs called to a council in Moscow, Avaakum wrote, fondly and familiarly: "You are a Russian, Alexei Mikhailovich" (*"Ty Rusak, Alexei Mikhailovich"*). Finally it had been said; a new dimension, national consciousness, was added to the mix that made up Russian identity. And if we take this symbolic instance seriously, national consciousness emerged as a popular reaction to the self-identity of the absolutist state, with the threat that those things which challenged it—the absolutist consciousness of tsar, empire, and Orthodoxy—could be excluded from Russian self-identity.

Certainly, one can test the validity of this hypothesis in the crucible of Petrine Russia, the epitome of change, reforms, and westernization. Great masses of the Russian people, Orthodox as well as Old Believers, seem to confirm our suppositions. One example may suffice. The Russian masses expressed their very serious opposition to Petrine policies—the growing exactions and repressions of the absolutist gentry monarchy—in many ways, but especially by the conviction that Peter was evil because he was a changeling, a foreigner. All those with him, his officers and servitors, in their foreign clothes and with their foreign manners, were foreigners also—not Russians but servants of Antichrist. Here at least is a true confirmation of national consciousness—xenophobia. To be a foreigner was an evil thing, the opposite of which was to be Russian.

But, as usual, things are not so simple: For Peter I and his gentry, with equal passion, also thought of themselves as Russians. Exactly because they *were* Russian, they felt they could borrow and utilize techniques, customs, and manners which were convenient or useful; for if they, the ruling class, defined "Russia," then everything they did was, by definition, Russian. At the same time, the Old Believers, and the peasants in general, began to insist on beards, traditional clothes, and old ritual—creating, in reaction, their own Russian identity. Ironically, one can pose, in historical terms, the emergence of a confrontation between two national consciousnesses: Ivan the Terrible, proud of his supposed Viking ancestry, accepted as the Orthodox natural tsar of all Russia; and Peter the Great, proudly insisting that he was a true and pure Russian, regarded as an illegitimate foreigner.

In conclusion, did these two national consciousnesses parallel Lenin's two cultures? Possibly. In any event, they were bound together, for they shared the same categories of consciousness—tsar, empire, Orthodoxy, Russia—and the tension between them continued, for each represented an identity which thrived best at the expense of the other. But the battle was curiously unequal. Affirming its self-identity in a national consciousness, the ruling class had all the power apparatus at its disposal to repress, compel, and even impose criteria of identity; yet, by the very nature of things it lacked the one power of consciousness—the power to exclude the masses from the national identity. And that was the one power that popular national consciousness possessed. The power of the ruling class allowed it to initiate, to conceptualize, to impose, and to pose, but always with the consciousness that the mass of the people were Russians and that this was the basic criterion to which the ruling class had to accommodate itself. Hence, the history of ruling class national consciousness is a history of endless searching, endless attempts to retain class identity and partake of Russian consciousness; in other words, it is a history of the perpetual question, "What is a Russian?" But the quest for national identity was made possible precisely by the power of the ruling class, by the ability to act, to create, and to take on an identity by an act of will. For popular national consciousness, the act of will and the possibility and need of choice were not available or necessary. Popular national consciousness was an affirmation of identity, national identity, in reaction to a social reality which it did not accept or legitimize. The confrontation within the emerging national consciousness of the seventeenth century remained; the ruling class cajoled, tried to compel, offered various dimensions of consciousness, and popular consciousness continued to deny it national identity.

Let me end with a symbolic representation of this. In 1881 Alexander II, the Tsar Emancipator (who freed the serfs) was assassinated. His son,

FIGURE 5. St. Basil's in St. Petersburg. Photo from the Bettmann Archive.

Alexander III, wished to commemorate his father with a monument symbolizing the reconciliation of the two national consciousnesses. Therefore, he built a church dedicated to Christ "on the Blood" (on the spot where the bombs were thrown at his father): a new St. Basil's, in the middle of secular, imperial St. Petersburg (see Figure 5). Aesthetically, at least, the solution did not work.

EDITORIAL NOTE: Professor Cherniavsky's decision to present his chapter without notes was accepted without hesitation by the editor. Scholars in the field of medieval and early-modern Russian history ought to have little difficulty in finding the citations should they wish to do so. Nonspecialists are referred to M. Cherniavsky, *Tsar and People: Studies in Russian Myths* (New Haven, 1961).

CHAPTER VI

SPAIN

HELMUT KOENIGSBERGER

On September 1, 1947, I was one of a huge crowd assembled in the main square of Salamanca to celebrate the fiesta of the Virgin of the Vega. The medieval silver image of the virgin was carried in solemn procession from the cathedral to the *ayuntamiento*, the town hall, and then a priest preached a sermon for the crowd. Spain, he said, was eternal. Spain had existed long before the national revival of the *caudillo*, Generalissimo Franco. It had existed under the Bourbons and the Hapsburgs and before the union of Aragon and Castile by the Catholic Kings, Ferdinand and Isabella. It had existed at the time of the Visigoths and of the Romans and of Tubal (a descendant of Cain and the first to settle in Spain); and it had existed even before that, before the creation of the world itself, in the mind of God.

This proud vision of Spain as a splendid Platonic idea lies at the base of a long tradition of Spanish literature and historiography, and it is closely connected with a favorite theme of Spanish writers, the nature of *hispanidad*, i.e., the essence of Spanishness. Its earliest form was the *laudes Hispaniae* of Orosius in the fifth century and of Saint Isidore of Seville in the seventh, in which Spain is celebrated as the richest, fairest, happiest land, and the cradle of the most valiant heroes and princes[1]— just as a dozen other European countries were similarly celebrated, following a well known classical genre.

With some gaps, this tradition continued through the late Middle Ages. Thus the thirteenth-century canon lawyer, Vincentius Hispanus, countered German claims to the empire by recalling the successful Spanish resistance to Charlemagne's invasion and the slaying of twelve of his paladins. Vincentius clinched a long argument by exclaiming:

[1] R. Menéndez Pidal, *The Spaniards in their History*, trans. W. Starkie (New York, 1966), p. 80.

144

"Who indeed, Spain, can reckon thy glories? Spain, wealthy in horses, celebrated for food, and shining with gold; steadfast and wise, the envy of all; and skilled in the law and standing high on sublime pillars."[2]

In the early-modern period, the style of such *laudes* became more sophisticated but the arguments remained essentially the same. The poet Quevedo, in the early seventeenth century, is not only roused to patriotic fury by the attacks of Joseph Scaliger ("a man of good letters but bad religion") on the Hispano-Roman authors, Quintilian, Lucan, and Seneca,[3] and by the geographer Mercator's deprecatory remarks on the Spanish language,[4] but he praises Spain in the traditional form of the *laudes*:

. . . there is no doubt that Spain, with its temperate climate and its serene sky produces similar effects in [our] humours and dispositions; for it is clear that neither does the cold make us phlegmatic and dull, like the Germans, nor does great heat make us incapable of working, like the Negroes and Indians; for, the one quality being tempered by the other, it produces well-chastened customs.[5]

In Spain, Quevedo continues, there is natural loyalty to the princes, a religious obedience to the laws, and love for generals and captains.[6]

More than three hundred years later, the distinguished twentieth-century writer and scholar, Menéndez Pidal, was still making essentially the same point:

Due to this instinctive influence of Seneca [i.e., of Stoicism], the Spaniard can as readily endure privations as he can withstand the disturbing temptations to greed and self-indulgence, for his innate soberness inclines him towards a certain ethical austerity. This shows itself in the general tenor of his life, with its simplicity, dignity . . . and strong family ties. The Spanish people preserve deep natural qualities unimpaired . . . , whereas other races which are more tainted by the luxuries of civilization find themselves constantly threatened by a process of wear and tear which saps their strength.[7]

---

[2] Quoted in G. Post, "Two Notes on Nationalism in the Middle Ages," *Traditio*, Vol. 9 (1953), p. 307. See also " 'Blessed Lady Spain'—Vincentius Hispanus and Spanish National Imperialism in the Thirteenth Century," *Speculum*, Vol. 29 (1954), pp. 198-209.

[3] F. de Quevedo y Villegas, "España defendida y los tiempos de ahora" (1609), *Obras completas*, Vol. 1 (Madrid, 1961), p. 489.

[4] *Ibid.*, p. 502.

[5] *Ibid.*, p. 521.

[6] *Ibid.* N.b. Quevedo writes, "Es natural de España la lealdad . . . ," not "para los españoles," as one would expect in a more modern writer.

[7] Menéndez Pidal, *The Spaniards*, p. 18.

Since the Middle Ages and the long, drawn-out struggle with the Moors for the control of the Iberian Peninsula, there was a strong religious component to Spanish patriotism. Santiago Matamoros, also known as the apostle St. James and "the Moor slayer," was the patron saint of the surviving Christians who fought the Moslems from their mountain kingdoms in Asturias, in northern Spain. They called themselves simply Christians; the word *español*, a Spaniard (though not the geographical term Spain) was a thirteenth-century importation from Provence, a convenient appellation invented by foreigners who were also Christians, and only slowly adopted by the Spaniards themselves.[8]

It is almost impossible to overemphasize this religious component in the Spanish concept of nationalism, for one might almost say that it alone provided the moral justification for patriotism. Quevedo clearly felt that it is only God who gives victories and that sin brings defeat and ruin in its train.[9]

> We were His militia at Navas de Tolosa [the great Christian victory over the Moors in 1212]. It was God's skill that won in the Cid and the same used Gama, Pacheco and Albuquerque as instruments in the East Indies to deprive the idols of peace. Who but God . . . upheld Cortés so that he might achieve famous deeds of daring whose prize was a whole New World. It was God's voice, which is obeyed by all things, by which Ximénez de Cisneros held back the night in the battle of Oran. . . .[10]

Cervantes, the volunteer who was wounded in the battle of Lepanto, thought in similar terms. In the *Exemplary Novels* Spaniards are occasionally mentioned as Spaniards, to distinguish them from Italians or Frenchmen or anyone else. But praiseworthy deeds derived mainly from Christian behavior, not from the fact of Spanish nationality. In *The Spanish Lady*, for instance, Englishmen are praised for their patriotic and chivalrous behavior; but the hero of the story is an English Catholic who, with his family, is described as Christian, in contrast to the rest of the English, including their queen, who, as Protestants, presumably could not be regarded as true Christians at all.

Perhaps the finest Spanish literary example of an essentially religious view of patriotism is Calderón's *El Principe Constante*. In this play the Infante Don Fernando of Portugal is taken prisoner in battle by the Moorish king of Fez. He is treated chivalrously, and eventually, his nephew, the king of Portugal, makes an agreement to redeem him by

---

[8] A. Castro, *The Spaniards: An Introduction to Their History*, trans. W. F. King and S. Margaretten (Berkeley, Los Angeles, London, 1971), pp. 10ff.

[9] Quevedo, "Politica de Dios y Gobierno de Cristo," *Obras completas*, Vol. 1, p. 683.

[10] Quevedo, "España defendida," pp. 523ff.

giving up Ceuta, which the Portuguese had captured some time before. The prince however refuses to allow the Christians to give up a city over which the cross had stood. All the ill treatment now inflicted on him by the Moors cannot make him change his mind. He dies, but his glorified spirit leads the Christian armies to victory. Calderón speaks highly of Portuguese valor—the crown of Portugal was worn by the king of Spain when he wrote—but so he does of the valor and chivalry of some of the Moors. The point at issue is, in fact, not national interest nor national honor; it is the cross versus the crescent.

One hundred and thirty years after Calderón wrote *El Principe Constante* (1629), Lessing wrote a short classical play, *Philotas*, on a similar theme (1759). Both the similarities and the differences between the two plays are very revealing for the understanding of the concept of nationalism. In Lessing's play, Philotas, a very young prince, is taken prisoner by the enemy in the very first skirmish in which he is allowed to participate. Just as Fernando, he is treated chivalrously; and he is told that the son of the king who captured him was also taken prisoner in the same skirmish. The two kings would now exchange their prisoners and make peace. Philotas' country would lose nothing because of his rash action in getting himself captured. Or so it is presented to Philotas. But he snatches up a sword and kills himself so as to give his country the advantage of holding the enemy prince prisoner without having to redeem their own prince. In this play religion is not a factor at all. Philotas talks only of the interest of his father and his country, and he sees this interest in the most stark terms of territorial aggrandizement and glory. He does not discuss any justification of the war, though he takes it for granted that his country is right and the enemy wrong.

The contrast between religious motivation and pure nationalism could hardly be clearer. Calderón undoubtedly accepted Prince Fernando's conduct and motivation as wholly admirable, though the play, written in the middle of the Thirty Years' War, may well have been intended to contain at least an implied criticism of war between Christians. Lessing, writing in the middle of the Seven Years' War, felt much more skeptical about his hero and his motivation, which he can make believable only by constantly stressing his youth or, perhaps, juvenility. The curtain line of the play is spoken by the king whose prisoner Philotas had been and who decides to abdicate: "In vain we have shed rivers of blood; in vain conquered provinces . . . Do you not think that one can become sick of being king?" If Lessing's play represents nationalism in its purest form, it is also a devastating indictment of its futility and moral emptiness.

According to most writers on the subject of Spanish national feeling, either during the early-modern period or since, the Spaniards avoided this futility precisely because of the religious content of their patriotic emotions. But such a view assumed that Spaniards, properly speaking, were always Christians and Catholics. It is the great merit of the work of the late Americo Castro to have insisted that this is not a tenable assumption. Spanish national consciousness and *hispanidad*, as he pointed out, so far from existing *ab initio* as a Platonic idea, were rather the strictly historical results of the interaction of Christian, Moslem, and Jewish peoples and traditions in the Iberian Peninsula.[11] The characteristically Spanish identification of the state or nation with religion, Castro claimed, "is a Judeo-Islamic characteristic of Oriental, not Occidental, civilization."[12] The first part of this statement, that identification of the nation with religion is a Judeo-Islamic characteristic, is evidently true, and it may well be that this tradition influenced Christian Spain. But it is not true, as Castro was driven to maintain, that other occidental nations, during their formative centuries, in the Middle Ages and the early-modern period, did not identify themselves in religious terms. The French and the French monarchy certainly did.[13] It was a question of degree and of circumstances. Most European states had to assert themselves against other Christian states and hence could not easily identify their cause with that of religion; but they certainly tried to do so when they had the opportunity. Only Spain, however, was a multiracial and multireligious country, which considerably influenced the development of self-identification.[14]

But the problem is more complicated. The Jews not only influenced Christian Spanish customs and attitudes, but the great majority of them were actually absorbed into Christian Spain, a process which certainly left its traces. Since Castro first pointed to the enormously important role of the converted Jews (the *conversos*, sometimes derogatorily called *marranos*) in the literary, theological, legal, and medical life of Spain, the hunt for a *converso* ancestry of the great names of the Spanish Golden Age has become an astonishingly popular and successful sport of historians.[15]

[11] Americo Castro, *España en su Historia: Cristianos, Moros y Judios* (Buenos Aires, 1948), with subsequent Spanish and English editions. The last is *The Spaniards*, trans. King, *passim*.

[12] Castro, *The Spaniards*, p. 15.

[13] J. R. Strayer, "France: The Holy Land, the Chosen People and the Most Christian King," *Action and Conviction in Early Modern Europe*, ed. T. K. Rabb and J. E. Seigel (Princeton, 1969).

[14] It is possible that a rather similar phenomenon occurred in Russia during the time of the Tatar domination.

[15] See A. Domínguez Ortiz, *Los Judeoconversos en España y América* (Madrid, 1971) and bibliographical indications contained therein.

Most of the *conversos,* and even a great many of the Spanish Jews before their expulsion in 1492, thought of themselves as Spaniards. Castro quotes a speech by Don Alonso de Cartagena at the Council of Bâle in 1434. Cartagena, a *converso* who had attained to the position of bishop of Burgos, argued for the right of precedence of Castile over England because

> Spaniards are not wont to prize great wealth, but rather virtue; nor do they measure a man's honour by the store of his money but rather by the quality of his beautiful deeds; wherefore riches are not to be argued in this matter (as the English argued them); for if we should mete out precedences according to riches, Cosimo de' Medici, or some other very rich merchant, mayhap would come before some duke.[16]

But such sentiments hardly marked Spaniards as off "by an abyss" from the rest of the European nobility, as Castro thought.[17] Cartagena's were only a somewhat extreme statement of quite common European aristocratic sentiments. Even Henry IV of France would still refer to Marie de Medici as "ma grosse banquière," even though by that time the Medici had provided two popes and had become grand dukes. And, of course, he had married her, just as the Castilian aristocrats of Alonso de Cartagena's time had married rich Jewish and *converso* women.

But if the *conversos* thought of themselves as Castilians or Spaniards, as Cartagena evidently did, the great mass of the population, and especially the lower classes, did not accept such an identification at all. They prided themselves on their *limpieza,* their purity of blood, and their descent from Old Christians, untainted by Jewish blood or, later, by the suspicion of heresy. In 1449 there were riots in Toledo against a new tax imposed by the constable of Castile, Alvaro de Luna. The riots turned into pogroms against Jews and *conversos* who were held to be the instigators of the new tax, and the rioters proclaimed a statute requiring purity of blood for holders of all public or private offices in Toledo.[18] From the middle of the sixteenth century, such statutes became common, especially in ecclesiastical institutions.

There was undoubtedly a considerable area in which the emphasis on *limpieza* overlapped with national sentiment in the minds of Spaniards. Nevertheless, the mania for purity of blood, with its strong anti-aristocratic overtones (for it was mainly the upper classes who had intermarried with Jews and *conversos*) was both a restrictive and a divisive force

---

[16] Castro, *The Spaniards,* p. 150.

[17] *Ibid.,* p. 151.

[18] A. A. Sicroff, *Les controverses des statuts de 'pureté de sang' en Espagne du XVe u XVIIe siècle* (Paris, 1960), pp. 32ff.

in Spanish society. The Count-Duke Olivares, first minister of Philip IV and a most ardent proponent of the greatness of Castile, certainly interpreted these emotions in this way, largely because he, too, like most of the Spanish high nobility and indeed the royal house itself, had *converso* ancestors.[19]

I have so far attempted to approach the problem of Spanish national sentiment by following the methodology of both the traditional writers of the *laudes Hispaniae*, from St. Isidore to Menéndez Pidal, and also of Americo Castro and his school. They tell us a great deal about Spanish history that is both true and perceptive, even if one does not always agree with their conclusions. There is, however, a fundamental limitation to this approach. By concentrating on a particular tradition, whether as a static characteristic of a national mentality, or as an evolutionary phenomenon, these writers have not accounted for large areas of human emotions and motivations which do not fit easily into the traditions and patterns they describe, regardless of the rich and varied ways in which they have conceived of their patterns. In other words, one can always find instances, and very important ones at that, where the pattern does not fit.

Take the case of the conquistadors in the New World. Here is Menéndez Pidal's characterization:

> It is . . . a natural trait in the Spaniard not to allow any calculation of gains and losses to prevail over considerations of another order. Columbus, a foreigner by birth, instead of allowing himself to be carried away by enthusiasm for his enterprise, kept postponing it while he negotiated interminably, and refused to risk the venture until he had secured for himself a dazzling series of profits and rewards. Whereas a host of Spanish explorers, despising material advantage, engaged in perilous exploits for the simple love of adventure, or with only problematic hopes of gain.[20]

Such an interpretation of national attitudes and motives reads strangely in the light of the actual history of the conquests of Mexico and Peru and even of the express views of many of the conquistadors themselves.[21]

---

[19] J. H. Elliott, "The Statecraft of Olivares," *The Diversity of History*, ed. J. H. Elliott and H. G. Koenigsberger (London and Ithaca, 1970), pp. 134ff.

[20] Menéndez Pidal, *The Spaniards*, pp. 19ff.

[21] A. Domínguez Ortiz, *The Golden Age of Spain 1516–1659*, trans. J. Casey, (London, 1971), gives a much more sober characterization of the motives of the conquistadors. On p. 289: "Ambition, the thirst for command, for acquiring nobility and renown, for leaving an honoured name behind—these were the ideals of the Renaissance Spaniard, and he found in the discoveries an opportunity to exploit them to the full."

"We came here to serve God and also to get rich," wrote Bernal Diaz, the chronicler of Cortés' expedition.[22] Pizarro, the conqueror of Peru, put it even more brutally, when an ecclesiastic in his band urged him not to rob the Indians but to bring them the Christian faith: "I have not come for any such reasons. I have come to take away from them their gold."[23]

No doubt, many of the Spanish conquistadors performed almost incredible feats of daring and were prepared to suffer hardships to the utmost limits of human endurance, and this, it is quite true, often with only problematic hopes of material gain. But does it detract from their personal achievements to wonder why such actions should be regarded as specifically Spanish or how they differed from the hardships endured by the Nansens and Amundsens, the Scotts, the Hillarys and the Tensings, and countless others of different nations and through many ages, who sought personal fame and satisfaction rather than material rewards through the performance of most hazardous quests? There were those, mainly Dominican and Franciscan friars, who genuinely thought of the Spanish conquests as opportunities to spread the word of God among the heathens. They did what they could to protect the Indians from exploitation and they gained the ear of the king of Spain. But in practice their efforts and those of the Spanish crown were outweighed by the rapacity of the Spanish settlers. If Spanish culture and the Catholic religion eventually pervaded large areas of the New World, the price paid for this by its original inhabitants was appallingly high. There is a rather horrible irony in finding that at least one of the reasons for the disasters which overtook the Indians was the fact that the Spaniards, who prided themselves so much on their indifference to material wealth, found the Indians' genuine indifference to gold and other possessions not only baffling but downright repellent.[24]

I am not trying to revive the "black legend" of specifically Spanish cruelty in the New World but simply trying to point to the inadequacy of using mainly literary sources for the understanding of human actions. If Spanish national feelings and the more admirable characteristics of *hispanidad* can be said to have manifested themselves in the conquest of the New World, then those were largely emotions recollected in tranquility, or, rather, in rhetoric after the event, and often, though not always, by those who stayed at home. If the "empire in which the sun never set" was a source of pride for Spaniards at home, it was not something for which

[22] Quoted in L. Hanke, *The Spanish Struggle for Justice in the Conquest of America* (Philadelphia, 1949), p. 7.

[23] *Ibid.*

[24] L. Hanke, *The First Social Experiments in America* (Cambridge, Massachusetts, 1935), p. 30.

most of them were prepared to make large sacrifices. In 1548, the Cortes of Castile petitioned the King to prohibit the export of Spanish manufactures to the colonies because this export raised prices to the consumer at home. Let the colonists manufacture their own goods from their own materials, they advised.[25]

My critical inquiry into the traditional views of Spanish nationalism is, however, as yet inconclusive. I have demonstrated that national feeling was not as universal and pervasive as has often been claimed. But I cannot, nor do I wish to, deny altogether the existence of national sentiment in Spain in the early-modern period. It should be stressed, however, that attitudes of mind expressed in literature or in the recorded remarks of individuals cannot tell us precisely *how* important such attitudes were and what role they played in the history of a country or a people.

A somewhat different but related problem arises with modern sociological theories of nationalism. Take, for instance, the conceptual framework used by K. W. Deutsch in his book, *National and Social Communication.*[26] Deutsch proposed a model of a world consisting of highly uneven cluster distributions of human settlement, held together and separated from each other by patterns of transport; barriers between markets; differences in wealth, language, caste, or class; institutions; and the uneven impact of historical events. The techniques of studying these partly overlapping problems have to be provided by all the social sciences, from demography to sociology and from economics to linguistics and history.[27]

So far, this is acceptable. In the process of working out his model, Deutsch makes some illuminating suggestions which are certainly applicable to the history of Spanish national feeling. For instance, the Spanish government's hopes for the assimilation of the *Moriscos*, the Christianized Moors, in the sixteenth century were doomed to failure because of the absence of any real communication between the Old Christians and the *Moriscos*, even when they lived side by side. Or again, there is Deutsch's suggestion—it is little more than that—of the importance for the growth of national feeling of assigning value to people as they are, i.e., whatever their origin and station in life.[28] It has recently been argued that the whole corpus of Spanish Golden Age drama was a sus-

---

[25] J. Carrera Pujal, *Historia de la Economía Española* (Barcelona, 1943), Vol. 1, pp. 142ff.

[26] K. W. Deutsch, *Nationalism and Social Communication: An Inquiry into the Foundations of Nationality* (New York and London, 1953).

[27] *Ibid.*, p. 161 and *passim.*

[28] *Ibid.*, p. 153.

tained and deliberate attempt to shore up the existing social structure by presenting on stage the dignity and sense of honor of members of all classes, of peasants and craftsmen as much as of nobles and princes.[29] But before this interpretation can be accepted, it should be noted that the great playwrights, from Lope de Vega to Tirso de Molina and Calderón, wrote what they thought *should* be, rather than what they thought actually *was*. Calderón's gentlemen officers in *El Alcalde de Zalamea* very evidently do not treat the peasants as if nobles and peasants were all members of a community which could be called a nation. The author needed a *deus ex machina*, the providential appearance of the king, in order to resolve the basically unresolvable class antogonism which he presents. And this his audience would understand, for the only real political emotion which nobles and peasants had in common was their personal loyalty to the king.

In the end, however, the theories of the sociologists, suggestive as they are, do not tell us enough. It looks plausible to analyze the problem of the assimilation of the *Moriscos* in terms of the problem of communication. But as soon as we compare it with that of the assimilation of the *conversos* the inadequacy of the technique becomes apparent. Between *conversos* and Old Christians, there was no communication problem whatever and no easily recognizable distinction, not in language, in social customs, nor in looks—in Spain at least. And yet, the doctrine of *limpieza* was directed both against *Moriscos* and *conversos*. The racialism of the Spanish Old Christians was therefore not primarily, if at all, a problem in social communication, even in the wide sense which Deutsch uses this term.[30] In other words, a sociological theory developed primarily from the observation of the contemporary scene is found to lack controls when introduced into a situation removed in time.

More serious still, however, is the excessive claim which Deutsch makes for his model. "The present distribution of sovereign states and blocks of states," he tells us, "was found necessary in its essential features, though not in its accidents."[31] Without even venturing into the morass of the taxonomic problems raised by this undefined distinction between

[29] J. A. Maravall, "Una interpretación historico-social del teatro barocco," *Cuadernos Hispanoamericanos*, No. 235 (1969).

[30] It would be possible to argue that this racialism was the result of a much earlier absence of communication in the period during which the separate Jewish, Christian, and Moslem traditions evolved. But such an argument would lead to further formidable problems about the spread of Islam during its expansionist period and also about the ethnic origins of Spanish Jews and Moslems, for none of which the Deutsch model is particularly illuminating.

[31] Deutsch, *Nationalism and Social Communication*, p. 161.

essentials and accidents, Deutsch's conclusion simply begs the question for the historian who is studying the early-modern period. Not only is the historian professionally interested in the accidents, but he has the strong suspicion that it may have been precisely what the sociologist would regard as accidents which determined the present distribution of sovereign states. The history of Spain in the early-modern period is very much a case in point, and it is now time to look more closely at this history, and to do so without the teleological preconceptions of either the literateur or the social scientist who has ventured into the territory of the historian.[32]

The history of modern Spain is usually held to start in 1469 with the marriage of Ferdinand and Isabella. This marriage, and the subsequent union of the crowns of Aragon and Castile, has traditionally been seen as an expression of a sense of Spanish nationality which antedated the political union. Some such feeling seems indeed to have existed in intellectual circles at the court of Ferdinand's father, John II of Aragon.[33] The motivation of the chief protagonists, however, was much more practical. John II desperately needed Castilian help to defend his Pyrenees provinces of Cerdagne and Roussillon against French attacks. For this purpose he negotiated with different Castilian factions until he found one which, for its own reasons, was willing to entertain the idea of the Aragonese connection. This was a section of the Castilian high nobility, led by Archbishop Carrillo of Toledo, who supported the succession claims of the Infanta Isabella, sister of King Henry IV, against the King and his daughter, Juana. This was a pure power struggle and its details were sordid. There had been civil wars and, at one stage, the grandees

[32] It is only fair to add that at least one stream of recent anthropological thought is moving away from the assumption that an ethnic unit is normally a discrete and homogeneous society. This assumption derived both from the nature of some primitive societies and from the post-Malinowskian methods of studying them. It is an assumption on which many anthropological and sociological generalizations appear to have been based but which, as I have tried to show, is not applicable to Spain. See R. A. LeVine and D. T. Campbell, *Ethnocentrism* (New York, 1972), chap. 7 and *passim*.

I do not, of course, mean to imply a blanket condemnation of social scientists. After I finished writing this paper, Professor Davydd Greenwood, of the Anthropology Department of Cornell University, drew my attention to *El mito del carácter nacional. Meditaciones a contrapelo*, (Madrid, 1970), by the eminent contemporary anthropologist, Julio Caro Baroja. This is an elegant and, often, ironical discussion of Spanish and non-Spanish views of the Spanish "national character" through modern history. Caro concludes on p. 112: "En suma, el del carácter nacional es un mito amenazador y peligroso, como lo fueron muchos de al Antigüedad pagana. Pero acaso no tenga la majestad y profundidad de aquéllos."

[33] J. H. Elliott, *Imperial Spain, 1469-1716* (London, 1963), p. 7, quoting R. B. Tate, *Joan Margarit i Pau, Cardinal-Bishop of Gerona* (Manchester, 1955).

had induced Henry IV to declare that his daughter had been fathered by a certain Beltrán de la Cueva—wrongly, as historians now believe. Isabella's supporters hoped to use the Aragonese alliance for their own purposes and, being the wooed rather than the wooers, were able to impose their own conditions on Ferdinand.[34] Ferdinand and Isabella, being cousins, forged a papal dispensation for their marriage. Because of the expected Castilian help against the French, news of this event was received with great jubilation in Zaragoza and Valencia and even in Palermo (where feelings of Spanish nationalism could not have been prominent); but the Castilians reacted with considerable coldness because they feared the renewal of civil war.[35]

It was not long in coming. Juana married Alfonso V of Portugal, and after Henry IV's death in 1474, both Aragon and Portugal immediately became involved in the renewed Castilian civil war. Alfonso and Juana were eventually defeated and the union of the crowns of Castile and Aragon was confirmed. It was a conclusion with far-reaching implications for the future. But it was not a foregone conclusion, nor was it inherently more national or Spanish than a victory for Juana and Alfonso would have been. Such a victory would have led to the union of the crowns of Castile and Portugal which, in the light of the previous traditions of the Iberian Peninsula, would have been just as natural, national, and Spanish as the actual union of the crowns of Castile and Aragon. It probably would have prevented the involvement of Castile in the Italian policy of Aragon and in the interminable and eventually ruinous wars with France.

If the union of the crowns of Aragon and Castile and the creation of what was called, mainly by foreigners, the kingdom of Spain were not primarily the result of national feeling, neither was much of the subsequent policy of Ferdinand and Isabella. The conquest of Granada certainly appealed to the traditional religious and, therefore one might say, national feeling of Isabella's subjects, and so did the setting up of the Spanish Inquisition and its policy of expelling Jews and persecuting *conversos*.

The Catholic Kings and their successors, moveover, continued King John II's patronage of Spanish historiography. Perhaps it was in this field, in which the feeling for Spanish nationality had already acquired a considerable and respectable tradition, that national awareness was given the strongest boost by the union of the crowns. This national sentiment showed itself particularly in the need felt by Spanish historians to pro-

[34] J. Vicens Vives, *Historia crítica de la vida y reinado de Fernando II de Aragon* (Zaragoza, 1962), pp. 242ff, 246ff, and *passim*.
[35] *Ibid.*, p. 263.

vide their country with antecedents as splendid as those traditionally claimed by the French and the English. Franco, the descendant of Aeneas, for France, and the Roman Brutus, for Britain, were now matched for Spain by Tubal and even by Hercules himself, not to mention such exotic figures as Osiris. The recent forgeries of Annius of Viterbo provided a particularly rich quarry for the Spaniards.[36] Charles V's court historian, Florián de Ocampo used a large part of his *Corónica general de España* (1544) to recount the pre-Roman history of Spain; in other words, he wrote a nationalistic historical fantasy. Even at the beginning of the seventeenth century, Juan de Mariana, a much more sophisticated historian than Ocampo, did not dare to dispense with the legends of Hercules in his *Historia de España*. The best Spanish historian of the early-modern period, however, Gerónimo Zurita, did not attempt to write a history of Spain at all, but confined himself to the history of Aragon in his *Annales de la corona de Aragón* (1562–80).[37] Spanish Renaissance historiography was therefore essentially a part of the tradition of the *laudes Hispaniae*; and if its critical understanding of Spanish history must be viewed as problematical, at least when compared with the Italian and French historiography of the period, it undoubtedly increased the national self-confidence of educated Spaniards. Apart from this, its effects on Spanish policy-making was practically nil.

Basically, the policies pursued by the Catholic Kings had two aims: the strengthening of the power of the monarchy and the pursuit of dynastic advantages, either through marriage alliances or through wars to conquer and maintain what Ferdinand claimed to be rightfully his. Neither of these aims was specifically inspired by national feeling, though such feeling was not necessarily absent. But even the official rhetoric of the Catholic Kings' diplomacy gives little basis for a nationalistic interpretation. For example, in 1473 Ferdinand set up Isabella as heiress

> in my said kingdoms of Aragon and Sicily, notwithstanding all laws, fueros, ordinances and customs of these said kingdoms which prohibit the succession of a woman . . . , and this not from ambition nor greed nor any excessive affection in which I hold the said princess, . . . but rather for the great benefit which the said kingdoms will derive from being united with those of Castile and Leon, and that one prince would be king, lord and governor of them all.[38]

[36] R. B. Tate, *Ensayos sobre la Historiografía peninsular de siglo XV* (Madrid, 1970), chap. 1.

[37] See E. Fueter, *Geschichte der neueren Historiographie* (3rd ed.; Munich, 1936), pp. 235ff.

[38] Quoted in F. Gómez de Mercado y de Miguel, *Dogmas Nacionales del Rey Catolico* (Madrid, 1953), p. 334.

The modern editor of this document comments that "the great statesman Don Ferdinand prepares the unity of all the medieval kingdoms in order to create the great Spanish nation."[39] But the document shows nothing of the sort. Not only does it not mention the Spanish nation at all, it expressly includes in the union of crowns, and in the benefits which are supposed to flow from it, the kingdom of Sicily. There is not the slightest hint that this Italian kingdom was in any way different from, or that it should be treated differently from, the Iberian kingdoms. The union which Ferdinand had in mind was a dynastic, not a national, union.

The case of Navarre was very similar.[40] In 1494 the Catholic Kings promised to marry their daughter, Anna, to a son of the king of Navarre. There was to be perpetual peace and an alliance between the countries for the mutual benefit of their respective subjects. But again the name of Spain is conspicuously absent from this document, as is any mention of a common tradition and language of the peoples of Castile and Navarre. As it happened, the marriage alliance was never concluded. In 1512, Ferdinand conquered Navarre by force of arms, again not on the basis of any national argument, but on the basis of the weak dynastic claim of his second wife, Germaine de Foix, and on the even more dubious authority of a papal excommunication of the actual king of Navarre.[41]

In 1504 Isabella died and almost all of the Castilian high nobility threw themselves into the arms of the Burgundian Philip, husband of Isabella's mentally disturbed daughter, rather than support the claims of the "national" king, Ferdinand. The Castilian grandees correctly calculated that Philip would be easier to handle than the old autocrat from Aragon. Ferdinand was furious, but it is unlikely that he was surprised by the Castilians' lack of national feeling. He expected men to act in accordance with more practical motives. This view was manifested in a letter he wrote to Emperor Maximilian in 1496, urging him to make war on France, in which he said the German princes would follow the Emperor if he prospered but would join the king of France if the Emperor hesitated.[42] Jumping on the band wagon, or as men put it during the Renaissance, the importance for a prince to have "reputation," was a well known phenomenon at the time and one to which judicious politicians attached a great deal more importance than to an abstract idea such as nationalism.

---

[39] Ibid., p. 337.

[40] L. Suarez Fernandez, Política Internacional de Isabel la Católica, Estudio y Documentos (Valladolid, 1971), Vol. 4, pp. 181-85, 197-99.

[41] R. B. Merriman, The Rise of the Spanish Empire (New York, 1918), Vol. 2, pp. 344-47.

[42] Suarez Fernandez, Política Internacional, Vol. 4, p. 569.

With the succession of Philip of Burgundy in Castile, the union of the crowns of Castile and Aragon was dissolved. Ferdinand acknowledged his son-in-law's succession in public, though privately he declared his agreement to have been obtained by force and hence to be null and void. But Ferdinand now contracted a second marriage, with Germaine de Foix, niece of Louis XII of France, in order to prevent a French attack on his kingdom of Naples, now bereft of Castilian support.[43] The expected son from this union would inherit all the realms of the crown of Aragon, in Spain and Italy. It has been argued that Ferdinand did not want to perpetuate the renewed division of the Spanish kingdoms, but rather intended to place his son by Germaine on the Castilian throne, as well as that of Aragon.[44] This is certainly plausible, though I still think Ferdinand thought more in dynastic than in national terms. Naples remained as important to him as Castile.

This became clear when Philip died and when Queen Germaine's son died immediately after birth. There would now be a Hapsburg-Burgundian dynastic claim to both Castile and Aragon. In the meantime, however, the union of the crowns was restored in the person of Ferdinand. For a short time, he left his regent in Castile, Cardinal Ximénes de Cisneros, free to pursue an essentially Castilian national policy, the conquest of the North African coast. It was then that the old cardinal, in the battle of Oran, was credited with having, like Joshua, held back the sun on its course to allow the Christians time to complete their victory. Ferdinand had not actively supported these endeavours; in fact, in 1510 he actually stopped them and switched Castilian resources back into his Italian policy.

It is little wonder that, at Ferdinand's death in 1516, the mutual antagonisms of the different Iberian kingdoms were as virulent as ever. Cardinal Ximénes, regent once again, painted a sombre picture of the mood of the country in his letters to the court of young King Charles in the Netherlands. The men of Navarra, old enemies of the Aragonese, would rather suffer a Turk than an Aragonese as governor of the fortress of Pamplona.[45] The Cardinal stated that the King's plan to send an Aragonese as his ambassador to Rome should be given up, for the many Castil-

---

[43] Treaty of Blois, October 12, 1505. See Baron de Terrateig, *Política en Italia de Rey Catolico 1507-1516* (Madrid, 1963), Vol. 1, p. 42.

[44] Merriman, *The Rise of the Spanish Empire*, Vol. 2, pp. 329, 332; Elliott, *Imperial Spain*, p. 128.

[45] Ximénes to Diego Lopez de Ayala in Flanders, Madrid, May 12, 1516, in P. Gayangos and V. de la Fuente, *Cartas del Cardenal Don Fray Francisco Jiménes de Cisneros* (Madrid, 1867), p. 129.

ians resident in Rome would never obey him. The ambassador, he added, should be a Castilian or a Fleming.[46]

As it turned out, the Castilians were not happy about the appointment of Flemings, either—at least, not in their own country. It has generally been held that the revolt of the *comuneros* in 1520 represented primarily a Castilian national movement against a foreign king and his foreign advisers. There was certainly considerable resentment against the Netherlanders in Charles V's court, and there were deliberate and much exaggerated campaigns against their "carpetbagging," even before they had set foot on Castilian soil.[47] There was also much resentment against Charles V's imperial title, and people said that it was better to be king of Spain than emperor of Germany.[48] Nevertheless, the *comunero* revolt was basically a civil war in which both sides claimed to represent the true interests of Castile. The economic antagonisms were old. The Mesta, the gild of sheep owners, and the merchants of Burgos had grown rich by the export of wool to the Netherlands. They welcomed the Burgundian connection and argued that grazing and the wool trade were "one of the principal resources [*haziendas*] of these kingdoms, employing a great part of its people and providing them with meat to eat, woolens to clothe themselves, shoes and many other necessities, without which these kingdoms could not survive and on which depend the greater part of the royal revenues. . . ."[49] Against this, the cloth manufacturers of Segovia, Toledo, and Valladolid had been arguing for years that the export of raw wool raised the price for the native manufacturer and ruined many poor people who had no other livelihood but weaving; that Flanders and England grew rich by working up Spanish wool into cloth;[50] and that the reason for the drain of money from Spain to other countries was the fact "that the goods which enter this country cost much, while those which are exported cost little."[51] Because the monarchy, for financial reasons, had always supported the Mesta and the wool exporters, it is not surprising to

[46] Ximénes to Diego Lopez de Ayala in Flanders; Madrid, September 27, 1516, in *ibid.*, p. 158.

[47] *Ibid., passim;* V. de la Fuente, *Cartas de los secretarios del Cardenal D. Fr. Francisco Jiménez de Cisneros durante su regencia en los años de 1516 y 1517* (Madrid, 1875), p. 18 and *passim.* See also J. E. A. Walther, *Die Anfänge Karls V* (Leipzig, 1911), *passim.*

[48] J. Sanches Montes, *Franceses, Protestantes Turcos: Los Españoles ante la Política de Carlos V.* (Madrid, 1951), p. 21, quoting Santa Cruz, *Cronica.*

[49] Memorandum of the Mesta, 1520, quoted in J. Pérez, *La révolution des 'comunidades' de Castille (1520-1521)* (Bordeaux, 1970), p. 43, n. 123.

[50] Memorandum by Pedro de Burgos, *ibid.*, pp. 103ff.

[51] Memorandum by Rodrigo de Luján, *ibid.* pp. 105ff.

find that Burgos remained royalist during the revolt, while Segovia and Toledo were the centers of the opposition.

The immediate cause of the revolt, however, was financial and political. There was an angry reaction to the government's demand for additional taxes and to its manipulation of the deputies of the Castilian Cortes to obtain consent for these taxes which were to pay for the King's journey to Germany. Though the economic antagonisms and the resentment of the foreign regent, Adrian of Utrecht, were important, the principal issue of the revolt rapidly became a constitutional and a social one: the political powers of the cities vis-à-vis the king, and the social and political position of the nobility, in the Cortes, in the cities, and even on their own estates. In these circumstances, the dislike of the Castilian nobles for the Burgundians and their sympathy for the cities were soon overshadowed by their fear for their social and political status. They raised an army and defeated the *comunero* movement and thus restored the authority of their foreign king.[52]

The subjects of the crown of Aragon were no more pleased with this foreign king and his Burgundian retinue than were the Castilians. Their Cortes were even less willing than the Castilian Cortes to pay for Charles V's German policy. But the government made no attempt to force the issue, as it did in Castile; consequently, the Catalans and Aragonese made no attempt to support the *comunero* movement. Common hatred of the foreigner was evidently not enough to produce a nationalistic Spanish policy. The Valencians did indeed have a rebellion of their own, the *Germanía*. But this was a lower class revolt, directed against the *Moriscos* and against the local nobility which protected them as a valuable and cheap labor force. So far from being in sympathy with the *comunero* movement, the *Germanía* loudly proclaimed its royalism. It mattered little. The crown inevitably allied itself with the nobility to suppress it.

During the remainder of Charles V's reign, the Castilian nobility and cities gradually came to accept the foreign king and his imperialist policies.[53] Charles, for his part, learned Castilian and made deliberate efforts to Castilianize himself. The word Castilian, rather than Spanish, is used deliberately, because the Emperor and his government made little effort to unify the Hispanic kingdoms further. Castile was, by far, the largest of

---

[52] The fullest modern account is in Pérez, *La révolution*. See also J. A. Maravall, *Las Comunidades de Castilla* (Madrid, 1963).

[53] In 1525, the Venetian ambassador in Spain, Gasparo Contarini, later the famous cardinal and church reformer, still thought that all classes of Spaniards disliked or even hated the emperor and that he reciprocated these sentiments but knew how to dissimulate. E. Albèri, *Relazioni degli ambasciatori veneti*, Series 1, Vol. 2, pp. 44ff.

his dominions and the one in which, after the *comunero* revolt, the crown had the most authority. Thus the Castilians were granted a monopoly on trade with the New World. While it was possible for the Catalans to engage in this trade by using Castilian cover firms, the same was true for the Genoese and Augsburgers; the non-Castilian Spanish subjects of the Emperor therefore had no advantage over foreigners. Empress Isabella, whom Charles left as regent in Spain during his long absences, was unwilling to leave Castile even to attend the Aragonese Cortes, a procedure which Aragonese law required her to follow.[54] Characteristically, she complained on one occasion that many Castilian grandees and caballeros wished to go to Barcelona to welcome the Emperor, who was expected to arrive there, which she said would lead to "the export of great sums of money and horses from these kingdoms,"[55] i.e., from the kingdoms of the crown of Castile to those of the crown of Aragon!

From Empress Isabella's correspondence with her husband it is possible to see that Charles V's imperial policy was not always what his Castilian subjects would have wished. But the differences were not fundamental. The Castilian grandees were coming to see the advantages of having a ruler who could dispense the patronage of so many countries. Sydney and Beatrice Webb once called the British empire of the early 1900s "a vast system of outdoor relief for the British upper classes." With its viceroyalties and governorships, with its colonelcies and captaincies of an ever-increasing army, with Italian bishoprics for Spanish ecclesiastics and councilorships in ever-proliferating councils in Madrid for educated hidalgos, Charles V's empire was becoming just such a desirable setup for the Castilian upper classes.

Discussions of high policy, in consequence, tended to turn upon the nature of the empire. The debates of 1544 are particularly revealing. After a reasonably successful campaign in France, Charles V concluded the peace of Crépy with Francis I because he had run out of money and because he wished to have his hands free to deal with the German Protestants. An important part of the treaty was a proposed marriage alliance between the houses of Hapsburg and Valois, in one of two alternative forms. The first possibility was that Francis I's second son, Charles, duke of Orleans, would marry Emperor Charles V's daughter Mary. The pair would receive the whole of the Netherlands, no less, and Franche Comté as their dowry, to rule with the title of governors until the Emperor's death, when they would get it in full sovereignty. The second was

---

[54] J. M. Jover, *Carlos V y los Españoles* (Madrid, 1963), p. 55.

[55] Empress Isabel to Charles V, Madrid, January 20, 1533, in M. del C. Mazarío Coleto, *Isabel de Portugal, Emperatriz y Reina de España* (Madrid, 1951), p. 372.

that the Duke would marry Anna, second daughter of the Emperor's brother, Ferdinand, king of the Romans, and receive as dowry the Duchy of Milan. The Emperor, in Brussels at the time, asked his Council of State in Spain to advise which alternative should be followed.

In December 1544, Prince Philip (later Philip II) reported to his father that the Council had been unable to agree.[56] One group of councilors, following the old cardinal-archbishop of Toledo, Juan Pardo y Tavera, took the traditional stance of opposing Castilian involvement in Italy and, more especially, in Milan, a province acquired only nine years before, but which had to be defended against the French at a high cost in blood and money. Equally important, the Cardinal was outraged by the very idea that Charles V should give up his hereditary Burgundian lands. The duke of Alva argued the opposite case. The Netherlands were difficult to hold because the supply lines from Spain, either by sea or across the Alps, were highly vulnerable. Without Milan, and hence northern Italy and the Alpine passes, the Netherlands were not really defensible at all. Conversely, Milan was entirely defensible without the Netherlands.

These diametrically opposed views have been characterized, quite correctly, as the Castilian and the Catalan-Aragonese traditions in foreign policy, regardless of the fact that Alva was an arch-Castilian.[57] They also represented the views of the traditionalists to whom dynastic loyalties were sacred and of the practical soldiers who made a hard-nosed assessment of the strategic and logistic problems involved in the two alternatives. Some twenty-five years later, Alva himself, as governor-general of the Netherlands, had the correctness of his analysis of 1544 proved to him by events, and this despite his deliberate efforts to prevent just such an eventuality. But neither Alva's nor Tavera's view in 1544 can be regarded as more Spanish than the other.[58]

[56] Philip's letter of December 14, 1544 is translated in *Calendar of State Papers Spanish*, Vol. 7, pp. 478-96. Further material and analysis of the discussions can be found in F. Chabod, "¿Milán ó los Países Bajos? Las Discusiones en España sobre la Alternativa de 1544," *Carlos V (1500-1558): Homenaje de la Universidad de Granada* (Granada, 1958), pp. 331-72.

[57] F. Chabod, "Contrasti interni e dibatti sulla politica generale di Carlo V," *Karl V. Der Kaiser und seine Zeit*, ed. P. Rassow and F. Schalk (Cologne, 1960), p. 56.

[58] Chabod thought Alva's view "assai più nazionale proprio dal punto di vista spagnuolo." *Ibid.* I doubt whether Alva himself saw it in such a light. It seems to me that Alva thought purely in terms of power and of military necessities for his sovereign. (Alva is perhaps the nearest character in modern European history to the Hagen of the *Niebelungenlied*.) His views were supported by the Italian Ferrante Gonzaga, Charles V's governor of Milan and otherwise no friend of Alva's. Gonzaga had in mind a strategically defensible Italo-Spanish Mediterranean empire. To achieve this he later even suggested an exchange of the Netherlands for Piedmont-Savoy. *Ibid.*, pp. 57ff. At the imperial court Gonzaga's proposals were rejected as being too Italian!

In the end Charles V predictably decided to give up Milan, rather than his hereditary Burgundian lands, and this certainly for dynastic and emotional, rather than for Castilian national reasons.[59] After all, he had never taken much notice of Tavera's repeated criticism of his Italian policy. But much to the relief of the imperial court, the duke of Orleans died, and the question of the first alternative died with him.

With the succession of Philip II in 1555, the Castilian ruling class more readily identified with an imperial policy that was thought of in religious terms but that was pursued in a very practical fashion, and this not least because Philip II himself was much more obviously a Castilian than his father. Officially, the King valued his Italian and Netherlands subjects as highly as the Spaniards. Italians from proud and ancient families, such as the Pescara and Colonna, served Philip loyally, even when they knew that he intrigued against them. Egmont never wavered in his personal loyalty, right up to the steps of the scaffold. Personal loyalty to the sovereign still outweighed national feeling for many of the European nobility, as in earlier times it had done dramatically for Pescara, victor of the battle of Pavia in 1525, who refused to listen when the chancellor of Milan, Girolamo Morone, used nationalistic arguments in an attempt to induce him to change sides and help free Italy from foreign domination.[60] Philip II even admitted that men might serve more effectively outside their own country. But instead of employing Netherlanders and Italians in Castile, as this statement would suggest, it meant that, whenever he could, he appointed Spaniards, or rather Castilians, throughout his empire. Cardinal Granvelle, a Franche-Comtois, suggested, as early as 1563, that the King appoint an occasional Netherlander to a Spanish ecclesiastical benefice, for even one such appointment would make hundreds serve more loyally, in hope of a similar favor. More particularly, Granvelle urged the King to offer the prince of Orange the viceroyalty of Sicily where he would serve well and also would no longer make mischief in the Netherlands.[61] This brilliant suggestion does not even seem to have been discussed by the government in Madrid. Philip was evidently unwilling to offend Castilian vested interests and found facile excuses not to act on Granvelle's proposals. Granvelle himself and all the other of Philip's non-Spanish servants in high positions—even his own nephew, Alexander Farnese, duke of Parma—found themselves faced with the

---

[59] See F. Walser, "Berichte und Studien zur Geschichte Karls V," Part VI, *Nachrichten von der Gesellschaft der Wissenschaften zu Göttingen* (Phil.-Hist. Klasse), 1932, Hft. 1, pp. 133-43, 167-71.

[60] K. Brandi, *Kaiser Karl V* (Munich, 1937/59), pp. 188ff.

[61] Granvelle to Philip II, March 10, 1563, *Papiers d'état du cardinal de Granvelle* (Paris, 1841), Vol. 7, pp. 53-55.

constant and unremitting hostility and uncooperativeness of the Castilians.

To the rest of the world it became clear quite rapidly that the universalist empire of Charles V had become a Spanish empire. In Spain itself the term did not come to be used until the 1590s.[62] But already in 1579, the Cortes of Castile had told the King that he should go ahead and acquire the crown of Portugal, even if he had no valid claims for it, for the succession of a foreign prince would be damaging to Castile and to the Christian religion.[63] The equation of Castilian reason of state with the good of Christendom became even clearer in 1587 when the Cortes argued that they were petitioning the King to lower taxes only so that they could serve him the better:

> for with their forces and substance, Your Majesty and your ancestors of glorious memory have conquered and maintained so many kingdoms, and Your Majesty has the obligation to preserve and maintain them and to conquer many others which God might give Your Majesty . . . as is needful for your subjects and vassals and for the Christian religion.[64]

During the last years of Philip II's reign, some doubts began to be raised about the effects of Castilian imperialism on Castile and on the common people who paid the taxes and provided the soldiers. One deputy of the Cortes wondered "whether France, Flanders and England would really be better if Spain were poorer."[65] Another detailed the

[62] From the reign of Philip II (1555-98), the phrase "Roi des Espagnes Catholique" or "Hispaniarum Rex" begins to appear in diplomatic documents. This is perhaps not surprising as, in view of the prevalent literary and rhetorical tradition, one would expect the Castilians to be claiming to speak to foreigners for the whole of Spain. But I don't think that too much weight should be attached to this convention. Nor was it followed at all consistently. At the very end of the reign, in the Treaty of Vervins, May 2, 1598, Philip II is still styled in the traditional form: "Roe Catholique, de Castile, de Leon, d'Arragon, des deux Siciles, de Hierusalem, de Portugal, de Navarres, des Indes," after which followed the ducal and other non-royal titles. There is not even any attempt here to group the Spanish titles together. J. Dumont, *Corps Universel Diplomatique du Droit des Gens* (The Hague, 1728), Vol. 5, p. 561. Internal documents seem to have followed the traditional style almost invariably: "Don Phelippe, segundo deste nombre, por la gracia de Dios rey de Castilla, de Leon, de Aragon, . . ." (e.g., a statute regulating the election of *regidores* in Toledo, March 17, 1566, quoted in *Privilegios Reales y Viejos Documentos*, Vol. I, Doc. XV (Madrid, 1963).

[63] For a more detailed discussion of this development and of these arguments, see my article, "The Statecraft of Philip II," *European Studies Review*, Vol. 1, no. 1 (1971).

[64] *Actas de las Córtes de Castilla* (Madrid, 1866), Vol. 8, p. 282.

[65] E.g., between 1567 and 1574 some 43,000 men were sent to Italy and the Netherlands. G. Parker, *The Army of Flanders and the Spanish Road 1567-1659* (Cambridge, 1972), p. 42, n. 3, and chap. 1, *passim*.

desperate effects of the King's policy on the common people and re-marked caustically that "today there exists no longer a common weal but a common misery for everyone."[66]

Such voices remained isolated, however. In his addresses to the Cortes the King stressed less and less the good of Christendom, as he had for-merly done, and more and more the benefit his subjects derived from his consistent attempts to meet the enemy outside their borders, rather than on their own soil.[67] Such appeals to patriotism and the need to defend the homeland evidently fell on receptive ears, especially after the Earl of Essex's raid on Cadiz.

The death of Philip II, the Prudent King who, as many Spaniards and almost the whole of the rest of Europe believed, had aimed at the domi-nation of Europe and the world, was followed by a period of introspec-tion and self-criticism in Spain. The *arbitristas*, who were the spokesmen of this mood, produced acute analyses of the Castilian economy and of Castilian customs and morality. Their proposals were similar to those of their contemporary mercantilist writers in other European countries. They shared a nationalistic concern for the wealth, and hence power, of their own country, with emphasis on the need to protect native industries; to improve transport; to encourage immigrants, especially those with tech-nical skills; and above all, to change the Castilians' dislike for productive economic work. But, apart from the advice to cut government expendi-ture and to spread the financial burden of supporting the empire over all the dominions of the crown, so as to relieve Castile, they made little attempt at a systematic analysis of the problems of empire and of the role the Spanish monarchy should play in Europe and in the world.

This was equally true of the historians of the time. The old Juan de Mariana, recounting how he had been persuaded to continue his *Historia de España* beyond the end of the War of Granada, rejoiced that the energies of his countrymen had, after 1492, come to be directed toward the conquest of foreign peoples and kingdoms and that "the name and valor of Spain, known to few and confined within the narrow limits of Spain, was in a short time, and with great glory, spread abroad, not only through Italy and through France and Barbary, but to the very ends of

---

[66] "No hay beneficio común, sino mal común, para todos en general." Rodrigo Sanchez Doria, deputy of Tordesillas, on 26 May, 1595. He also made the remark that "the reason why taxes have been raised without noise is because they have not fallen on the rich who are those who have a voice and are heard in republics, and the sweetness which they find, that is the blood of the poor." In "The Statecraft of Philip II" (p. 20), I mistakenly attributed this remark to Pedro de Tello of Seville. *Actas de las Córtes*, Vol. 14, pp. 52-59.

[67] *Ibid.*, Vol. 15, pp. 444-45.

the earth." It was the conquest of this empire and the resultant greatness of Spain which he was persuaded to describe.[68] In this work at least, Mariana was concerned only with the question of Spanish reputation and he did not even begin to inquire what effects the winning of this reputation might have had on his country and countrymen or on the rest of the world. Even to the spread of Christianity, the usual justification for the Spanish overseas conquests, Mariana allows in all his long work just two sentences: "God gave them [the American Indians] great benefits and showed them great mercy in delivering them into the power of the Christians. . . . Above all, he gave them knowledge of himself, so that they would cease living as savages and live as Christians." At this point, Mariana seems to have become aware that he may have omitted something in his characterization of the effects of the Spanish conquests, for as if Las Casas or Vitoria had never discussed the intricacies of this problem, he added quickly, "They derived greater benefit from being subjected than from continuing in their liberty."[69]

The Castilian grandees, in whose hands lay the guidance of Spanish policy during the reign of Philip III, and who not only continued to occupy the Spanish viceroyalties and embassies abroad but now also dominated all the central councils of the government, were not given to such basic analysis either. Brought up in the later, expansionist, years of Philip II's reign, they took three things for granted: that the Spanish monarchy, even if not necessarily aiming at world empire, should still play a predominant role in Europe; that this role was synonymous with the cause of the Catholic Church and, hence, of God himself; and that the Castilian ruling classes should have the running of it. They differed only over tactics. The duke of Lerma—Philip II's *privado*, or principal minister—and the Council of State in Madrid, conscious of the precarious financial position of the monarchy, settled the English and Dutch wars (the latter at least temporarily) and tried in general to keep Spain out of further wars. It was they, however, who took the decision to expel the *Moriscos* from Spain in 1611, a decision that was undoubtedly popular and that did relatively little harm to the economy of Castile, but a great deal to that of Aragon and Valencia.

The Castilian viceroys and governors-general in Italy and the ambassadors in Rome, Venice, Prague, and Brussels felt themselves under no such restraints as Lerma, nor were they restrained by him. By usurpation, bullying, and intrigue they greatly extended Spanish power and influence in Italy and Germany. For two decades, from 1610 to 1630, Spain for the last time dominated the politics of Europe.[70]

[68] J. de Mariana, *Historia de España*, book 26, chap. 1.
[69] *Ibid.*, chap. 3.
[70] See the brilliant description of this position, especially of the first of these two

The events of those years were wholly disastrous for Spain. To a much greater degree than most contemporaries realized, the Spanish domination of Europe rested on default because of the temporary weakness and disunity of her enemies and, more especially, of France in the twenty years following the assassination of Henry IV in 1610. There were those, such as the count of Gondomar, Spanish ambassador in England, who still felt Spain could be a world empire if only England were conquered, a matter which Gondomar did not regard as exceptionally difficult. The majority of the Council of State who in 1621 debated the question of the resumption of the Dutch war were more restrained. The Dutch had used the Twelve Year Truce (1609–21) to capture the carrying trade of western Europe and the Baltic to Spain. If they continued their piracy and interloping of the Spanish-American trade as they were now doing, then first the Indies would be lost, then the rest of Flanders, the Spanish dominions in Italy, and finally, Spain herself.[71] Here was a clear identification of the national interest, even of the problem of national survival, with the empire. Tactically, the argument used was what I have on other occasions called the argument of the escalation of potential disasters. The strength of this position is that it is defensive in form (for it is the enemy who is credited with all positive action) but aggressive in intent. It seemed an unanswerable case, and Spain decided on war.[72] Gustavus Adolphus used the same argument to persuade a reluctant but patriotic Riksdag to support the entry of Sweden into the German war a few years later (1628).[73]

Both Castilians and Swedes were to experience the same disillusionment. What looked like the exertion of the national will in the defense of the monarchy's legitimate rights and in the service of God's cause (though, of course, differently interpreted) was seen by the rest of Europe, even by Spain's and Sweden's allies, as naked and aggressive power politics. It was the nemesis of Castile, and it was a shattering demonstration of the weakness of a genuinely Spanish nationalism, as against a Castilian-aristocratic imperialism, that the non-Castilian kingdoms of Spain were no more convinced by the claims of the Spanish monarchy than were non-Spaniards.[74]

Olivares, Philip IV's *privado*, was aware of this problem; at least, he

---

decades, by H. R. Trevor-Roper, "Spain and Europe 1598-1621," *New Cambridge Modern History*, Vol. IV, chap. 9.

[71] *Ibid.*, pp. 279-82.

[72] See H. G. Koenigsberger, *The Habsburgs and Europe 1516-1660* (Ithaca, 1971), pp. 228ff.

[73] *Ibid.*, p. 247.

[74] J. H. Elliott, *The Revolt of the Catalans* (Cambridge, 1963), pp. 200-203. See also my "The Catalan Revolution of 1640," *Estudios de Historia Moderna*, Vol. 4 (1954), pp. 278ff.

saw it in terms of the need to spread the burden of imperial policy from Castile to the King's other dominions. He also realized that these dominions would only agree to accepting such burdens if they could be made to feel part of the monarchy's cause, i.e., if they could be given a share of the benefits of empire. In a secret memorandum to the King in 1624, Olivares outlined his plan: the laws of Portugal, Aragon, and the Italian kingdoms should be assimilated to those of Castile, but the King should frequently visit these kingdoms to dispense patronage to their inhabitants, who should be given important imperial offices and honours, hitherto reserved to the Castilians. But this was precisely what the Castilian ruling classes would not accept, and Olivares did not even dare to propose his plan openly. In the 1560s, Philip II's failure to implement a similar plan, proposed by Granvelle, for integrating the Spanish empire had left the Spanish government no alternative but Alva's policy of repression, which caused the revolt of the Netherlands. In the 1620s, the failure of Olivares' attempt left him no alternative but the formation of the "Union of Arms," which caused the revolts of Catalonia and Portugal. The "Union of Arms" was a scheme for the creation of a reserve army of 140,000 men, for which all the dominions of the Spanish crown were to pay in proportion to their estimated resources. But the non-Castilians disliked this proposal because it infringed on their laws and liberties and because, with some justice, they distrusted the government in Madrid. When the ever-increasing demands of the war forced Olivares to be insistent, he set Madrid on a collision course with Catalonia and Portugal. The Catalans and the Portuguese (whose crown had passed to the kings of Spain in 1580) had certain feelings of loyalty to the person of the king. They had none for a Spain which, during the preceding one hundred years, had come to be identified with the imperial ambitions of the Castilian ruling classes. The Portuguese proclaimed their independence in 1640 and were never reconquered. The Catalans, finding themselves too weak for such a course, transferred their allegiance to the king of France, "as in the time of Charlemagne" (January 1641). Emotionally, it meant little. When the French armies withdrew during the civil wars of the Fronde, the Castilians were able to reconquer Catalonia in 1652. The Catalan upper classes, at least, were relieved. They had found the French even less congenial masters than the Castilians. Madrid did not repeat its former mistakes and restored all Catalan liberties and privileges. But, as subsequent history, right into the present century, was to show, the integration of Catalonia into a Castilian-dominated Spain remained highly problematical.

The history of Spain during the remaining years of the house of Austria, i.e., until the end of the seventeenth century, is a sad one. The decline of Spain, or at least of Castile, observed by contemporary visitors and debated by later historians, is an undeniable fact. It is visible in demography, in economic activity, in national and international politics, and even in literature and painting, for Calderón, Velázquez, and Murillo had no successors of comparable stature. Only national consciousness and pride did not decline. In the face of successive disasters, of the defeat and ineffectiveness of Spanish arms, and of the contempt with which Spain came to be treated in the councils of Europe, the Castilian nobility refused to face reality, just as they had refused to face it in the days of their triumph. Alexander Stanhope commented in 1699:

> The scarcety of money here is not to be believed but by eye-witnesses, notwithstanding the arrival of so many flotas and galleons, supplies not to be expected again in many years, for the last flota went out to India empty, and *ex nihilo nihil fit*. Their army in Catalonia, by the largest account, is not 8000 men, one half of the Germans and Walloons, who are all starving and deserting as fast as they can. When I came first to Spain [in 1690] they had eighteen good men-of-war; these are now reduced to two or three, I know not which. A wise council might find some remedy for most of these defects, but they all hate and are jealous of one another; and if any of them pretends to public spirit to advise anything for the good of the country, the rest fall upon him, nor is he to hope for any support from his Master. . . . This is a summary account of the present state of Spain; which, how wretched soever it may seem to others, they are in their own conceit very happy, believing themselves still the greatest nation in the world, and are now as proud and haughty as in the days of Charles the Fifth.[75]

The Castilian temperament always had something of the Quixotic.

It was the hubris of the Castilian ruling class, convinced of the God-ordained justice of their monarch's dynastic power politics, which had led Spain into two centuries of European war. It was the wars which devoured her, even though they were fought mostly beyond her borders. They never created an effective Spanish national feeling. Such a feeling did not appear until the Spaniards found themselves fighting a foreign invader on their own soil, during the Napoleonic wars.

SUMMARY AND CONCLUSIONS

The history of Spanish national feeling in the early-modern period is complex and ambivalent. The concept of nationalism itself is protean, and the attempt to give it clear definitions is not necessarily illuminating, nor perhaps even possible. The rather definite statements which follow are intended to serve primarily as debating points.

[75] Alexander Stanhope, British Minister at Madrid, to the Marquis of Normanby, January 6, 1699. *Spain under Charles II, or Extracts from the Correspondence of The Hon. Alexander Stanhope* (London, 1840), pp. 120ff.

1. There was a literary, rhetorical, and historiographical tradition of Spanish nationalism, mainly in the form of *laudes Hispaniae* which went back to Roman times and which was still very much alive in the early-modern period. It did not differ in essentials from similar traditions in other European countries. It is, however, doubtful whether it penetrated much beyond the relatively small literate section of society, and its political effects were slight.

2. There was a strong feeling of religious purpose. It was developed during the centuries when Spain struggled to free herself from Moorish domination, and it came to be identified with a national purpose, even when there was little or no objective basis for such an identification. This sentiment affected all classes of society.

3. The problem of Spanish nationalism, or even of a feeling of Spanish identity, was vastly complicated by the fact that the population of the Iberian Peninsula was multiracial and multireligious. Christians, Moslems, and Jews influenced each other's customs and sensibilities, though the exact degree to which this happened is a matter for controversy. Nearly all baptized Jews (*conversos*) and probably even a majority of the unbaptized Jews seem to have considered themselves Spaniards (n.b. They were literate.) This identification was, however, not accepted by large sections of the Old Christians, especially the lower classes, who developed a strong feeling of racial identity, "purity of blood." Nevertheless, successive generations of *conversos* were gradually absorbed in and assimilated to the Christians. This did not happen to the baptized Moors, the *Moriscos*, and this despite deliberate governmental policy to try to effect such assimilation. The *Moriscos* were eventually expelled from Spain (1611).

4. The word *español*, and the concept of the Spaniards as a nation distinct from other Christian nations, derived from non-Spanish Christians and from the relations of the Spaniards with them. A rather similar phenomenon occurred in other European countries.

5. In Spain, as everywhere else in Europe, there was a strong feeling of xenophobia. This was an old story, voiced very neatly in an anonymous Czech pamphlet of 1325:

> Oh, my God, the foreigner is favored; the native is trampled upon. The normal and proper thing is for the bear to stay in his forest, the wolf in his cave, the fish in the sea and the German in Germany. In that way the world would have some peace.[76]

[76] Quoted in S. Harrison Thompson, *Czechoslovakia in European History* (Princeton, 1953). I wish to thank Mr. Kenneth Dillon for drawing my attention to this quotation.

Appeals to this feeling were sometimes effective when an actual enemy invasion threatened the homeland, such as Philip II's appeals toward the end of his reign. It was not, however, the same as a feeling of nationalism. It was often, or perhaps even usually, directed against a neighbor in the peninsula. Sometimes, but not invariably, it coincided with differences in language (Castilian, Catalan, Galician, Basque, etc.). It was often institutionalized by custom or law so as to allow only the natives of a province to hold public offices or ecclesiastical benefices. Such customs and laws existed everywhere in Europe, though the degree to which they were enforced varied with time and place.

6. Closely connected with the previous point is the importance of political loyalties. In the Middle Ages these had been largely personal, and this continued to be a most important element in the early-modern period. Only gradually was it supplanted by a feeling of loyalty for an abstraction, such as the state, and then it tended to be for one's local kingdom, rather than for the whole of Spain.

7. The unification of the neighboring medieval principalities into so-called national monarchies was primarily the result of the dynastic policies of ruling houses. These policies, to a large extent, created the modern nations—a different process than that which gave existing nations political unity, as happened in Germany and Italy in the nineteenth century. This is very evident in the Netherlands and in Switzerland in the early-modern period. It is also evident in the Iberian Peninsula, where dynastic and tactical considerations created Spain by the union of the crowns of Aragon and Castile, rather than by the union of the crowns of Castile and Portugal. To Ferdinand of Aragon the union of the crowns of Aragon, Sicily, and Naples was equally important. Neither a historical determinism, based on the pre-existence of a Spanish nation as a self-conscious political force, nor a sociological determinism, based on a theory of communication, seems to me to offer an acceptable explanation of Spanish history.

8. The Spanish monarchy, from Ferdinand and Isabella to Charles II, was singularly ineffective in promoting either institutional or emotional unity among its Spanish kingdoms. This is not really very surprising. Because the Spanish monarchs ruled non-Spanish countries, notably in Italy and the Netherlands, by hereditary right, they were precluded largely for psychological reasons from feeling in national Spanish terms. In effect, they pursued the politically easiest line, that of deferring to the feelings of the ruling groups of the largest of their kingdoms, Castile.

9. The alliance of the Castilian ruling classes with the dynastic and

religious ambitions of the Hapsburgs—which began in the reign of Charles V, was consummated in that of Philip II, and was never given up after that—produced a Castilian imperialism that can only very marginally be identified with Spanish nationalism. Genuine Spanish nationalism, as an effective political force, does not seem to have appeared before the Napleonic Wars in the early nineteenth century.

INDEX OF
NAMES

173

Library of Congress Cataloging in Publication Data
Main entry under title:

National consciousness, history, and political culture
in early-modern Europe.

(The Johns Hopkins symposia in comparative history, 5)
Based on the 1973 Schouler lectures, sponsored by
the Dept. of History of the Johns Hopkins University.
Includes bibliographical references.
1. Europe—Politics—1492–1648—Addresses, essays,
lectures.   2. Europe—Politics—1648–1789—Addresses,
essays, lectures.   3. Europe—Civilization—Addresses,
essays, lectures.   I. Ranum, Orest, ed.
II. Series.
D217.N37 1975   320.9′4′02   74-6837
ISBN 0-8018-1619-X